Becoming a Microsoft Dynamics 365 Marketing Functional Consultant

Learn to deliver enterprise marketing solutions and insights to exponentially grow your business

Malin Martnes

BIRMINGHAM—MUMBAI

Becoming a Microsoft Dynamics 365 Marketing Functional Consultant

Copyright © 2022 Packt Publishing

Group Product Manager: Alok Dhuri

Publishing Product Manager: Akshay Dani

Senior Editor: Nithya Sadanandan

Technical Editor: Pradeep Sahu

Copy Editor: Safis Editing

Language Support Editor: Safis Editing

Project Coordinator: Manisha Singh

Proofreader: Safis Editing

Indexer: Rekha Nair

Production Designer: Alishon Mendonca

Developer Relations Marketing Executive: Deepak Kumar and Rayyan Khan

Business Development Executive: Uzma Sheerin

First published: December 2022

Production reference: 1251122

Published by Packt Publishing Ltd.
Livery Place
35 Livery Street
Birmingham
B3 2PB, UK.

ISBN: 978-1-80323-460-1

www.packt.com

To my son Nicolai, for all the love in the world.

To my partner Mark, for always believing in me.

- Malin Martnes

Contributors

About the author

Malin Martnes is the CEO of MaCoTra AS, a company focusing on Dynamics 365 and the Microsoft Power Platform. The Malin has been working with Microsoft technology for 10 years, but before that, she got a degree in marketing and has had this subject as an interest for many years. Microsoft awarded her with the title of Most Valuable Professional in 2019 and has re-awarded her every year since. Microsoft **Most Valuable Professional** (**MVP**) is an award for individuals who have exhibited exceptional technical expertise and a talent for sharing knowledge within their technical community.

I want to thank my son and my partner, for giving me the energy and push I needed. And the technical reviewers, Dilyana and Vivian, for giving great feedback and making the book even better.

About the reviewers

Vivian Voss is a functional solution architect with 7 years of experience with CRM and Dynamics products. Starting off as a technical consultant on Dynamics CRM 2011, she has followed Microsoft's development to the now-known Dynamics 365 and most of the products within it. In 2022, she got rewarded as a Microsoft Business Applications MVP for her blogging about Dynamics 365 Marketing and organizing or volunteering at various Power Platform and Dynamics 365 events. Being part of the Dynamics365/Power Platform community, and especially the people within it, is what keeps her passion for the area burning.

Dilyana Radulova works as a technical specialist for Microsoft, focusing on Dynamics 365 Marketing and Customer Insights. Dilyana has years of experience working with the Microsoft stack as a functional consultant and running projects as the functional lead.

Dilyana is one of the leaders in the Dynamics 365 Customer Experience User Group, a user group focusing on Dynamics 365 Marketing.

Table of Contents

3

What Are Segments and Lists?   69

Part 2 – Core Features of Dynamics 365 Marketing

4

Managing Marketing Forms, Pages, and Websites   93

5

Creating Marketing Emails   121

6

Outbound Customer Journeys   157

7

Real-Time Marketing Journeys   185

8

Managing Events   221

Part 3 – The Microsoft Ecosystem Adding Value

9

Dynamics 365 Customer Voice   257

10

Power Platform   293

Assessments   333

Index   343

Other Books You May Enjoy   352

Preface

Dynamics 365 Marketing is Microsoft's solution to help companies achieve more with marketing. This book will guide you through learning about and using Dynamics 365 Marketing to better your company's marketing automation efforts.

The first part of the book is all about getting the foundation correct so that you have a solid ground on which to keep building your marketing. Understanding the basis of how the system is built and the configuration is important before you start using it.

The second part of the book gives you an in-depth walk-through of the core functionalities of Dynamics 365 Marketing and gives you the *dos and don'ts* of the functionality.

The third part explores one of the biggest advantages of choosing a Microsoft system: the surrounding environment and the large ecosystem. From extending the marketing system to having an event portal and asking customers for their feedback, there is a solution in the Microsoft world to fix it.

This book will guide you through everything you need to know to have a flying start in your implementation or when working with Dynamics 365 Marketing.

Who this book is for

This book is for both marketing consultants doing implementations and marketers using the system, who are interested in learning all about Dynamics 365 Marketing. This book is ideal if you want to learn all about the system, to implement it from end to end, to pass the MB-220 certification, or just to get more knowledge about Dynamics 365 Marketing.

What this book covers

Chapter 1, The Basic Configuration of Dynamics 365 Marketing, covers the prerequisites before you start implementing Dynamics 365 Marketing and what kind of setup you will need before you can start using the system.

Chapter 2, Managing Leads, Accounts, and Contacts, covers how Dynamics 365 Marketing defines your customer. We'll go through what accounts, contacts, and leads are and how they are connected. We'll also look at active marketing customers, who you can send information to, and learn what the lead life cycle is.

Chapter 3, What Are Segments and Lists?, goes through the creation and administration of segments, subscription centers, and lists.

Chapter 4, Managing Marketing Forms, Pages, and Websites, covers how to create marketing forms, pages, and websites. We will have a look at what they are and some use cases for them.

Chapter 5, Creating Marketing Emails, explains how you can create a good email, what different layouts are available, and how you can create your own with templates. We'll also go through the analytics of emails and how you can read these to improve your emails.

Chapter 6, Outbound Customer Journeys, combines all of your efforts together in journeys. There are two different types of customer journeys: outbound and real-time. In this chapter, we'll go through the outbound customer journeys. Lastly, we will look at the analytics and how we can read them to create even better journeys.

Chapter 7, Real-Time Marketing Journeys, goes through the more modern real-time marketing journeys. Lastly, we will look at the analytics and how we can read them to create even better journeys.

Chapter 8, Managing Events, covers one of the features that make Dynamic 365 Marketing stand out most: the event module. We go through the setup of both in-person events and webinars. We look at the event journeys and see how we can use Power Pages as the event website.

Chapter 9, Dynamics 365 Customer Voice, covers an important part of marketing: getting responses, feedback, and information from your customers. Dynamics 365 Customer Voice is tightly connected to Dynamics 365 Marketing, and is the system where you create surveys to send to your customers, potential customers, and event participants.

Chapter 10, Power Platform, covers the ecosystem of the Microsoft Power Platform. No system is created perfect but the possibility to make changes and customize the system to your company's needs is key, and the Power Platform can help with this. In this chapter, we'll go through all the applications that are relevant to the system and how you can use them to get even better usage of Dynamics 365 Marketing.

To get the most out of this book

To get the most out of the book, I highly recommend you have a Dynamics 365 solution set up. If you do not have this set up, you can easily create a trial from `https://dynamics.microsoft.com/en-gb/dynamics-365-free-trial/` and select Dynamics 365 Marketing. You will then get a 30-day free trial, where you can test everything we go through in the book.

You can read more about the prerequisites for setting up a system on this site: `https://learn.microsoft.com/en-us/dynamics365/marketing/purchase-setup#prerequisites-and-requirements`.

Download the color images

We also provide a PDF file that has color images of the screenshots and diagrams used in this book. You can download it here: `https://packt.link/yJxeH`.

Conventions used

There are a number of text conventions used throughout this book.

`Code in text`: Indicates code words in text, database table names, folder names, filenames, file extensions, pathnames, dummy URLs, user input, and Twitter handles. Here is an example: "If you have a list of contacts to which you should never send any emails, that's an important block to add to any segment that you'll use to send an email, in the form of a `but not` segment block."

Bold: Indicates a new term, an important word, or words that you see onscreen. For instance, words in menus or dialog boxes appear in **bold**. Here is an example: "On the **Usage limits** screen, you can see the fair use policy usage limits."

> **Tips or important notes**
> Appear like this.

Get in touch

Feedback from our readers is always welcome.

General feedback: If you have questions about any aspect of this book, email us at `customercare@packtpub.com` and mention the book title in the subject of your message.

Errata: Although we have taken every care to ensure the accuracy of our content, mistakes do happen. If you have found a mistake in this book, we would be grateful if you would report this to us. Please visit `www.packtpub.com/support/errata` and fill in the form.

Piracy: If you come across any illegal copies of our works in any form on the internet, we would be grateful if you would provide us with the location address or website name. Please contact us at `copyright@packt.com` with a link to the material.

If you are interested in becoming an author: If there is a topic that you have expertise in and you are interested in either writing or contributing to a book, please visit `authors.packtpub.com`.

Share Your Thoughts

Once you've read *Becoming a Microsoft Dynamics 365 Marketing Functional Consultant*, we'd love to hear your thoughts! Scan the QR code below to go straight to the Amazon review page for this book and share your feedback.

https://packt.link/r/1803234601

Your review is important to us and the tech community and will help us make sure we're delivering excellent quality content.

Download a free PDF copy of this book

Thanks for purchasing this book!

Do you like to read on the go but are unable to carry your print books everywhere?

Is your eBook purchase not compatible with the device of your choice?

Don't worry, now with every Packt book you get a DRM-free PDF version of that book at no cost.

Read anywhere, any place, on any device. Search, copy, and paste code from your favorite technical books directly into your application.

The perks don't stop there, you can get exclusive access to discounts, newsletters, and great free content in your inbox daily

Follow these simple steps to get the benefits:

1.   Scan the QR code or visit the link below

https://packt.link/free-ebook/9781803234601

2.   Submit your proof of purchase
3.   That's it! We'll send your free PDF and other benefits to your email directly

Part 1 –
The Foundation of
Dynamics 365 Marketing

This first part of the book is all about creating the foundation to build your marketing on. Understanding the basics of how the system is built and its configuration is important before you start using it. The following chapters are included in this part:

- *Chapter 1, The Basic Configuration of Dynamics 365 Marketing*
- *Chapter 2, Managing Leads, Accounts, and Contacts*
- *Chapter 3, What Are Segments and Lists?*

1

The Basic Configuration of Dynamics 365 Marketing

Welcome to the world of Dynamics 365 Marketing! We're going to have a lot of fun with this book, and you will learn all about how to use the system the right way, taking advantage of all the features of this amazing system.

This first chapter of this book is a fragmented chapter about setting up the system correctly. If you're brand new to Dynamics 365 Marketing, you might want to skip this part and circle back to it when you're done with this book and keep it as a reference for when you're doing implementations. This chapter will tell you all about what you need to set up to use the system effectively and efficiently.

You will learn about the following main topics in this chapter:

- Prerequisites of Dynamics 365 Marketing
- Setting up and managing Dynamics 365 Marketing
- Configuring marketing settings
- Templates
- Asset library

By the end of this chapter, you'll know what all the different settings are for and how you can use them to get your Dynamics 365 tailored to your needs.

Prerequisites of Dynamics 365 Marketing

Before we start using the system, we need to make sure you can access **Dynamics 365 Marketing**, so the first thing we need to go through is how to get access to the system.

The first thing you should check is that Dynamics 365 Marketing is available in your region. The easiest way to do that is by going to `https://dynamics.microsoft.com/en-us/availability-reports/georeport/` and checking if it's listed as generally available in your region.

In this section, we'll go through Microsoft 365 tenants and which licensing you need to use the system.

Microsoft 365 tenants

The first thing you need is an existing **Microsoft 365 (M365)** tenant. An M365 tenant is a location where all your organization's data is stored. If you're located in Europe, you will most likely have a tenant localized in the European data centers. To create an environment for Dynamics 365 Marketing, you'll need to have your M365 tenant already set up. If this is not something your company has already done, it will need to be created before you can continue creating your Dynamics 365 Marketing environment. To learn more about administrating Microsoft 365, I highly recommend the book *Microsoft Office 365 Administration Cookbook* by Nate Chamberlain, available at `https://www.packtpub.com/product/microsoft-office-365-administration-cookbook/9781838551230`.

License

Once you have your tenant in place, you need a license. If you're familiar with the world of **Microsoft licensing**, you might know that this isn't always the easiest area to explain, but let's see if we can make sense of it.

The first thing you need to check is if you have 10 or more licenses for other Dynamics 365 applications such as Sales, Customer Service, Field Service, Supply Chain Management, Finance, or Commerce. If you have 10 or more of these licenses, then you qualify for an attach license, which is half the price of the normal full-price Marketing license. Marketing isn't licensed per user, but per app, so you don't have to buy multiple licenses because you have multiple users.

When you've purchased the base license, you get 10,000 **marketing contacts** and 100,000 **marketing interactions** included in the price. Now, let's dig deeper into what this means.

A marketing interaction is a personalized message sent through a customer journey (where all messages from the system are sent from). No matter what channel you send this information through, it's a marketing interaction.

A marketing contact is anyone with at least one marketing interaction registered in the past 12 months.

If you need more marketing contacts or marketing interactions than those included in the base license, you can buy additional packs for both. If you want to have more than one production environment or a sandbox or development environment, you can buy additional licenses for that as well.

The world of licensing is always changing. You can read all about pricing on the pricing page at `https://dynamics.microsoft.com/en-us/pricing/` or the licensing guide at `https://go.microsoft.com/fwlink/?LinkId=866544&clcid=0x409`.

Now, you're ready to start installing Dynamics 365 Marketing!

Setting up and managing Dynamics 365 Marketing

If you're a Global admin or Service support admin, you can install the system on your tenant. If you already have a Dynamics 365 Marketing app installed, you won't be able to install a new one, but you can do a reinstallation. Each Marketing app can only be used with one Dynamics 365 environment. Let's begin:

1. Go to `https://admin.powerplatform.microsoft.com/` and choose **Resources | Dynamics 365 apps** from the left menu. On the **Dynamics 365 apps** pane, you need to find **Dynamics 365 Marketing Application** and click the three dots, then choose **Manage**, as shown in *Figure 1.1*:

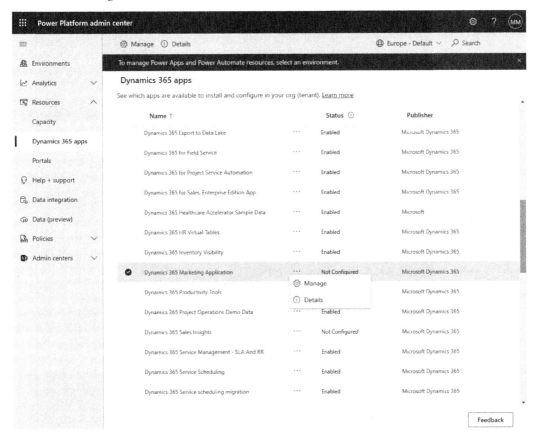

Figure 1.1 – Power Platform admin center – Dynamics 365 apps

2.   This will start the setup wizard, where you can choose which environment you want to set up and the web hosting you want to use (you can change this after the setup), as shown in *Figure 1.2*:

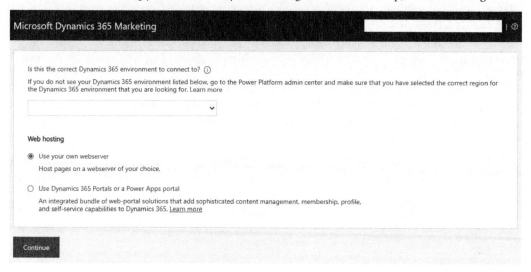

Figure 1.2 – Connecting to the Dynamics 365 environment and web hosting

If you have a web server, you can create pages and link them back to Dynamics 365 Marketing. If you use Power Apps Portals (now called Power Pages), you can use the out-of-the-box functionality of marketing pages. We will cover all of this in *Chapter 4, Managing Marketing Forms, Pages, and Websites*.

3.   When you've selected your environment and hosting, you must accept the Microsoft terms and conditions and put in your company's physical street address. There are several laws and regulations in different countries that state that you need to add your company's physical street address, so this needs to be done in the setup. It will take about 3 hours for everything to be set up so that you're ready to start configuring.

Configuring marketing settings

When you set up a new Dynamics 365 Marketing system, you have a lot of links to go through on the **Settings overview** page, as shown in *Figure 1.3*:

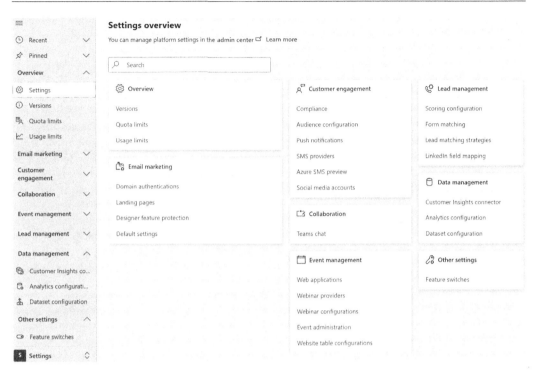

Figure 1.3 – Settings overview

We're going to go through all of these so that you know what each one does and how you can use them to tailor your system in the best way possible.

Overview

The first area we start with is the **Overview** area. Here, you can see the available versions, quota limits, and usage limits.

Versions

About once a month, the team from Microsoft comes out with a new version. Some of these contain lots of new stuff, while others just contain bug fixes and minor changes. The **Versions** area is where you make sure that your Dynamics 365 Marketing is up to date with all the new features. I highly recommend updating the system outside of normal business hours to make sure that you don't interfere with the usage of the system.

If you set up your system before March 2022, the **Versions** area is where you activate the real-time marketing features. This book will dive deeper into the features of real-time marketing in *Chapter 6, Outbound Customer Journeys,* and *Chapter 7, Real-Time Marketing Journeys.* If you don't see it on your system, go to **Settings** | **Versions** and activate it. This will take a couple of hours.

Quota limits

As we discussed in the first part of this chapter, you get a set of interactions and marketing contacts with your license. In the **Quota limits** area, you get an overview of what you have used every month based on the licenses you have. You can see how many emails, text messages, or push notifications you have used that month and how much you have left on your quota. You can also see how many marketing contacts you have in Dataverse. If you have gone over your limit of marketing contacts or your interaction quota, then you can buy additional licenses. The contacts in your system with which you haven't done marketing for the last 12 months move over to regular contacts and no longer count against the quota of your marketing contacts.

Usage limits

On the **Usage limits** screen, you can see the fair use policy usage limits. Dynamics 365 uses cloud resources for data and processing that are shared with other organizations, and to avoid taking up all the capacity of the tenant, there are limits per organization. You can see these limits in *Figure 1.4*:

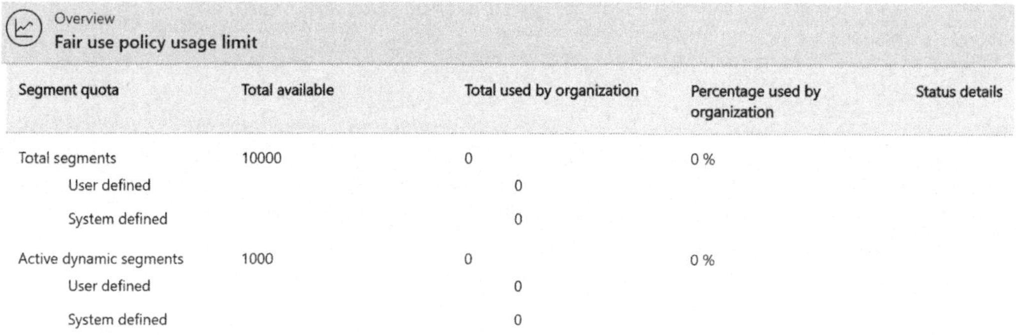

Overview Fair use policy usage limit				
Segment quota	**Total available**	**Total used by organization**	**Percentage used by organization**	**Status details**
Total segments	10000	0	0 %	
User defined		0		
System defined		0		
Active dynamic segments	1000	0	0 %	
User defined		0		
System defined		0		

Figure 1.4 – Fair use policy usage limit

Email marketing

For many, email marketing is a fundamental part of their marketing. Email marketing is how a lot of companies share their information with both established and potential customers. There are several settings you should go through to tailor your system to your company's needs as much as possible.

Domain authentication

When sending an email to a customer or hosting a form, you want the sender to be your organization and the sender's email to be your company's email. To be allowed to do this, you need to register your domain in Dynamics 365 Marketing. First, you need to claim your domain through a method called **DomainKeys Identified Mail (DKIM)**. DKIM is an authentication method that tells your users that this is a safe domain and is not used for phishing or email spam. **Domain authentication** is implemented through the internet's DNS system; you will need to own your domain before you can claim it in Dynamics 365 Marketing, as shown in *Figure 1.5*:

Figure 1.5 – Domain authentication

This means that you cannot send an email in Dynamics 365 Marketing from another domain that you do not own. This is for security reasons – you can only use a domain that you own; otherwise, it will automatically be flagged as spam and will not be sent out by the system. When you start with Dynamics 365 Marketing, you get a default domain that you can use. While it won't look as pretty as your domain, it gives you a place to start.

Landing pages

The settings area for **landing pages** is where you create a record for configuring your landing pages. You need to have one record that will act as the default configuration for your landing pages, as shown in *Figure 1.6*, but you can have multiple configurations for landing pages. Maybe your company has several departments, or you might have multiple companies in the same organization:

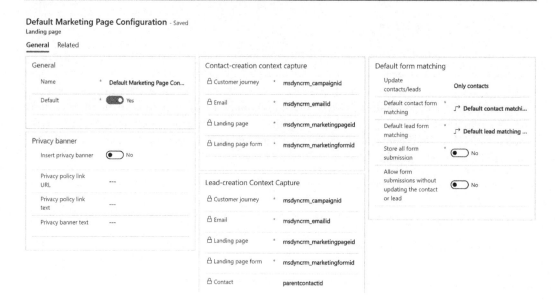

Figure 1.6 – Default Marketing Page Configuration

In the record, you can specify if you want a privacy banner and what links you want in that banner. You can also set the form matching and whether you want to store form submissions and allow submissions where you don't update the contact or lead. All these settings will impact how your landing pages will behave.

Designer feature protection

There is at least one of these people in every company. You know the ones I'm talking about – the ones that always break the design guidelines or just tweak the email a bit so that it becomes exactly as they wanted. With **designer feature protection**, you can add a team or a user and block them from using either the HTML features or the Litmus integration (preview functionality for emails you create). This can be great when you need to make sure that everyone in your company is using predefined templates for their emails or landing pages.

Default settings

You can have multiple default settings, but you can only have one default setting record that is the default and will be used as a standard. These are confusing names, but I will make sense of it all later in this book when we go through how you use these settings.

In the **Marketing email** tab (*Figure 1.7*), you need to connect to features such as default content settings and default sending domain, which we'll go through in depth in this chapter:

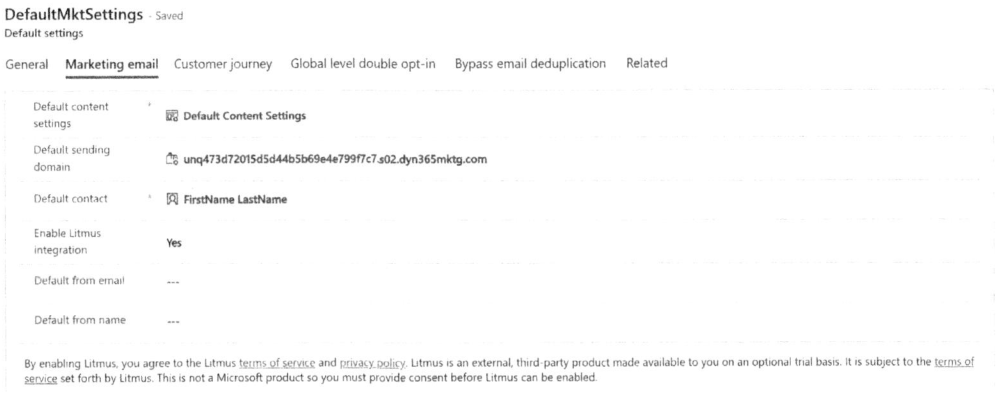

DefaultMktSettings - Saved
Default settings

General   **Marketing email**   Customer journey   Global level double opt-in   Bypass email deduplication   Related

Default content settings	🔳 **Default Content Settings**
Default sending domain	🔳 unq473d72015d5d44b5b69e4e799f7c7.s02.dyn365mktg.com
Default contact	🔳 FirstName LastName
Enable Litmus integration	**Yes**
Default from email	---
Default from name	---

By enabling Litmus, you agree to the Litmus terms of service and privacy policy. Litmus is an external, third-party product made available to you on an optional trial basis. It is subject to the terms of service set forth by Litmus. This is not a Microsoft product so you must provide consent before Litmus can be enabled.

Figure 1.7 – Default settings – the Marketing email tab

Another important feature to enable here is Litmus integration. Litmus allows you to preview your emails in different browsers and systems. A limited number of previews are included in your Marketing license, but you can always buy more previews directly from Litmus if that's needed.

In the **Customer journey** tab, you can set the preferred time zone.

Double opt-in is when you send an email to have the customer confirm that they want to sign up for your newsletter, as you need to confirm that it's them that signed up for it. The global level double opt-in option allows you to set this for the entire tenant, and you can change the settings for it in the **Global level double opt-in** tab (*Figure 1.8*):

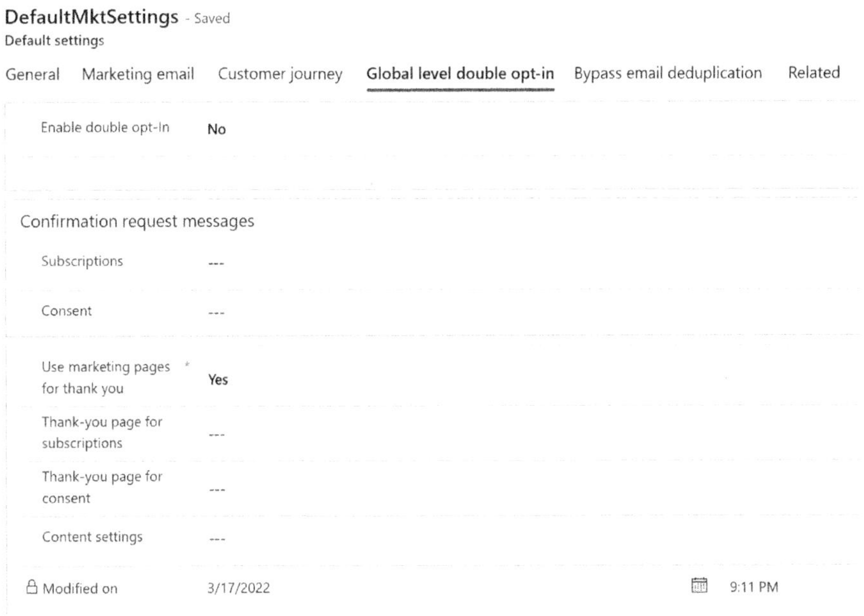

DefaultMktSettings - Saved
Default settings

General   Marketing email   Customer journey   **Global level double opt-in**   Bypass email deduplication   Related

| Enable double opt-In | **No** |

Confirmation request messages

Subscriptions	---
Consent	---
Use marketing pages for thank you	**Yes**
Thank-you page for subscriptions	---
Thank-you page for consent	---
Content settings	---

| 🔒 Modified on | 3/17/2022 | 📅 9:11 PM |

Figure 1.8 – Default settings – Global level double opt-in

> **Important note**
>
> I don't recommend using this feature – there are only a few customers I've met that need to use double opt-in, and I've never come across any that should use **Global level double opt-in**.

The **Bypass email deduplication** tab is also a rare feature for my customers to use, but some special customers need it. One of my customers is a bank; their customers are parents and their children, often with the same email address. If they want to send out an email that's personalized to each of their customers, they can use **Bypass email deduplication** so that only one of these emails is sent out, even if it is supposed to go to each contact, so long as it's the same email. They need to change this setting to **Yes** if they want multiple emails to be sent to the same email address.

Customer engagement

In the **Customer engagement** section, we can find areas for compliance, audience configuration, push notifications, SMS providers, Azure SMS preview, and social media accounts. Let's take a look at all of these.

Compliance

With the importance of the **GDPR** and **privacy**, you need good features to help you make sure you use the system correctly. There are different options for this, including **Outbound consent** and **Real-Time consent**. Let's take a look at what the different options are.

Real-Time consent

In the **Real-Time consent** part of **compliance** (*Figure 1.9*), you can decide if you're going to use a **restrictive** or **non-restrictive consent model**. If you're somewhere where the GDPR is in play, you need to use the restrictive model, which means you can't send anything to customers without their consent to do so. The non-restrictive model means you can send commercial information to every customer until they opt out.

You can also specify whether you want to get tracking consent from customers and fill out the physical postal address for your company:

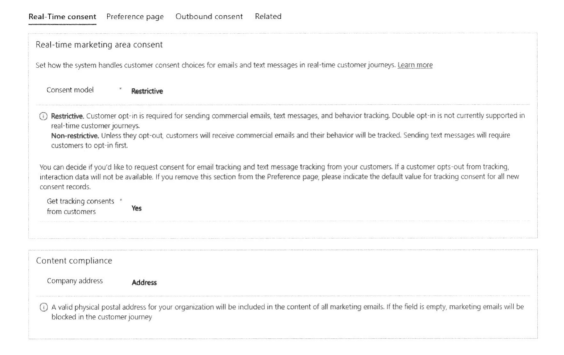

Figure 1.9 – Compliance – Real-Time consent

Preference page

The **Preference page** options (*Figure 1.10*) are where you edit the page your customers go to so that they can change their preferences for things such as whether you can send them information or not via email and/or SMS:

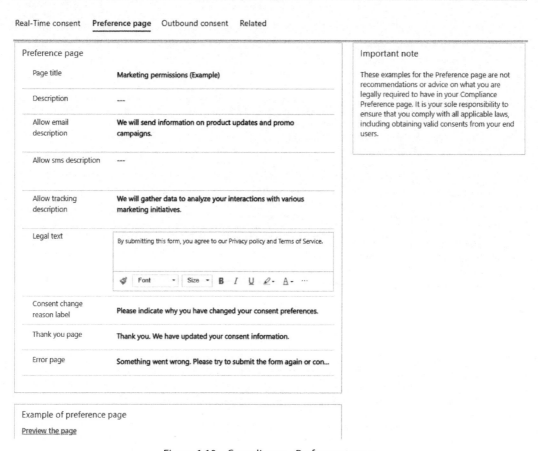

Figure 1.10 – Compliance – Preference page

You can also preview the page to see how the page will appear to your customers, as shown in *Figure 1.11*:

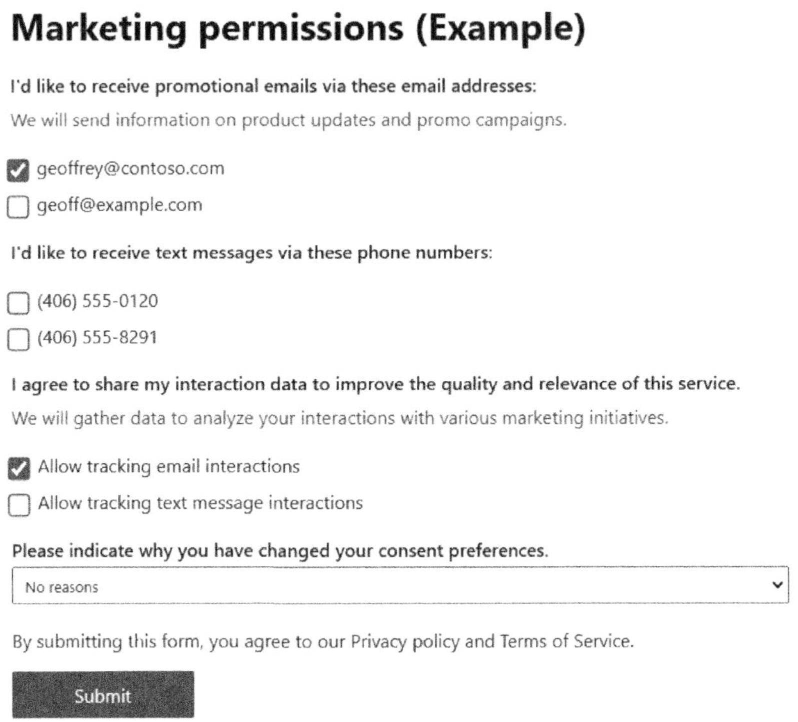

Marketing permissions (Example)

I'd like to receive promotional emails via these email addresses:

We will send information on product updates and promo campaigns.

☑ geoffrey@contoso.com

☐ geoff@example.com

I'd like to receive text messages via these phone numbers:

☐ (406) 555-0120

☐ (406) 555-8291

I agree to share my interaction data to improve the quality and relevance of this service.

We will gather data to analyze your interactions with various marketing initiatives.

☑ Allow tracking email interactions

☐ Allow tracking text message interactions

Please indicate why you have changed your consent preferences.

No reasons ⌄

By submitting this form, you agree to our Privacy policy and Terms of Service.

Submit

Figure 1.11 – Compliance – Preview of Preference page

Outbound consent

In the **Outbound marketing consent** area (*Figure 1.12*), you must decide if you want to enable a dropdown in the outbound customer journey and if you want to log the changes on that field:

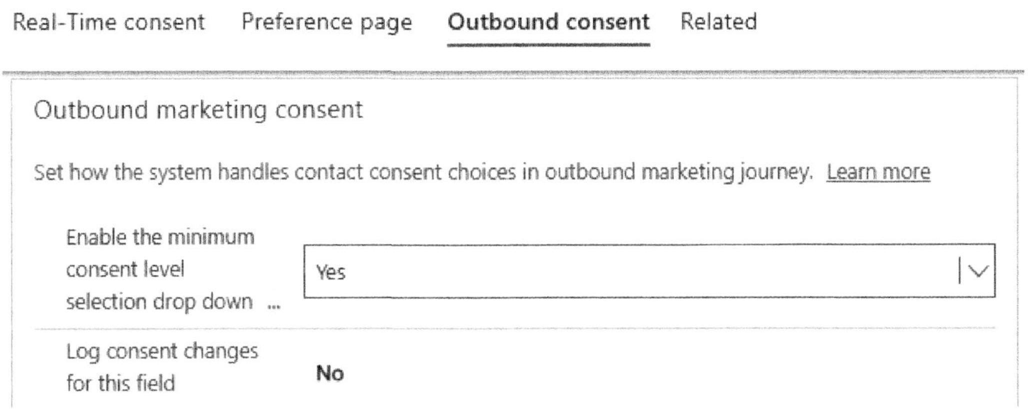

Real-Time consent   Preference page   **Outbound consent**   Related

Outbound marketing consent

Set how the system handles contact consent choices in outbound marketing journey. Learn more

Enable the minimum consent level selection drop down ...	Yes ⌄
Log consent changes for this field	**No**

Figure 1.12 – Compliance – Outbound consent

Audience configuration

In real-time marketing, you can send information to contacts, leads, and/or customer profile entities. Both contacts and leads use the default fields for email and phone numbers, so if you aren't using the default fields for email and phone, you'll have to go into the audience data configuration options (*Figure 1.13*) and edit the recipient fields:

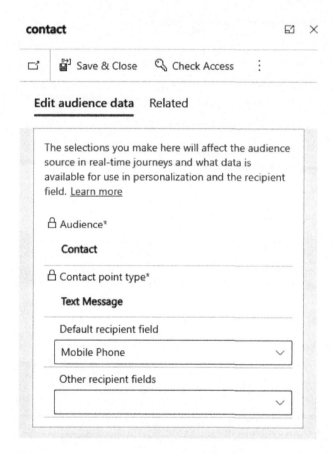

Figure 1.13 – Audience configuration

Push notifications

To use **push notifications** in Dynamics 365 Marketing, you will have to have a complete app already available on the iOS App Store and/or Google Play. To connect the app and Dynamics 365 Marketing, you need to create a new mobile app configuration, as shown in *Figure 1.14*:

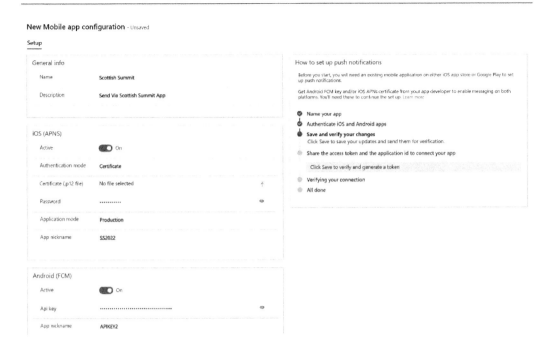

Figure 1.14 – Mobile app configuration

In the configuration, you need to get the Android FCM key and/or the iOS APN certificate from your developers. When you've created a new mobile app configuration, you get the access token and application ID you will need to connect your app to the system. Now, you can start using push notifications directly from Dynamics 365 Marketing in your app.

SMS providers

In Dynamics 365 Marketing, you have the option to connect to two out-of-the-box **SMS** providers, either TeleSign or Twilio, as of October 2022. From October 2022 you have the option of creating a custom channel where you can connect to your local provider. To use either provider, you must become a customer of them, after which you can connect the provider to your Dynamics 365 Marketing instance, and then use the provider to send your text messages. After you become a customer, you need to fill in the details shown in *Figure 1.15* to connect with your SMS provider:

SMS number setup

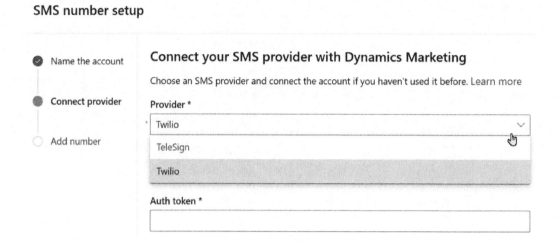

Figure 1.15 – SMS number setup

You will need some information from your provider so that you can register your number. Then, you'll be ready to start sending SMSs from the system.

Azure SMS

The third choice of SMS provider is the SMS functionality in the **Azure communication services**, which lets you send out text messages in bulk, have a two-way conversation, and get access to analytics. To see where the data from Azure communication services is available, along with any geographical restrictions, check the page at `https://docs.microsoft.com/en-us/azure/communication-services/concepts/privacy`.

To learn more about subscription eligibility and number capabilities, visit `https://docs.microsoft.com/en-us/azure/communication-services/concepts/numbers/sub-eligibility-number-capability`.

Social media accounts

Social media is a big part of marketing, and Dynamics 365 Marketing gives us the functionality to work with social media through the platform. To create **social media posts** directly from Dynamics 365 Marketing, you will have to set up the connection between the system and your social media profile, which you can do by accepting the terms and conditions and giving the configuration a name (*Figure 1.16*). When you click **Create**, you need to sign in to the social media account:

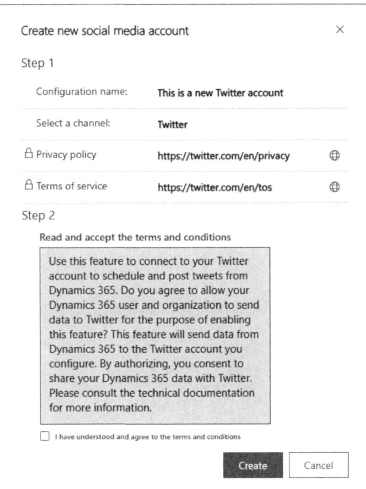

Figure 1.16 – Create new social media account

You will need to sign in to your Facebook, Twitter, LinkedIn, or Instagram account before you can utilize the social media posting feature.

With LinkedIn, you can also connect your account with LinkedIn Lead Gen Forms. Be aware that the LinkedIn user profile (*Figure 1.17*) is set up a bit differently than other social media, as you always need to connect to it with your own personal LinkedIn that is connected to your company's LinkedIn site. If you have any campaigns or Lead Gen Forms, the information from these can be automatically sent to your system:

Figure 1.17 – LinkedIn user profile

Collaboration

Collaborating with your colleagues is getting more and more important and Dynamics 365 Marketing has features to help you with this.

Teams chat

Over the last couple of years, **Microsoft Teams** has become increasingly popular across the globe. In the **Teams chat settings** area, you can turn on the ability to link your records to different Microsoft Teams channels, which allows you to pin records and views in your Teams channel from Dynamics 365. Another feature allows you to turn on confidential labels so that you can create private teams that only you and selected users have access to.

If you and your team want to chat about the new campaign you are creating in Dynamics 365 Marketing in Teams, this Teams chat can be linked to a record in Dynamics 365, thus storing all the information about this specific customer journey in one place. These two systems working together makes it even easier for marketers to collaborate and share information about the marketing efforts they do for your company.

Event management

The **Event management** module is one of the features that most separates Dynamics 365 Marketing from other marketing automation tools, so naturally, there are some settings you need to go through before you can start using it. We will look at some of these in the following sections.

Web applications

If you are using APIs to interact programmatically with events, you need to register them in web applications.

Webinar providers

If you want to use another third-party **webinar** host, you can use On24, for which there is a record already set up, but you rarely need to go into this setting.

Webinar configurations

To use On24 as your webinar host, you need to set up a webinar configuration where you can add your credentials to On24 and connect the two systems.

Event administration

The most important setting in **New event administration** is **Match contact based on**, as shown in *Figure 1.18*.

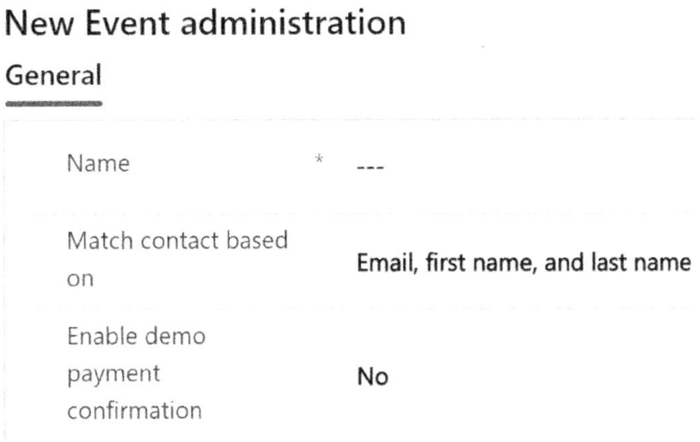

New Event administration

General

Name *	---
Match contact based on	**Email, first name, and last name**
Enable demo payment confirmation	**No**

Figure 1.18 – New Event administration

When a customer registers for an event, this is the field that defines the matching criteria for contacts. If the event participant registers their details, and these match in terms of email, first name, and last name, then the registration for event participation will be connected to the contact. All of these attributes need to match to deem it a contact match. If you have duplicates in your system, then it also makes sense to match on email, first name, and last name to ensure it's the correct contact.

If you're in your production environment, you should never enable the demo payment confirmation. This is only meant to be used if you're doing a demonstration.

Website table configurations

If you want to connect with the event API and expose custom fields, you need to set up website table configurations.

Lead management

Leads are an important part of your system. You can read more about this in *Chapter 2, Managing Leads, Accounts, and Contacts*. To work with leads and utilize the leads you have in your system properly, you have several settings to do in lead management. Let's go through the most important aspects of lead management.

Scoring configuration

If you want to use **lead scoring** in Dynamics 365 Marketing, you must have one scoring configuration. One possible setup is shown in *Figure 1.19*:

Figure 1.19 – Scoring configuration

When you set **Automatic sales ready** or **Automated marketing qualification** to **Yes**, this will change the out-of-the-box Business Process Flow for the lead. If the lead is Sales-ready, it's ready for the sales team to take over to work with the lead. If it's automatically marketing qualified, this means that marketing has approved the lead and the status in the Business Process Flow changes automatically.

The **Automatic lead scores cleanup** option allows you to specify what will happen with the calculated scores if you stop a lead-scoring model – that is, whether it will remove or keep all the scores of existing leads.

Form matching

Nobody wants duplicates in their system. The **Form matching** area of the settings is where you set up how you want to match your contacts and leads from forms. You can specify which attributes need to match to map new leads or contacts coming into the system, as shown in the following screenshot:

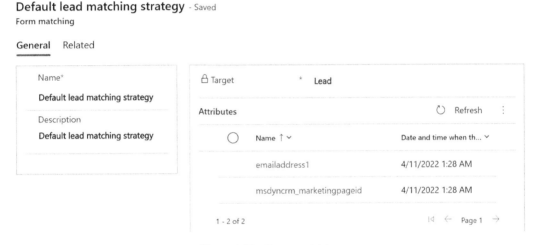

Figure 1.20 – Form matching

Commonly used matching strategies include email addresses and/or phone numbers. You always have one default contact matching and one default lead matching strategy, but you can also have multiple types of strategies that you can use on different landing pages.

Lead matching strategies

In the **Email Lead Matching Strategy (Default)** area (*Figure 1.21*), you define how to connect the leads coming from **LinkedIn** into your system, with the choice of always creating a lead or enabling contact creation. You need to set which matching leads fields you want to use:

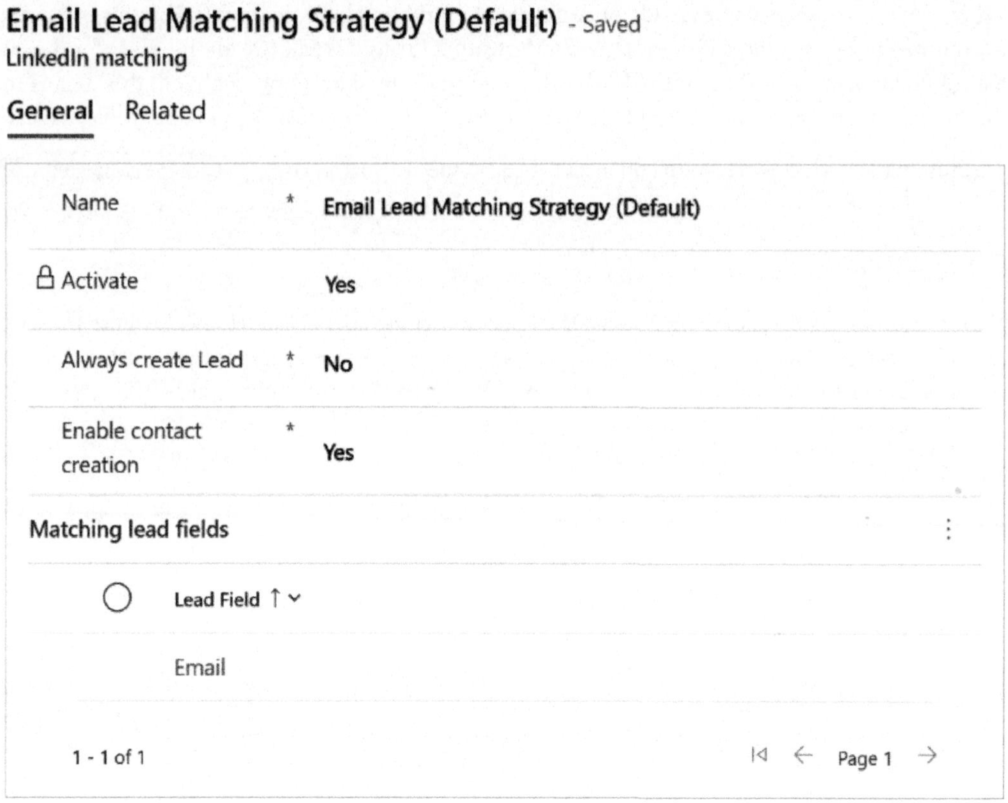

Email Lead Matching Strategy (Default) - Saved
LinkedIn matching

General   Related

Name	*	**Email Lead Matching Strategy (Default)**
🔒 Activate		**Yes**
Always create Lead	*	**No**
Enable contact creation	*	**Yes**

Matching lead fields   ⋮

○	Lead Field ↑ ˅
	Email

1 - 1 of 1 |◁ ← Page 1 →

Figure 1.21 – LinkedIn matching

LinkedIn field mapping

In the **Active LinkedIn Field Mappings** area (*Figure 1.22*), you define which field from LinkedIn is connected to which field in Dataverse. The reason you do this is to be able to collect all the data from LinkedIn and place it in the correct fields in Dynamics 365 Marketing. If you don't map them, the system doesn't know where to store the information and just ignores it:

Active LinkedIn Field Mappings* ⌄   ⊞⚙   ▽

○	Name ↑ ⌄	Lead Field ⌄	Created On ⌄
	City	City	10/30/2022 2:21 PM
	Company name	Company Name	10/30/2022 2:21 PM
	Company size	Company size	10/30/2022 2:21 PM
	Country	Country/Region	10/30/2022 2:21 PM
	Degree	Degree	10/30/2022 2:21 PM
	Email	Email	10/30/2022 2:21 PM
	Field of study	Field of study	10/30/2022 2:21 PM

1 - 19 of 19

Figure 1.22 – Active LinkedIn Field Mappings

Data management

One of the big advantages of working in the Microsoft ecosystem is the possibility to connect to other Microsoft systems. In this section, we're going to go through the Customer Insights connector, analytics configuration, and dataset configuration.

Customer Insights connector

The **Customer Insights** connector (*Figure 1.23*) lets you connect Dynamics 365 Marketing to Dynamics 365 Customer Insights. Customer Insights is a system that gives you a 360-degree view of your customers using data coming from multiple systems across your company. This gives you a unique opportunity to get insights and helps create segments that you can use in Dynamics 365 Marketing. You will learn more about Customer Insights and the benefits of integrating it into Dynamics 365 Marketing in *Chapter 10, Power Platform*:

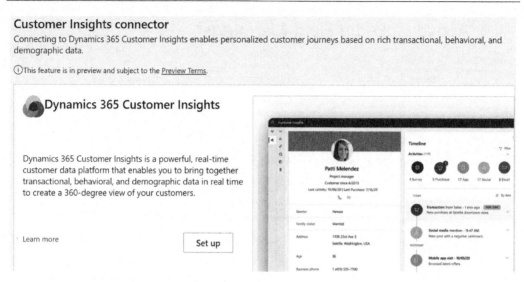

Figure 1.23 – Customer Insights connector

Analytics configuration

In the **Analytics configuration** area, you can add your existing **Azure Blob storage**. Many companies connect multiple systems with their Azure Blob storage, such as Power BI or other analytics systems.

Dataset configuration

Imagine you have a lot of custom tables in **Dataverse**, and you want to do any of the following:

- Use those custom tables in queries in your segments
- Want to show them as dynamic data in your email messages
- Want to use the column values of these tables in lead scoring
- Want to export data to Azure Blob storage

To do so, you have to go into your **Dataset configuration** area (*Figure 1.24*) and add your custom tables:

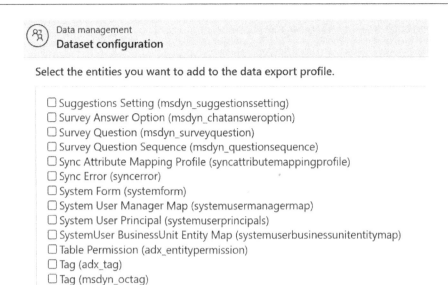

Figure 1.24 – Dataset configuration

It's important to know that if you add tables to the configuration, you cannot remove them again later. To be able to synchronize these tables, you will need storage space and processing time, so you should never sync tables that you will not use. Be sure that you know which specific tables you need for your work with analytics, dynamic email content, segmentation criteria, and lead scoring.

Other settings – Feature switches

In the **Feature switches** area (*Figure 1.25*), you can enable or deactivate several features such as integration with **Customer Voice**, the usage of event registration forms, and the required consent level to use the smart scheduler. Remember that after you've made changes in the settings for the different features, you need to click **Save** in the top-right corner.

The feature switches are always changing with the new features that are coming. As of August 2022, the following features are available:

- **Business unit scoping**: If your company has several business units (or perhaps you have two different companies in one system), you can differentiate between the marketing process and data for the different business units.

- **Event registration forms**: The event registration forms are useful if you're using event management in Dynamics 365 Marketing and want to have participants register through your forms and fully utilize the system.

- **Updated customer journey designer**: This offers new features for designing customer journeys.

- **New canvas experience and content blocks**: When you enable this feature, you get the new and improved version of creation and content blocks.

- **Brand profiles**: Brand profiles are great if you have different brands that you do marketing for. When you turn this option on, you get the choice to simply choose different brand profiles for a marketing email, for example.

- **Conditional content in email editor**: This feature is only available in real-time marketing. You can now create personalized messages much more easily than previously.

- **Data sharing program**: You need to be very careful with this feature if you're in the EU. This gives Microsoft permission to review and access your customer data to develop better AI models.

- **Customer voice integration**: This is the feature that enables Dynamics 365 Customer Voice integrations with Marketing.

- **Smart scheduler**: This lets you specify which level of consent is required from your customers to use the smart scheduler, which allows you to send emails to your different customers at their preferred times:

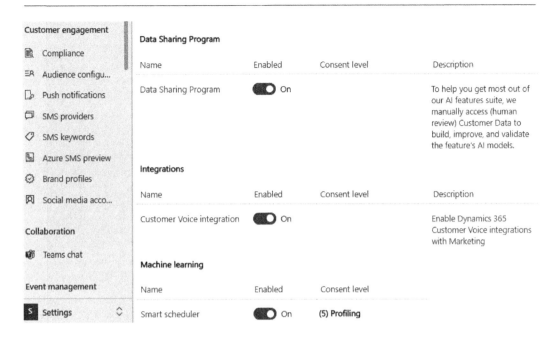

Figure 1.25 – Feature switches, parts one and two

With that, we've gone through all the system settings and made sure our system is set up correctly. We've tailored the setup to our company's needs. Now, we're ready to start using it. One of the first things we should create is templates.

Templates

Templates will make your life easier once you start using the system. Every time I do training or talk to customers, I always stress the importance of creating **templates**, whether it's email templates, customer journey templates, or landing page templates. It's a way to make sure that everyone is using the same layout and graphic design and just generally makes it easier to not have to start from scratch every time.

There are some important settings in this area we're going to go through – that is, content settings, form fields, and email templates. We will also take a look at some templates specifically for outbound and real-time marketing.

Content settings

Content settings is where you register companies' addresses, social media URLs, subscription center, and **Forward to a friend** details. We'll go through the subscription center and **Forward to a friend** in depth in *Chapter 4, Managing Marketing Forms, Pages, and Websites*. These will then be used when you send out your marketing emails. If you have multiple companies using the same Marketing solution, you can use different content settings (*Figure 1.26*) for the different companies:

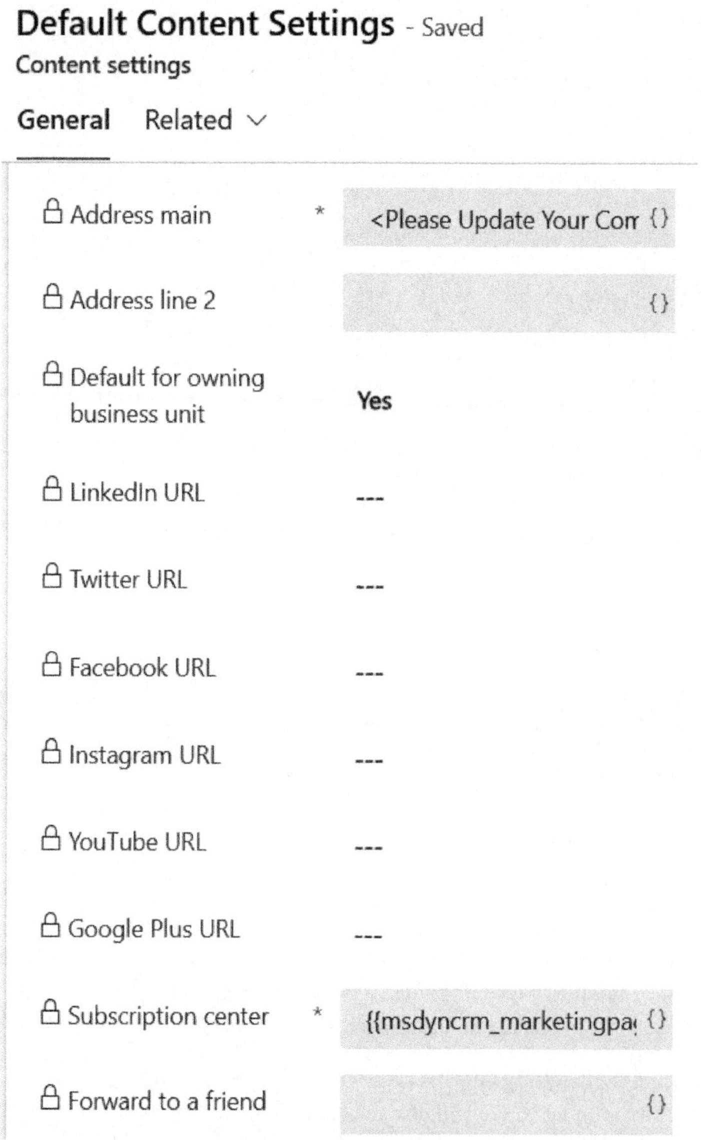

Default Content Settings - Saved
Content settings

General　Related ∨

🔒 Address main ＊ `<Please Update Your Com {}`

🔒 Address line 2 `{}`

🔒 Default for owning
business unit **Yes**

🔒 LinkedIn URL ---

🔒 Twitter URL ---

🔒 Facebook URL ---

🔒 Instagram URL ---

🔒 YouTube URL ---

🔒 Google Plus URL ---

🔒 Subscription center ＊ `{{msdyncrm_marketingpa {}`

🔒 Forward to a friend `{}`

Figure 1.26 – Content settings

Form fields

To be able to store information in a form, you need to create a form field and connect this to the correct field on your contact or lead table (*Figure 1.27*). Several of the most used fields (such as name, email, and address) are already created by default, but if you want to add others, you need to create the relevant form fields before you can use them in your marketing forms:

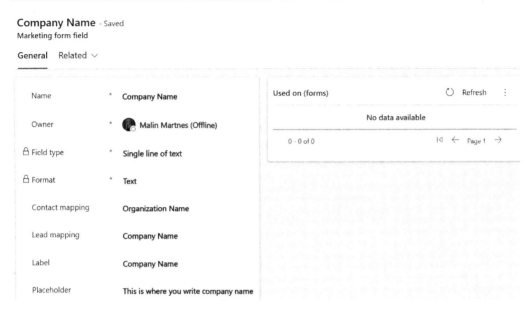

Figure 1.27 – Form fields

Email templates

Your emails are one of the most important places to create templates. You want all your emails that are sent out to look somewhat the same, in line with your company's established graphical profile, and templates are a good way of making sure of this. You can create template emails with different layouts ready for use by everyone who needs to create any type of email (*Figure 1.28*). This way, you can just focus on creating relevant content and not have to worry about the actual layout of the email each time:

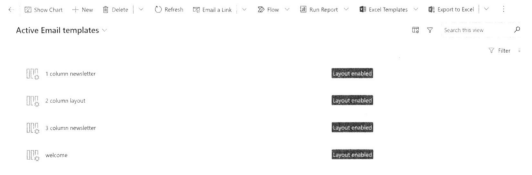

Figure 1.28 – Email templates

Outbound specific

As of November 2022, most templates are created in the **Outbound** section of Dynamics 365 Marketing. Let's go through which templates you can create from the outbound area.

Customer journey templates

Let's say you want to create a simple **customer journey** based on how you run your events and how you communicate with the attendees from Dynamics 365 Marketing. If you use templates (*Figure 1.29*), you can have all of this set up for you so that you don't have to start from scratch. If you start from nothing, it is easy to miss some important steps in your communication – you might miss a reminder the day before the event starts, or you might miss the evaluation afterward. If you create a customer journey template, then you can make sure that everyone follows and creates the same type of journey for all the same types of events:

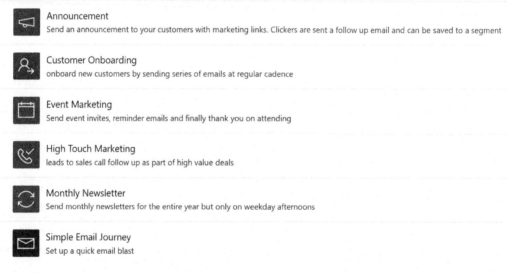

Figure 1.29 – Outbound customer journey templates

Forms, pages, and websites

Other types of templates you can make are **forms, pages, and websites** (*Figure 1.30*). For example, if you do a Christmas campaign each year with the same form, the same page, and the same website, that's a perfect reason to create a template:

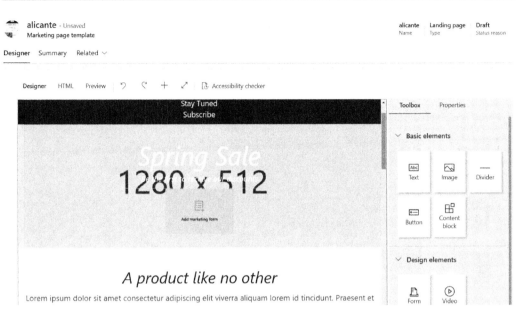

Figure 1.30 – Marketing website template

I often use event-form templates (*Figure 1.31*) to make it easier for people to register for events. Other contact forms are also good to have templates for:

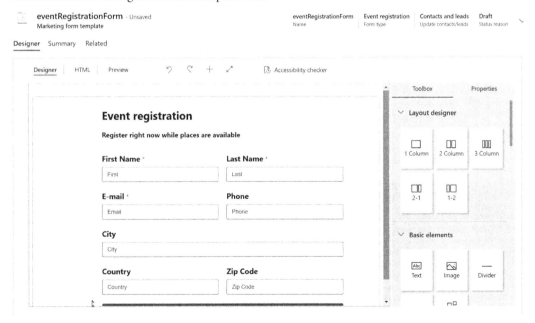

Figure 1.31 – Event form template

Segments

Segments are another type of template you can create, as shown in *Figure 1.32*. There are some segments that you will likely want to use several times, such as to find out who attended an event. If you create a template with the most used segments, it will make it easier to create that segment in the future:

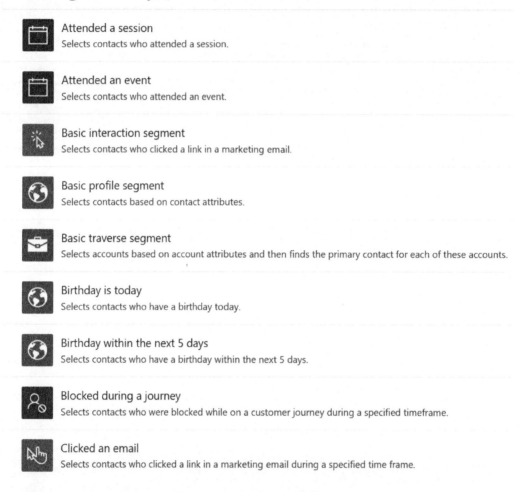

Active segment templates ∨

Attended a session
Selects contacts who attended a session.

Attended an event
Selects contacts who attended an event.

Basic interaction segment
Selects contacts who clicked a link in a marketing email.

Basic profile segment
Selects contacts based on contact attributes.

Basic traverse segment
Selects accounts based on account attributes and then finds the primary contact for each of these accounts.

Birthday is today
Selects contacts who have a birthday today.

Birthday within the next 5 days
Selects contacts who have a birthday within the next 5 days.

Blocked during a journey
Selects contacts who were blocked while on a customer journey during a specified timeframe.

Clicked an email
Selects contacts who clicked a link in a marketing email during a specified time frame.

Figure 1.32 – Segment templates

Maybe you have one core criterion you always want to have in all your segments. You can have that as your template and create all your new segments from that template, making sure the base criterion is always in place.

Activities

You can also create **calls, tasks, and appointments** as templates. This way, you can use them in a customer journey. If, for example, you have a customer journey that starts with a lead coming into your system, then you want to automatically register a call to the new potential customer to get more information on their needs, and this process will use a call template. Another use for this is if you want to make sure you run credit checks on all potential customers, and you have one person that does this whenever a new lead comes into the system. In this context, you can create a task for each lead that comes in for the credit checker to go through.

As you can see, there are several templates you should consider setting up in your system before you start using it. All of these templates can make it easier for you to work with the system in the future.

Asset library

Pictures, videos, and graphical content are very important for anyone working in marketing, and your asset library is where you control all this. Let's go through how Dynamics 365 Marketing lets you work with pictures, videos, documents, and content blocks in outbound and real-time marketing.

Outbound

Because outbound and real-time marketing are different, there are different ways of working with graphical content. We're going to dive deeper into the differences in *Chapter 6, Outbound Customer Journeys*. First, let's go through the outbound way of working with this.

Keywords

Keywords are a terrific way of keeping track of your pictures in outbound marketing. You will have to tag each picture with the correct keyword. To search for a picture, you can either use the keyword or search for the name of the picture.

Pictures

In outbound marketing, you can add **pictures** you want to use in your emails or pages. You can add keywords for pictures to make sure you can easily find the different pictures.

Video

You cannot host a **video** directly in outbound marketing; you can only link to a video that's hosted somewhere else.

Content blocks

To make it even easier for your marketers to create content, you can create **content blocks** (*Figure 1.33*) they can reuse. If you always want to use the same type of picture in the header, then you can create a content block to be used in emails with the right format for the picture, or maybe you want to create a footer to be used on all pages with the correct information. This can be created with a content block; you must go live with a content block before you can use it.

You need to specify where the content block will be available – that is, out of email, forms, and/or pages. You can also specify if the content block is protected, meaning that only certain security roles will be able to edit the content block:

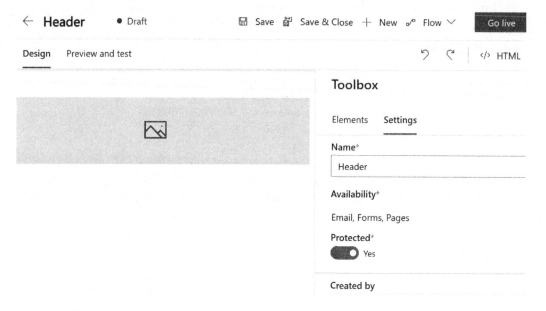

Figure 1.33 – Content block

Real-time marketing-specific configuration

Now that we've taken a look at how to work with graphical content in outbound marketing, let's go through how this is done in real-time marketing.

Tags

In the real-time marketing **asset library**, it has been made a lot easier to find your pictures by using tags. Dynamics 365 Marketing uses an AI to automatically tag your pictures, and you can also add your own tags if needed.

Pictures

Pictures are probably the main focus of your asset library. These are the images you want to add to your emails, forms, landing pages, and websites. You can upload one picture, several pictures at once, or a whole folder. You can see the pictures in my asset library in the following screenshot:

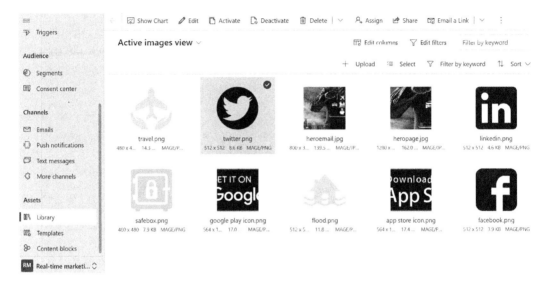

Figure 1.34 – Asset library

You're most likely going to have a lot of pictures, but your tagging will make sure that you can find them again when you need them. If you make sure you name your pictures correctly and you tag them with something that makes sense, then other people will be able to access them efficiently and use the correct format of, for example, your logo without difficulty.

Video

In real-time marketing, you can upload your videos and use them in your marketing efforts. This will upload the **video** to your marketing Azure Blob storage, so you don't have to worry about where to store your video so that your customers can access it.

Documents

There are so many use cases for **documents** in marketing. You might create a white paper that you want to send to your customers or a presentation that needs to be sent to your event participants, or maybe you want to send some meeting minutes to your potential customers. All of this is possible by uploading your documents to the asset library.

Copying files from outbound

Because companies already use the outbound marketing library, Microsoft has made it easier to copy all content from outbound marketing over to the real-time marketing asset library. From outbound marketing, you can click on the **Copy all files into Real-time marketing** option. You can just copy all your files – there's no need to select the ones you want to copy.

With that, you've seen how Dynamics 365 Marketing works with pictures, video, and other elements you can use in your emails and other content. Having control over these elements will make it easier for you to have oversight over the creation and presentation of graphics for your company.

Summary

There are many settings you should go through in Dynamics 365 Marketing to make sure you have the best possible system set up before you use the system in production. You need to go through and be familiar with each of these settings. This chapter is good to keep in mind and come back to when you're doing an implementation or before you go live with your system, to make sure you've remembered all the important settings.

In this chapter, you learned about the different settings you need to go through. You saw how you need to set up Dynamics 365 Marketing to use it properly. We also went through how you can work with templates to make future content creation easier. All of this is information you will need every time you implement Dynamics 365 Marketing. If you go through everything you've learned in this chapter every time you implement Dynamics 365, you're going to create a fully functioning system that is tailored to each company.

In the next chapter, we're going to dig deeper into the data of your system and take a look at leads, contacts, and accounts. We're going to look at what they are and how they are set up out of the box.

Questions

The following are some questions that will help you gauge your understanding of the topics discussed in this chapter. The answers are available in the *Assessments* section at the end of the book.

1. Can you turn off the tables you don't need for synchronization on data tables?

    (a) Yes

    (b) No

2. What are the different types of templates in outbound marketing?

    (a) Email

    (b) Form

    (c) Pages

(d) Websites

(e) Event

(f) Segment

(g) Customer journeys

3. What tables can a landing page update?

(a) Contacts

(b) Leads

(c) Contacts and leads

(d) Contacts, leads, and custom tables

4. Can you send emails from any domains in Dynamics 365 Marketing?

(a) Yes

(b) Yes, but you need to connect the domain first

(c) No

5. Do you have one consent center for both outbound and real-time marketing?

(a) Yes

(b) No

6. Which social media sites can you connect to?

(a) Facebook

(b) Google Plus

(c) Google Ads

(d) Twitter

(e) Pinterest

(f) LinkedIn

(g) Instagram

7. Which third-party webinar provider can you connect to?

(a) On24

(b) Microsoft Teams

(c) Zoom

(d) Slack

8. If you have a LinkedIn Lead Gen Form and want to add that to your system, what do you need to do, and in which order?

    (a) Sign in to LinkedIn with your company profile, then connect to the correct LinkedIn Lead Gen Form

    (b) Sign in to LinkedIn with your profile, then connect to the correct LinkedIn Lead Gen Form

    (c) Sign in to LinkedIn with your profile that's connected to your company's profile and the LinkedIn Lead Gen Form

9. Which fields can you define your lead matching strategy on?

    (a) Email

    (b) First name

    (c) Last name

    (d) First and last name

    (e) Email, first name, and last name

    (f) Any field you want

10. You can only have global double opt-in.

    (a) Yes

    (b) No

11. When is a lead sent to Sales?

    (a) When a lead gets a lead score of 100 points

    (b) When a lead comes into the system

    (c) When a lead hits the sales-ready score set by lead scoring

    (d) When a lead is set as sales-ready by marketing

12. You can store documents in outbound marketing.

    (a) Yes

    (b) No

13. You can store videos in real-time marketing.

    (a) Yes

    (b) No

2
Managing Leads, Accounts, and Contacts

How do you make sure that everyone you need to market to is in your database, that everyone is registered correctly, and that you are allowed to have everyone registered? How do you know whether someone is a potential customer or an existing customer? Would you target your marketing differently at these two different types of people? The answer, by the way, should be yes. Yes, you absolutely would do marketing differently for a potential customer and an existing customer.

Microsoft, together with Adobe and SAP, is part of the **Open Data Initiative** (**ODI**), and they have all agreed on a **Common Data Model** (**CDM**). The ODI and CDM are a way to make sure that a lot of systems that are used in IT are based on the same types of tables and named in the same way, making it easier to do integrations even when you have two systems from different companies.

One of the first things I always do when going to a new customer is write down what information they need on **contact**, **lead**, and **account**. Almost no customer I have ever dealt with has just used the standard columns. Every company has something unique to their customers that they want or need to register in their system.

In this chapter, we will go through what leads are and how you create and manage them. We're going to look at contacts and why they're so important for the system. How businesses are registered in the system, and how can you use companies to do marketing? Because Dataverse is a relational database, we're also going to look at relationships, and how leads, contacts, and accounts are all connected.

Last but not least, we're going to take a look at the lead life cycle and see what happens to a person from the second they contact us until they are an existing customer; we continue to do marketing from start to finish.

This chapter covers the following areas:

- Understanding and managing leads
- Understanding and managing contacts

- Understanding and managing accounts
- Relationships
- The lead life cycle

By the end of the chapter, you'll have a good understanding of what leads, contacts, and accounts are. You'll also know how to manage these in relation to each other and understand the lead life cycle and how that affects your leads process.

Understanding and managing leads

Your leads table is important whether you're talking about sales or marketing, but there are some differences between how the two use leads. Let's take a closer look at leads, how they're important in the system, and how to create them.

Defining leads

In **Dynamics 365**, there are different definitions for leads depending on which applications you are working with. In Dynamics 365, you have a **sales lead** and a **marketing lead**. Let's go through the definition for both of these.

A sales lead

A sales lead in **Dynamics 365 Sales** is someone that has an interest in your company's offerings, nothing concrete. You know they are interested in something, but you're not sure what. You might not have information about the customer or the company, and you might not know which product they are interested in. All you know is that they have expressed some sort of interest in your company.

A marketing lead

In **Dynamics 365 Marketing**, a marketing lead is someone who has an interest in getting information from your company. This might be a person that will be interested in your offerings in the future, or maybe they just want to gain knowledge about your company and your company's offerings. A marketing lead can be qualified as a sales lead. A sales lead is a lead that salespeople should prioritize in their list. A lead that comes from marketing has most likely got information from you and has some knowledge about your company and products, thus having a shorter sales cycle.

Creating a lead

Before we start looking deeper into what a lead can contain, let's first look at how we can manually create a lead:

1. In the **Outbound Marketing** area of Dynamics 365 Marketing, you will find **Leads** under **Lead management**, as shown in *Figure 2.1*:

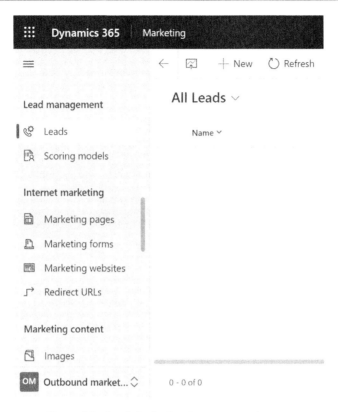

Figure 2.1 – Leads in the Lead management menu

2. When you've found the area for leads, you can create a new lead manually by clicking the + **New** button in the top menu, as shown in *Figure 2.2*:

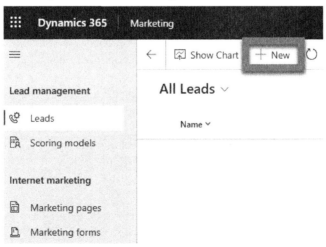

Figure 2.2 – Clicking + New to create a new lead

3. When you click the **+ New** button, a new form will open, and you will be able to add all the information you have on your lead and save the lead to your Dataverse environment.

You can have different forms for different areas of the business, and you can customize these forms to best suit your company. Let us take a look at what you get out of the box in Dynamics 365 Marketing.

The out-of-the-box form in Dynamics 365 Marketing

Because there are so many varieties of needs from different companies, I'm going to go through the out-of-the-box-form for a lead (*Figure 2.3*), so you can see how much information there is before you start customizing the system:

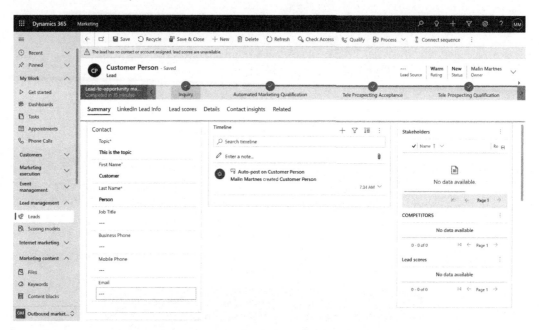

Figure 2.3 – The out-of-the-box form for a lead

On the left side of the form (*Figure 2.4*), you have information about the person and company for this lead. You need to fill in the name of the person, which is mandatory information. You can register information about the company, but that's not required information. Another mandatory column is the topic, which is a short description of the lead. This column will also be copied to the opportunity record when the lead is qualified and becomes an opportunity:

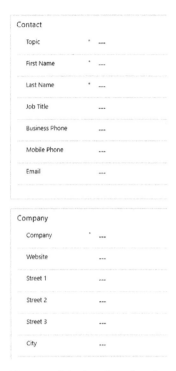

Figure 2.4 – The out-of-the-box form for a lead – left side

In the middle of the form (*Figure 2.5*), you have the timeline where all activities are registered. If a person registers a phone call or an appointment, or any kind of activity, it will show in the timeline:

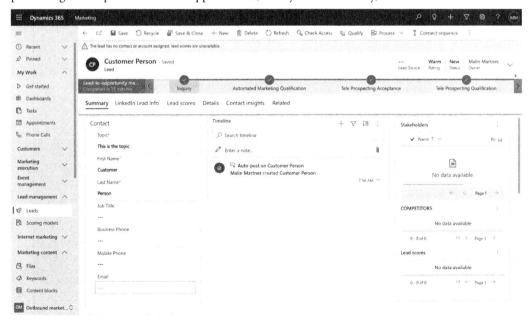

Figure 2.5 – The out-of-the-box form for a lead – middle

In the timeline, you can see interactions from both outbound and real-time marketing. So all the emails that you send and other interactions will show on the timeline together with other activities.

The right side of the form is for all the related tables, as shown in *Figure 2.6*. Here, you'll find stakeholders and competitors and see the lead scores:

Figure 2.6 – The out-of-the-box form for a lead – right side

You also have different tabs where you can see different information, such as LinkedIn lead info, digging deeper into lead scores, more details, and contact insights. **Contact insights** (*Figure 2.7*) is where you can find all the interactions the lead has from your marketing efforts in the system from outbound marketing:

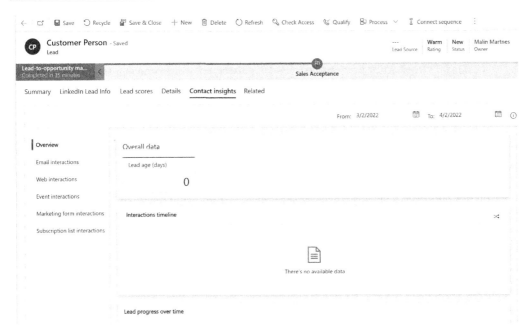

Figure 2.7 – Lead – Contact insights

Now we've gone through the out-of-the-box lead form; you can see that there is a lot of information you can register. Make sure you get all the information needed for your company to have the relevant information for capturing your leads. Next, let's move on to contacts and take a look at what's relevant there and how that differs from leads.

Understanding and managing contacts

Contacts are the core focus of your company. These are all the most important people that you have registered. They are your customers, event participants, competitors, and every other person you need to keep track of. Let's take a look at how we define a contact, how we create a contact, and how the contact form looks out of the box.

Defining contacts

In Dynamics 365, every person in your system is registered as a **contact**. However, in Dynamics 365 Marketing, you have to know who your marketing contacts are because they impact your licensing. If you've worked with Dynamics 365 for years, you might not agree with me. You might say that a person can also be just a lead. In the Microsoft world, a lead is an interest, not a person. A lead can be connected to an existing contact or create a new contact, but it always creates an opportunity when it's qualified. Before you can know who your marketing contacts are, you need to be aware of what a marketing contact is. In this section, we're going to go through both **regular contacts** and the information you have on those and **marketing contacts** and how to know who they are.

A regular contact

A **regular contact** is any person that you have registered in your system. If you're in Europe, you will have to consider GDPR rules and legislation and cannot register everyone you want in your system. You need to have a reason to have them in your system, and you have to ask before you add them. A regular contact can be someone that has bought something from your company, someone who you have exchanged business cards with from a trade fair and registered, someone you're working together with on a project, someone who's been at your event, and everyone who is a customer of the company.

A marketing contact

A **marketing contact** is someone you have had a marketing interaction with in the past 12 months. A marketing interaction can be an email, SMS, or push notification. You can have thousands of regular contacts in your system, but only the marketing contacts are counted when it comes to licensing. Every marketing contact in Dynamics 365 Marketing is also always a regular contact. If you have 1,000 contacts in your system but only have marketing interactions with 300 of them, then your license only needs to cover the 300 marketing contacts.

Creating a contact

Before we continue looking deeper into what a contact can contain, let's see how we manually create a contact:

1. In the Outbound Marketing area of Dynamics 365 Marketing, you will find **Contacts** under **Customers**, as shown in *Figure 2.8*:

Figure 2.8 – Contacts in the Customers area

2. When you've found the area for contacts, you can create a new contact by clicking the + **New** button in the top menu, as shown in *Figure 2.9*:

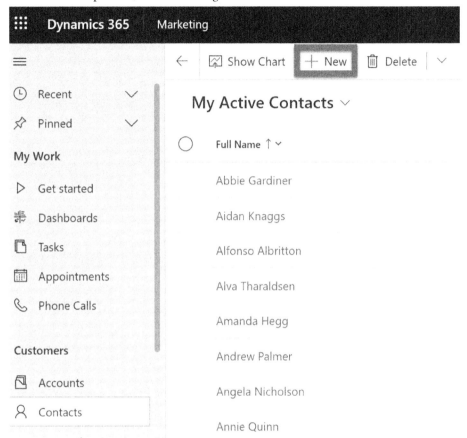

Figure 2.9 – Clicking + New to create a new contact

3. When you click the + **New** button, a new form will open, and you will be able to add all the information you have on your contact and save the contact to your Dataverse environment.

You can have different forms for different business areas, and you can customize all forms to best suit your company. Let us look at what you get out of the box in Dynamics 365 Marketing.

The out-of-the-box form in Dynamics 365 Marketing

As it is with leads, contacts also have a lot of information in the out-of-the-box form, even more so than leads. Let's take a look at the out-of-the-box form (*Figure 2.10*) and see what kind of information we have and the different uses for it:

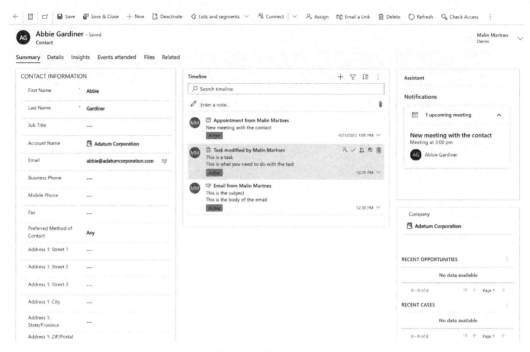

Figure 2.10 – The out-of-the-box contact form

The **Last Name** field is mandatory; you can't save the form without knowing the last name of the contact. **First Name** is recommended, but not mandatory. You should register as much information as you need to have on each contact; if **Fax** is relevant to your company, keep it; otherwise, delete the column from the form.

As with leads, you have the timeline in the middle of the form, as shown in *Figure 2.11*:

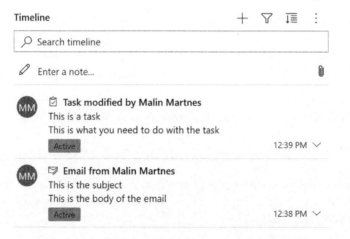

Figure 2.11 – The out-of-the-box form timeline on a contact

At the top right, you have the assistant. This is an AI feature from Microsoft that will notify you when something relevant happens. In *Figure 2.12* you can see that you have a notification about a new meeting with a contact. The Assistant gives you information about relevant activities to make it easier for you to keep track of your activities with the customer.

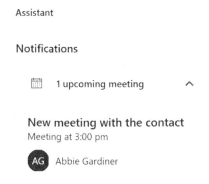

Figure 2.12 – The out-of-the-box form assistant

You also have other related information, such as which company the contact is connected to and some information from the company. You can also see opportunities, cases, and entitlements, as shown in *Figure 2.13*:

Figure 2.13 – The out-of-the-box form-related tables

Now you've seen all the information that is in the out-of-the-box form for a contact. You should always go through all the columns and be sure you're registering all the information that your company needs to know about the accounts.

Understanding and managing accounts

If you're only working with private customers, you most likely won't have much need for accounts. However, you might want to use them to register information about your partner companies or suppliers. If you're working with companies, then it's crucial to register the correct information about your accounts. Let's take a closer look at how Microsoft defines accounts in Dynamics 365 Marketing, how to create an account, and how it looks out of the box.

Defining accounts

Your accounts are all the companies in your system. These can be your customers, business associates, companies you work together with, or your suppliers. Even businesses that purely work in the **business-to-consumer (B2C)** market might need to create accounts. If you do **business-to-business (B2B)** marketing, your focus area will be accounts, as this is a very important table in your system.

Creating an account

As we've done with contacts and leads, let's see how we can manually create an account before looking at the out-of-the-box form:

1. In the Outbound Marketing area of Dynamics 365 Marketing, you will find **Accounts**, above **Contacts**, in the **Customers** section, as shown in *Figure 2.14*:

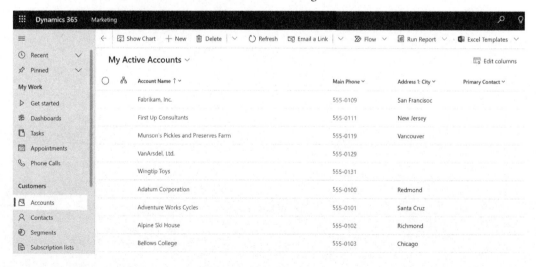

Figure 2.14 – Accounts in the Customers area

2. When you've found the area for accounts, you can create a new account by clicking the + **New** button in the top menu, as shown in *Figure 2.15*:

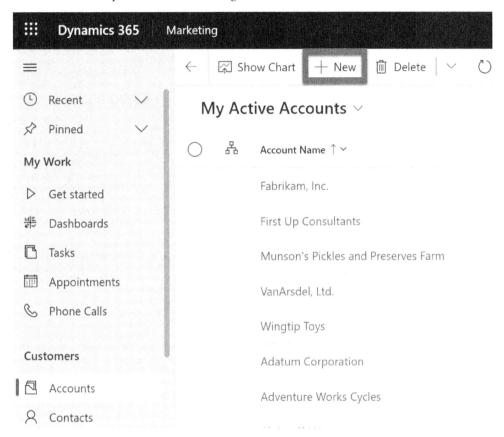

Figure 2.15 – Clicking + New to create a new account

3. When you click the + **New** button, a new form will open, and you will be able to add all the information you have on your account and save the account to your Dataverse environment.

As with leads and contacts, you can have different forms for different needs, and you can customize all forms to best suit your company. Let us look at what you get out of the box in Dynamics 365 Marketing.

The out-of-the-box form in Dynamics 365 Marketing

Once again, accounts also have an out-of-the-box form, as shown in *Figure 2.16*, so let's dig deeper into it:

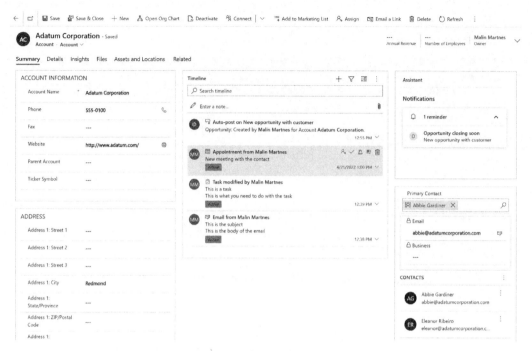

Figure 2.16 – The out-of-the-box form for an account

For an account, the account name is the only mandatory field, but I highly recommend registering more information, such as contact information or address, which you can find on the left side of the form. Your timeline for activities is in the middle. It's important to know that the activities you register to a contact connected to the account will also show on the account timeline. If you send an email to a contact, this will be shown on the timeline, as shown in *Figure 2.17*:

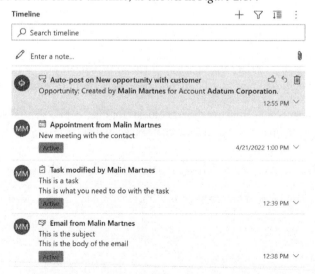

Figure 2.17 – The out-of-the-box form account timeline

Accounts, the same as contacts, have the AI assistant and related tables on the right side, as shown in the following screenshot:

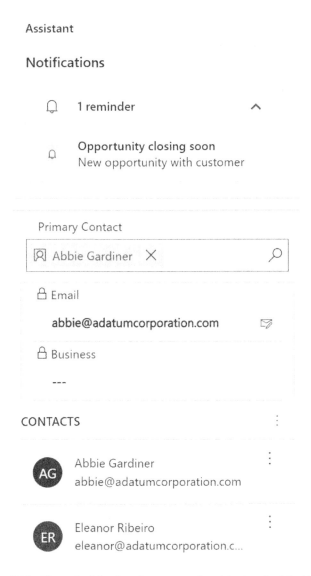

Figure 2.18 – The out-of-the-box form account assistant and related tables

As you can see, there are a lot of similarities in the way the forms are built for leads, contacts, and accounts. Once you understand one setup, it's easy to understand the others. In accounts, you should gather all the information you need to have about the companies you work with. Now, let's take a look at how all of these are connected with relationships.

Relationships – connecting everything

All the previous tables we've talked about are connected through **relationships**. A contact can be employed and connected to one account, and an account can have several contacts employed and associated with it. One contact can be connected with many events, and all the events will have several contacts related to them. Dataverse is your **relational database** and has every possible relationship available. Let's take a closer look at the different types of relationships you can find in Dataverse.

One-to-many or many-to-one (1:N/N:1)

One-to-many and **many-to-one** are two sides of the same relationship. It's when one row can be connected to just one other row, but the other row can be connected to several rows from the same table. One contact can only be connected to one account, but on the account row, we can have many contacts connected to it, as shown in *Figure 2.18*:

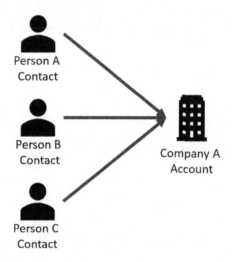

Figure 2.19 – The relationship between contacts and accounts

On an account, you have one lookup field for a primary contact. Only one person can be the primary contact and can be connected to the account through a lookup field, as shown at the top of *Figure 2.20*. All other contacts related to this account are shown at the bottom, as shown in *Figure 2.20*. This way of showing related tables is called a subgrid. For example, it's when an account has many contacts registered to it.

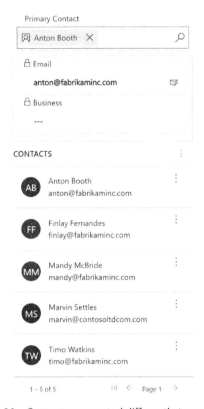

Figure 2.20 – Contacts connected differently to an account

Many-to-many (N:N)

When you want to connect events with contacts, you need to be able to connect many events with many contacts. This works by creating a **many-to-many** (**N:N**) relationship. If you're running an amusement park and you want to register which contacts go on which rides, many contacts can be registered to many rides, and every ride will have many contacts registered to it, as shown in *Figure 2.21*:

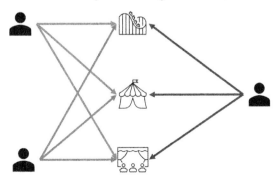

Figure 2.21 – Contacts connected to rides

The N:N relationship actually consists of two N:1 relationships combined into an intersect table, as shown in *Figure 2.22*. These two tables are connected with one table where you get two relationships to be able to connect the two:

Figure 2.22 – Contact and ride connected with an intersect table

As you can see, there are many different ways of connecting different tables together. This is one of the biggest advantages of having a relational database, such as Dataverse. When your tables are connected, it's easier to see how everything works together. You can see that a contact is working for a specific account, or that they've been to an event. This helps you get a complete picture of your contacts and everything they're connected with.

The lead life cycle

Once your marketing lead has been **sales qualified**, **salespeople** have to contact them. When the salespeople have gained more insight and have more concrete information about the lead and their needs, they can qualify them.

A lead can be connected to an existing contact and/or account. If it's not connected to existing contacts or accounts, new ones are created. When you qualify a lead in Dynamics 365 Sales, it will always create an **opportunity** where salespeople will work further on the sales process and make sure that the lead goes through the company's sales process and becomes an actual sale.

One very important feature of the lead life cycle is lead scoring. Let's take a deeper look at how this works in Dynamics 365 Marketing.

Lead scoring

In order to prioritize the leads you have in your system and to know which lead you need to do more work with, you can implement **automated lead scoring**. **Lead scoring** can be helpful for your marketers to know what information you need to send to each lead. It can also be helpful for salespeople to know how interested each lead is in your company and your company's offers. To be able to use lead scoring on a lead, it needs to be connected to a contact or an account.

For each condition, you have to specify the properties to say what should trigger the action (increasing or decreasing points). You can use one or several expressions to get the criteria you want.

You need to give the condition a display name. This is just so you will recognize it. You then find the entity (table) you want to apply the expression to. In *Figure 2.23*, you can see that we've chosen the lead's parent account (**Lead.Parent account**), which is the account this lead is connected to. We then find the **Industry** field (column) and say that it should equal **Business Services**. As seen in the following screenshot, every lead connected with an account in the Business Services industry will get a five-point increase in lead scoring:

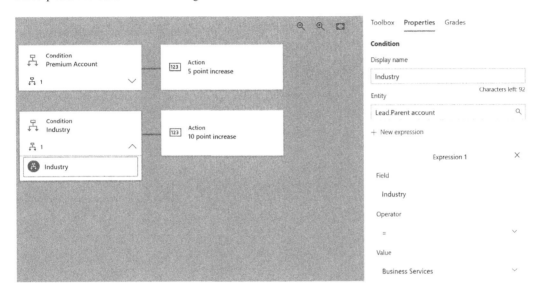

Figure 2.23 – Lead scoring model condition properties

It's important to know that the entity list only includes relevant entities that can be related to a lead record and the lead itself. Say you want to add points for every contact that has registered for an event and has registered their phone number. First, you find the table event registration in the entity list, then type a period (this is how you find the related table), and then find the contact. This way, you find the event registration and can get information that is registered on the contact. You can now find expressions if the contact has registered for an event.

If you have several expressions, your model will go through each of the expressions and score accordingly. You can set different grades for lead scoring, as you can see in *Figure 2.24*. When the lead is ready for sales, you can add new score levels and different points to each different scoring model you use:

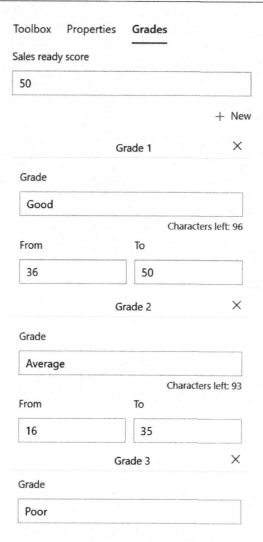

Figure 2.24 – Lead scoring grades

It is important to note that a lead scoring model needs to go live before the scores start to gather.

Now, let's take a look at the different lead scoring models and how you can use them.

Different lead scoring models

Different companies require different types of lead scoring. If you work with B2C, you might want to differentiate between geographic areas, but if you work with B2B, you might need to differentiate between the accounts' geographic areas. You need different lead scoring models to cover your various needs. Let's go through some of the most used styles of models.

Behavior lead scoring model

A lead scoring model focusing on behavioral information, such as whether you have clicked a link or opened an email, is a behavior-type lead scoring model. In *Figure 2.25*, you can see some conditions, such as **Evaluate Email Engagement** and **Evaluate Disengagement**, which increase and decrease the lead scoring:

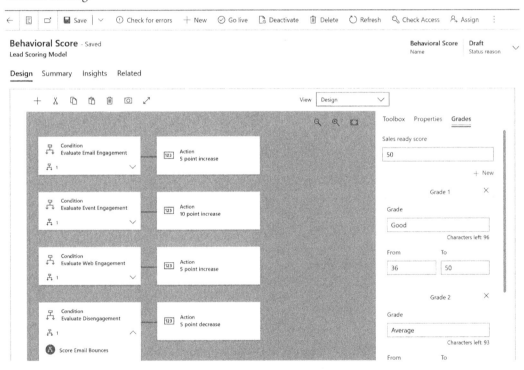

Figure 2.25 – Lead scoring – a behavioral scoring model

Demographic lead scoring model

If you want to differentiate your leads based on where they live or which industry they work in, use a **demographic-type lead scoring model** (*Figure 2.26*). Maybe your preferred person to work with is a **chief technical officer** (**CTO**) working in a private company of over 2,000 employees. You want to give them a high score because these are your preferred leads to work with. This can be achieved with a demographic-type lead scoring model:

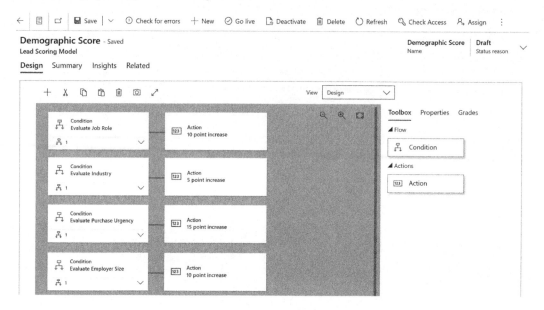

Figure 2.26 – Lead scoring – a demographic scoring model

Firmographic lead scoring model

If your work is focused on B2B sales, you might need to score your leads based on the information registered on the account. If a new lead is registered in your system and the company is a gold partner in a preferred industry, this will automatically give your lead extra points, as you can see in *Figure 2.27*. This is a person you want to talk to, and you want to have a high score so that they are prioritized and contacted:

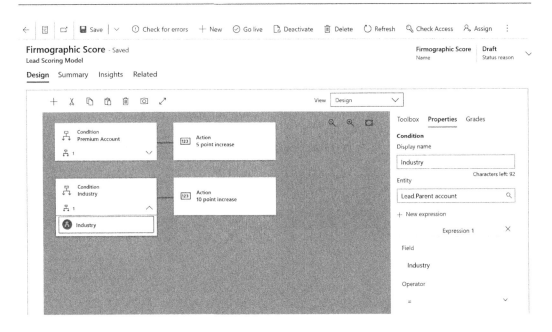

Figure 2.27 – Lead scoring – a firmographic scoring model

When the lead scoring model is live, you can see all the scores from the related tab – **Lead scores**, as shown in *Figure 2.28*:

New Lead - Saved
Lead Scoring Model

Design   Summary   Insights   **Lead scores**   Related ∨

🖾 Show Chart   ○ Refresh   ⚙ Flow ∨   📲 Excel Templates ∨   📲 Export Lead scores | ∨

Lead score associated view ∨

○	Lead ↑ ∨	Lead scoring model ↑ ∨	Score ↓ ∨	Score status ∨	Grade ∨
		New Lead	15.0	Up to date	Freezing
		New Lead	30.0	In progress	Freezing
		New Lead	5.0	In progress	Freezing
		New Lead	55.0	Up to date	Cold
		New Lead	5.0	In progress	Freezing
		New Lead	5.0	In progress	Freezing
		New Lead	5.0	In progress	Freezing
		New Lead	260.0	In progress	Hot Hot Hot

Figure 2.28 – Lead scoring with scored leads

As Figure 2.28 shows, you can see the scores of each lead and see the grade they have. A lead can be part of multiple lead scoring models.

Lead-to-opportunity marketing sales business process flow

When you create a new lead, you get a process bar called a **business process flow (BPF)**. The out-of-the-box one is **lead-to-opportunity marketing sales business process flow (BPF)**. As you can see in *Figure 2.29*, the process contains five different stages where you add different types of data:

1. The first stage is where you see whether the lead should be connected to an existing contact or account.

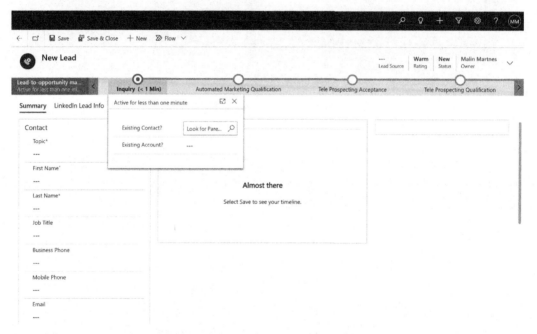

Figure 2.29 – Lead-to-opportunity BPF stage one

2. The next stage is the automated marketing qualification, as you can see in *Figure 2.30*. It contains two checkboxes to see whether the lead is ready for sales or tele prospecting:

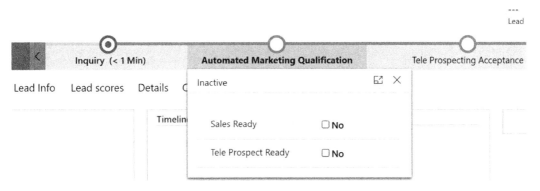

Figure 2.30 – Lead-to-opportunity BPF stage two

3. The third stage is for tele prospecting. If your company doesn't do tele prospecting, you'll want to edit this process and go straight to the sales stage. As you can see in *Figure 2.31*, the tele prospecting team will need to accept the lead to start working on it:

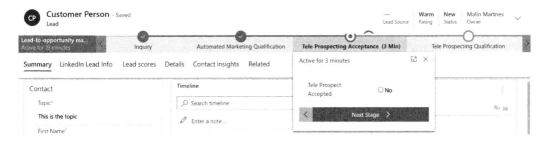

Figure 2.31 – Lead-to-opportunity BPF stage three

4. The fourth stage of the BPF is the tele prospecting qualification (*Figure 2.32*). This has several fields you need to fill out to move to the next stage. This is the stage where you're on the phone with the lead, gathering information about the needs of the potential customer:

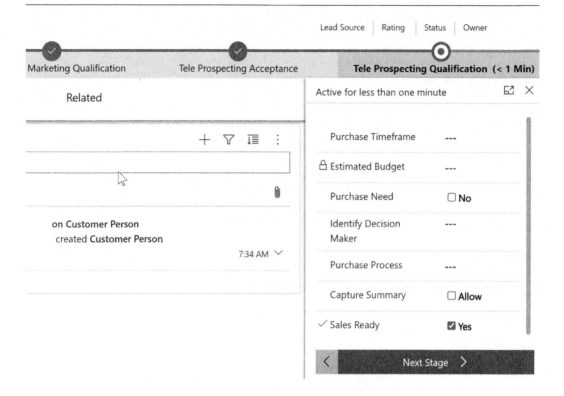

Figure 2.32 – Lead-to-opportunity BPF stage four

5. The fifth and final stage of the BPF is the sales acceptance stage, where your salespeople accept the lead and start working with it from a sales perspective. When sales have accepted the lead, you can click on the **Finish** button to complete the marketing side of the leads process (*Figure 2.33*):

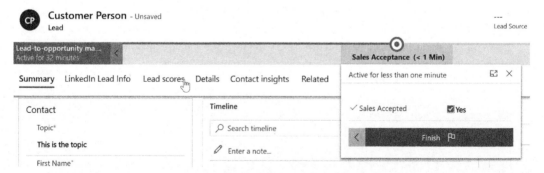

Figure 2.33 – Lead-to-opportunity BPF stage five

You can now see, as shown in *Figure 2.34*, that the process is finished and when it was completed:

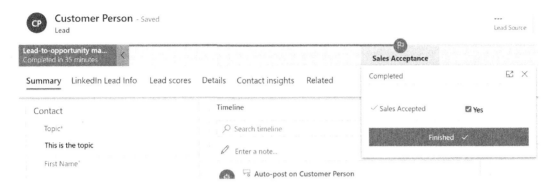

Figure 2.34 – Lead-to-opportunity BPF finished process

As you can see, the BPF is a very good way of keeping track of your company's process when it comes to leads. It will help you to put in the same effort for all your leads.

Summary

We have now gone through some of the most important tables in Dynamics 365 and Dataverse; leads, contacts, and accounts. These tables are the foundation of everything you do; these are the people you talk to, your potential customers, and the companies you are working with or selling to.

If you do not spend some time getting to know the structure of your company's data, you will have a hard time understanding and getting good analytics or creating a better system. Structure in your data should be your priority; you want to generate and understand analytics, know how your company is doing, and improve your company. It is a lot harder to do this and become better if you do not know your data.

We've looked at relationships and seen how all the tables are connected. We've also gone through the lead life cycle and looked at the different lead scoring models. We have also looked at the lead-to-opportunity marketing sales BPF and seen how this can help us structure our leads and make sure that all our leads are treated equally.

Because leads and contacts are where all your marketing efforts will be focused, it's important to have control of these tables. To have control over your leads, contacts, and accounts, you first need to know how they work and how they're connected. If you don't have control over your data, you will not succeed.

In the next chapter, we'll review segments and lists and see how you can group and categorize your leads and contacts.

Questions

The following are some questions that will help you gauge your understanding of the topics discussed in this chapter. The answers are available in the *Assessments* section at the end of the book.

1. Why are leads important?

    (a) To generate sales

    (b) To have someone to market to

    (c) To have somewhere to register "fussy" interest

    (d) To know your customers

    (e) To know your companies

2. Which contact type is considered in licensing?

    (a) Sales-ready contact

    (b) Marketing-ready contact

    (c) Regular contact

    (d) Marketing contact

    (e) Event contact

    (f) No contacts are relevant to licensing

3. What type of relationship do contacts and accounts have out of the box?

    (a) 1:N

    (b) N:N

    (c) They're not related

4. If you want to do lead scoring based on "If a lead has clicked on an email," what type of lead scoring model will that be?

    (a) Behavior

    (b) Demographic

    (c) Firmographic

5. Can a lead be scored with multiple lead scoring models?

    (a) Yes

    (b) No

What Are Segments and Lists?

In *Chapter 2, Managing Leads, Accounts, and Contacts*, you learned about **leads**, **contacts**, and **accounts**. Now, let's see how we can use these in **segments** and **lists**.

Segments and lists are used as a way to group contacts. You can use these groups to specify who you want to focus your marketing efforts on. We're going to look at how you can use subscription centers to follow privacy rules and legislations, such as GDPR, and make sure you're marketing to the right people. In this chapter, we're going to cover the following:

- Understanding and managing segments
- Understanding and managing subscription centers and lists

By the end of the chapter, you'll understand what segments and lists are, what the differences between them are, and when to use them. Let us start with what segments are and see how they are created and managed.

Understanding and managing segments

As mentioned before, segments are a way to group your contacts based on their registered information. Any type of column can be used to specify your segments. You can also use the information in related tables to create your segment. In this section, we're going to take a look at the different types of segments and how you can specify which contacts to target.

What are segments?

A segment is a list of contacts, not any other table. You can use the information on, for example, an account or a lead to decide what contact you'll use, but there will only ever be contacts in your segment. You can set **criteria** on the segments to find the **specific selection of contacts** you want. The only required field of any segment is its name. In dynamic segments, you will find the name at the top of the form, as shown in *Figure 3.1*:

Figure 3.1: Name in a dynamic segment

In your static segments, you will find the name of the segment in a side panel, as you can see in *Figure 3.2*:

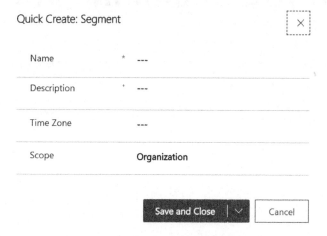

Figure 3.2: Name in a static segment

Make sure you give your segments suitable names so that people can understand what they're used for.

You can create as many segments as you want in Dynamics 365 Marketing; they are essential when you start talking with your customers. You can read more about how segments are used in a customer journey in *Chapter 6, Outbound Customer Journeys*, and *Chapter 7, Real-Time Marketing Journeys*.

You can create a dynamic or a static segment. You choose between them when you're creating the segment, as you can see in *Figure 3.3*:

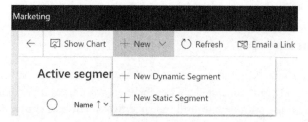

Figure 3.3: Choosing a dynamic or static segment

Let's start going through what a dynamic segment is.

Dynamic segments

A **dynamic segment** is a collection of contacts with a matching set of criteria. The segment will automatically add or remove a contact when it matches the criteria. You define the dynamic segment criteria with **queries** that you build in the **segment designer**. How do we build these queries? Let's dive into queries in the segment designer.

Segment designer

The first thing you should do when working with segments is to select what view you want: the natural view or the tree view. This doesn't in any way change the functionality; it's just about how your mind processes the queries best. In *Figure 3.4*, you can see how the **natural view** looks:

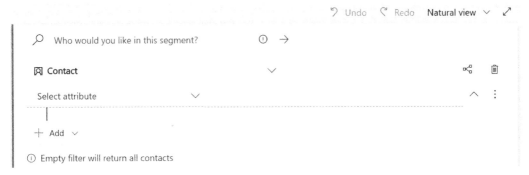

Figure 3.4: Natural view in a dynamic segment

In *Figure 3.5*, you can see how the **tree view** looks. As you can see, the differences between the two aren't that big; it's just about picking the one you feel most comfortable with:

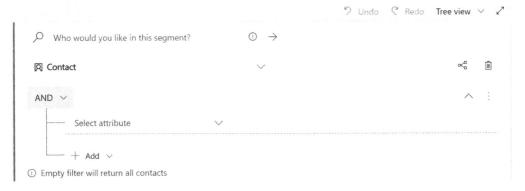

Figure 3.5: Tree view in a dynamic segment

A query in a segment can contain one single criterion or a long list of criteria. There are three different segment blocks that you can use in your queries. We'll go through what you can do with each of them.

Query blocks

In **query blocks**, you can select the tables that contain the attributes you want to filter by. If you don't specify any filters, you'll get all the contacts in Dataverse as members of the segment. As you can see in *Figure 3.6*, you can choose any of the tables that are related to the contact:

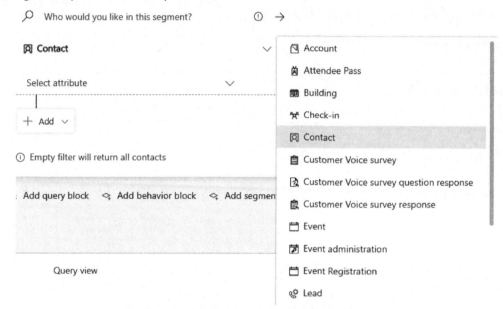

Figure 3.6: Selecting the tables in a dynamic segment

To see how all the tables are connected, you can click on the icon marked in red in *Figure 3.7*:

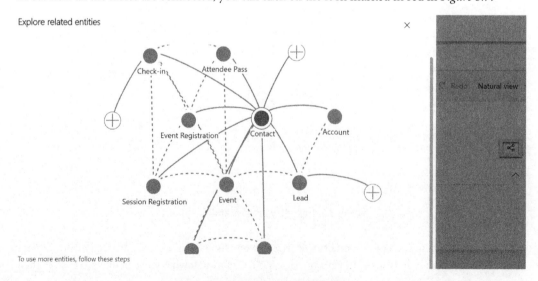

Figure 3.7: Exploring related tables

In the popup that you can see in *Figure 3.7*, you can see how the different tables in Dataverse are connected to the **Contact** table. This can make it easier to understand the underlying data structure and how everything is connected to the **Contact** table.

Moving back to the query blocks, we can select an attribute (a column on the table you chose). As you can see in *Figure 3.8*, I've started to type in em and attributes containing em come up:

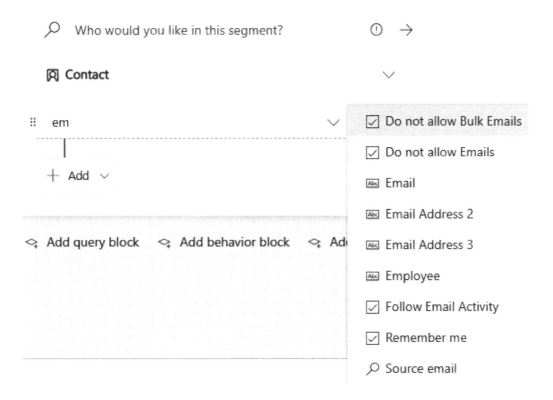

Figure 3.8: The columns you can choose as attributes in a segment

Once you've chosen the **Email** attribute, you can specify the **operator**. The operator can be 1 of 10 set **variables**, as shown in *Figure 3.9*:

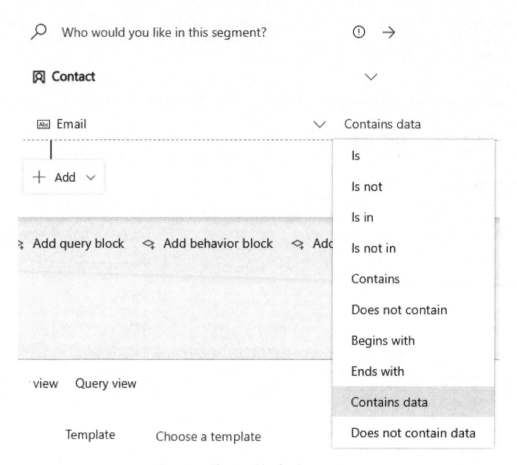

Figure 3.9: The variables for the operator

Here, you can choose whether the **Email** column contains data. There's no use in sending an email to someone that doesn't have the email field filled out – or you might want to create a segment for contacts whose email contains a specific domain. Another way of writing your queries is by using **natural language**.

Natural language is writing what you want to query with normal text, without knowing the name of the columns in your data. This works for English as a language as of November 2022.

In *Figure 3.10*, you can see that I've written a sentence saying I want to see all the contacts that live in Oslo. I am then getting a suggestion of the **address1_city** column and that it should be **Oslo**. It then also puts this query in the segment, and it has translated what I asked into a query:

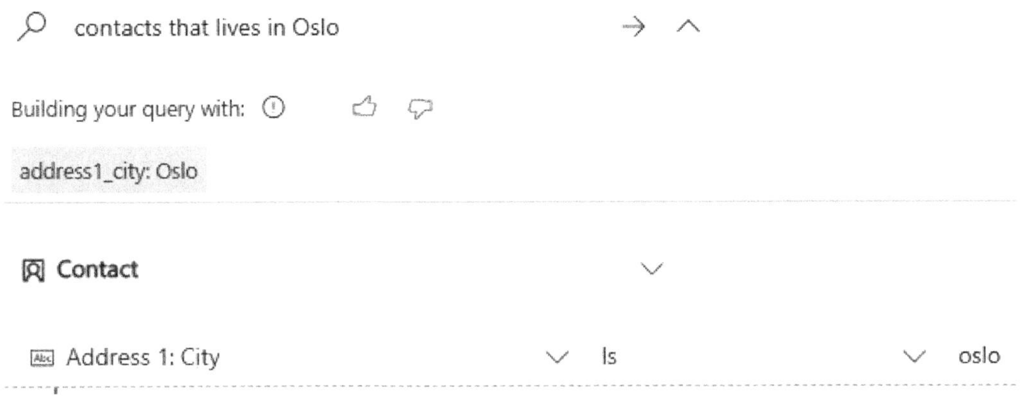

contacts that lives in Oslo

Building your query with: ⓘ   👍 👎

address1_city: Oslo

🔲 **Contact**   ⌄

Abc Address 1: City   ⌄   Is   ⌄   oslo

Figure 3.10: Natural language in a segment

Now that we've seen how we can ask questions and use the query blocks to make our segments as specific as we need them to be, let's take a look at another way of querying with **behavioral blocks**.

Behavioral blocks

In **behavioral blocks**, you create queries based on the behavior of the contact. You want to have a segment of all the contacts that have checked into an event, to make sure they get a follow-up email thanking them for being there. This is done by choosing the **Event check-in** interaction and then further specifying which event you want the customer to have checked into, as you can see in *Figure 3.11*:

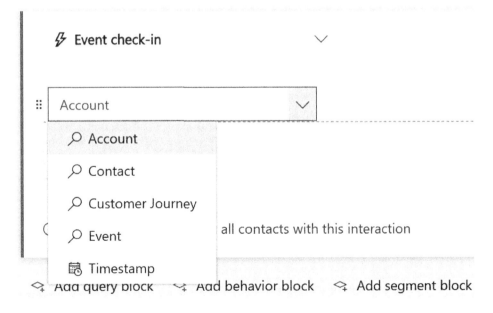

Figure 3.11: Event check-in interaction chosen

There are several **interactions** you can build a query on, such as the following:

- Form submitted or visited
- LinkedIn form submitted
- Marketing list subscribed or unsubscribed to
- Activity on a contact
- Customer Voice answered
- Website visited or clicked on
- Several interaction options for emails

If you don't have any filters on the query blocks, a blank filter will give you all the contacts for the interaction specified.

We've now gone through the query blocks and the behavior block. Let's take a look at the last type of block we have in the system, the **segment block**.

Segment blocks

The segment block is a block where you can find other segments to use in a query. You might want to find all the contacts that are your active customers, but if you don't want to create that filter every time, you can add it to a segment block, as you can see I've done in *Figure 3.12*:

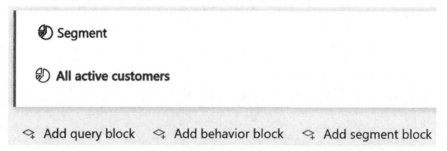

Figure 3.12: A segment block with the All active customers segment chosen

So far, we've created **simple segments**, but in real life, we usually have more complex requests. Let us go through some more complex ways of using these queries.

Complex queries

Now, we've gone through the query blocks, the behavior blocks, and the segment blocks; however, a lot of the time, we will actually use a combination of these. We have three different options when it comes to combining our queries, **or**, **and also**, and **but not**, as you can see in *Figure 3.13*:

Figure 3.13: The three different ways of combining our queries

Let's have a look at these options more closely:

- **or** gives you all the contacts that are in one or another block. If we want to build a list of all our contacts that live in Oslo or have signed up for the Oslo local newsletter, we can create our query to include contacts from both of these blocks, as you can see in *Figure 3.14*:

Flow view   Query view

Figure 3.14: The flow of a query with or

- **and also** gives you contacts that meet the query of two or more queries. We might want to have a segment with all contacts from Oslo that have clicked on a link in an email. As we can see in *Figure 3.15*, both queries bring contacts into the query, while some are not included:

Flow view   Query view

Figure 3.15: The flow of a query with and also

- **but not** gives you contacts that meet one query but are not in another query. If we want to find our contacts that are in Oslo but have not visited our website in the past year, then we use the **but not** operator to exclude everyone that has visited our website and that also lives in Oslo. The flow of the **but not** query is shown in *Figure 3.16*. You can see that some contacts are incorporated into the blue line, and the purple line represents the contacts excluded by the **but not** query:

Figure 3.16: The flow of a query with but not

If you have a list of contacts that you should never send any emails to, that's an important block to add to any segment to which you'll send an email as a **but not** segment block.

To include members in your dynamic segment, you have to save it and go live. You cannot use a segment anywhere until it's gone live. Once you've gone live with a segment, you have to click the **Edit** or **Stop** button to be able to make any changes to the segment. You'll also get a list of members in your segment once it's live. You can see the list of members under the **Members** tab for your segment, as you can see in *Figure 3.17*:

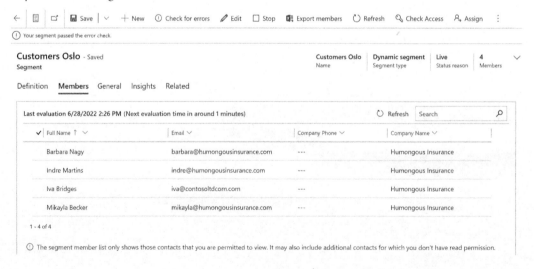

Figure 3.17: A live segment with a list of members in it

We've now taken a look at all the different options for how to build a dynamic segment. The dynamic segment changes based on the criteria you put in the query and is a living, changing segment. Let's take a look at how we build a static segment.

Static segments

A **static segment** is a segment that will not update automatically. If you add a contact, they will never appear or disappear as they would on a dynamic segment. In a static segment, the contact can either remove themselves or you can remove them. As you can see in *Figure 3.18*, you can add a member manually or with a query, and you can remove members with a query or by selecting the ones you want to remove and clicking **Remove**:

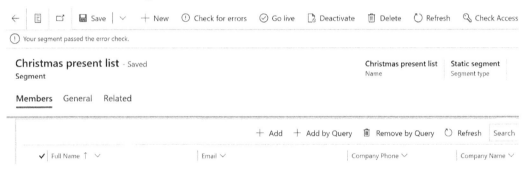

Figure 3.18: Static segment – adding members

Let's see how you can add or remove them manually.

Adding or removing members manually

You can pick contacts manually for your segment. You might have a group of contacts that will receive a Christmas present from the company. This is a list to which only certain, handpicked people will be manually added. You can add these manually by clicking on the **Add** button; a side panel appears and you can select the contacts you want to add, as you can see in *Figure 3.19*:

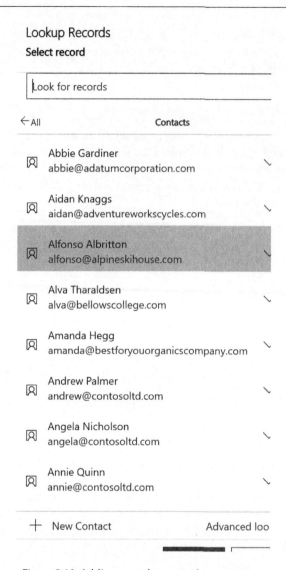

Figure 3.19: Adding records to a static segment

Let's take a look at an easier way of adding contacts, with queries, much like the queries in dynamic segments.

Adding or removing members by query

Now that you've gone through dynamic segments, the method for building queries should be familiar to you. In static segments, you can use query blocks or segment blocks to build your queries. In *Figure 3.20*, we can see how we build these queries. We find the contact table and then we find the attribute, which is **Address 1: City**. We then specify what city we want to filter by – in this case, **Oslo**:

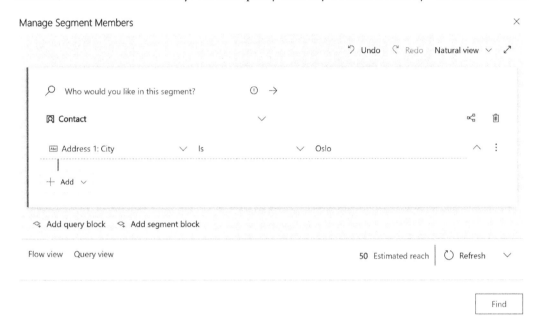

Figure 3.20: Building queries in a static segment

We will also get an estimated reach of the segment. Here, there are an estimated 50 people in the segment. When we click **Find**, we move to another page. As you can see in *Figure 3.21*, we get a list of all the contacts and we can choose the members we want to add, edit the query, or add all members to our segment:

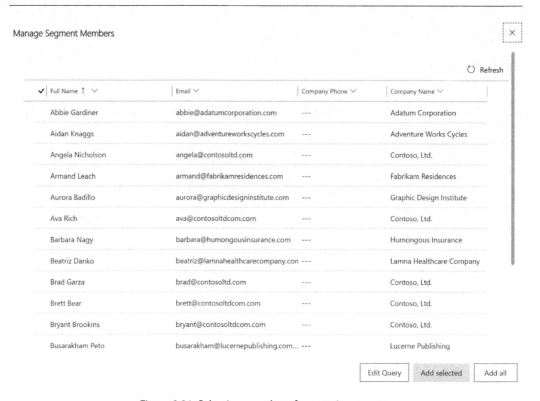

Figure 3.21: Selecting members for a static segment

If you want to remove members from the segment using a query, you can click on the **Remove by Query** button, add your query, and remove the contacts.

Now that we've looked at dynamic and static segments, let's take a look at a more automated type of segment created with the help of AI: **Customer Insights (CI)** segments.

CI segments

Dynamics 365 CI is a system you will learn more about in *Chapter 10, Power Platform*. One of the benefits of CI is that it can **automatically create segments** that you can use in Dynamics 365 Marketing. These segments will change when they're updated from CI, so they behave differently from other segments. Every time a segment is pushed from CI, the entire segment will update in Dynamics 365 Marketing. A customer of mine uses an external system to manage their consent. This consent is pushed to CI and from there, it's pushed to Dynamics 365 Marketing, where they can utilize these segments.

Real-time marketing segments

Since the wave 2 2022 release in October, there is a new way of creating segments in Real-time marketing. Let's go through this.

When you create a new RTM segment, you give it a name, choose the target audience (**Contact** or **Lead**), and give the segment a description as shown in *Figure 3.22*:

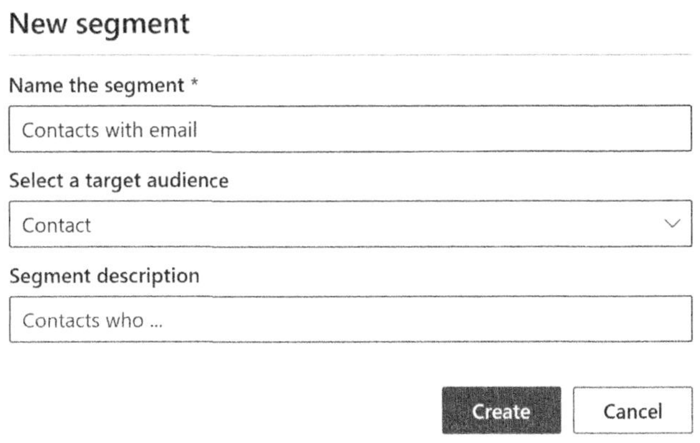

Figure 3.22: Creating a new real-time marketing segment

When the segment is created, you get a new screen where you can edit your segment as shown in *Figure 3.23*:

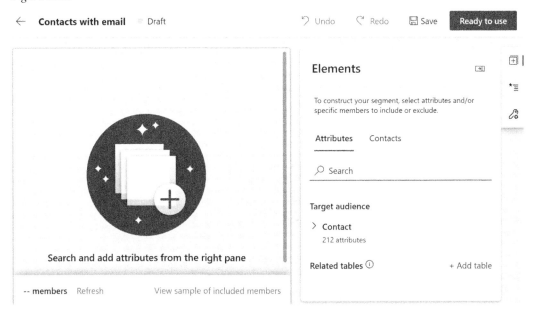

Figure 3.23: RTM segment builder

You can select the attributes and set the conditions to create your segment as shown in *Figure 3.24*:

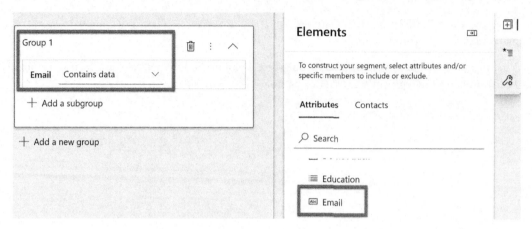

Figure 3.24: Selecting attributes and groups

You can also create subgroups and add multiple groups where you can have different conditions to create your segment. This way, you can create your segment according to your needs exactly.

On the right-hand side, you have three menu areas; the second is **Query Assist**, where you can use natural language to help build your segment, as shown in *Figure 3.25*:

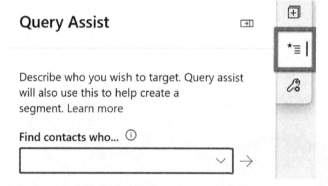

Figure 3.25: Query Assist

You can write which contacts you want to find, and the assistant helps you create the queries needed for the segment.

In the **Settings** area, you can say whether you want to automatically refresh the segment (dynamic), or have a static segment as shown in *Figure 3.26*:

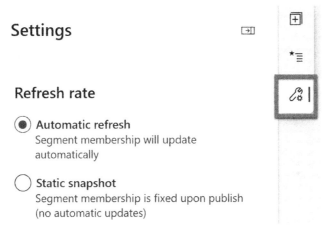

Figure 3.26: Settings for the segment

When you're satisfied with the segment, you must set it as ready to use and the segment will go live and find all the contacts or leads that match the conditions you set in the segment.

Now that we've gone through the different segments there are and how you can create queries to find the contacts you're looking for, let's take a look at subscription centers and marketing lists and how these are created and used in Dynamics 365 Marketing.

Understanding and managing subscription centers and lists

Now, we've seen what the different segments are and how we can find the different segments we need to market to. According to GDPR, we can't just send information to anyone we want; we need to control to whom we can send information. We control all of this through subscription centers and lists of people we can contact.

Subscription centers

A subscription center is a marketing page where your contacts can see what type of communication preferences they have and change their contact details. You cannot send out any email messages in Dynamics 365 Marketing without a link to a subscription center. Those of you who live in Europe are probably familiar with GDPR and know that there are legal requirements to adhere to in order to send emails to a customer. What you might not know is that an unsubscribe link will also help you with your deliverability, as many spam filters and internet reputation monitors will give you a bad score if you don't have an unsubscribe link.

With every Dynamics 365 Marketing instance, you will always get a default subscription center out of the box. It is important to never delete the default subscription center page, as you cannot create it again. As you can see in *Figure 3.27*, there is a lot of information on the automatic **Default Marketing Page** already set up for you out of the box:

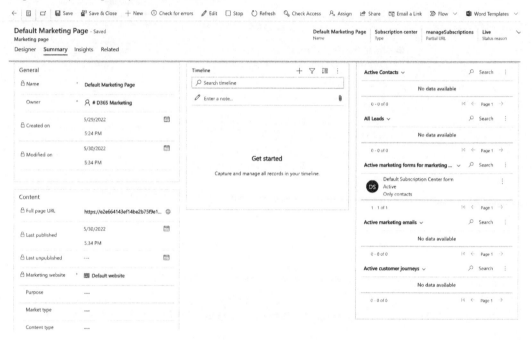

Figure 3.27: Default Marketing Page

You will learn more about marketing forms and marketing pages in *Chapter 4, Managing Marketing Forms, Pages, and Websites*. You can also create different subscription centers and subscription lists tailored to your company's needs.

Your subscription centers can contain several subscription lists. Let us take a look at how we create subscription lists.

Subscription lists

A subscription list is a list where contacts register or unregister, for example, to a weekly newsletter. The actual setup for subscription lists is simple, as you can see in *Figure 3.28*. You give the list a name; it is always a static list and it always goes to contacts. Once you've saved the list, you can see the members and add or remove members manually or wait for your contacts to register themselves:

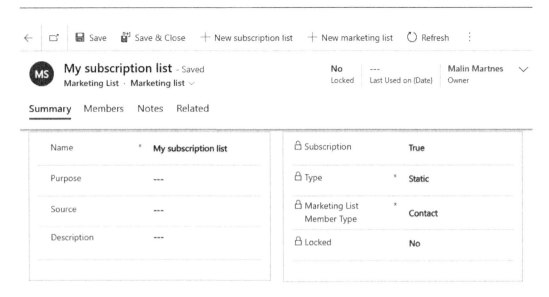

Figure 3.28: Marketing list

When you've created the subscription list, it's time to create your marketing form. Your marketing form needs to be a **Form**-type subscription center. You need to add your subscription list to the subscription form. You can have one or several subscription lists on a single subscription form. In *Figure 3.29*, you can see the default subscription center form with just the **Email** field and the **Do not email** checkbox:

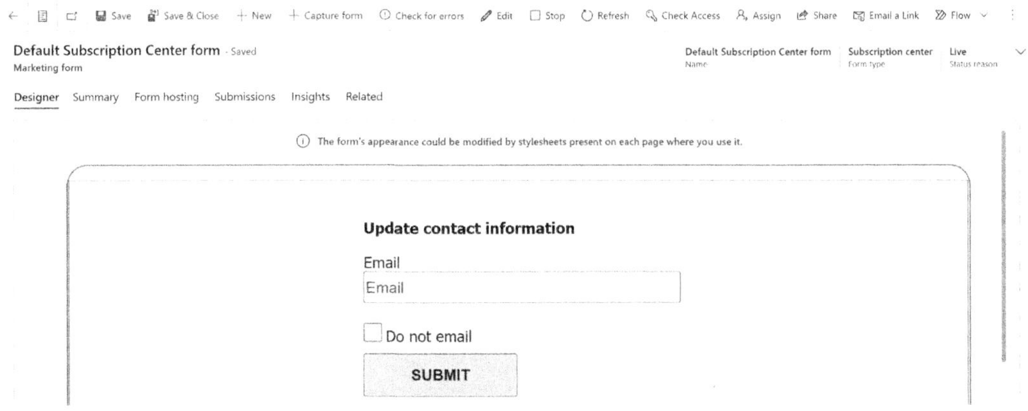

Figure 3.29: Default marketing form-type subscription

Once your marketing form is done, it is time to create your marketing page. Your marketing page needs to be a **Subscription Center**-type marketing page. You can only add a **Subscription**-type marketing form to a **Subscription**-type marketing page. As you can see from *Figure 3.30*, the marketing page looks the same as the marketing form. That's because the page contains the marketing form and nothing has been added to the page. You can style your marketing page to look more like your company's style:

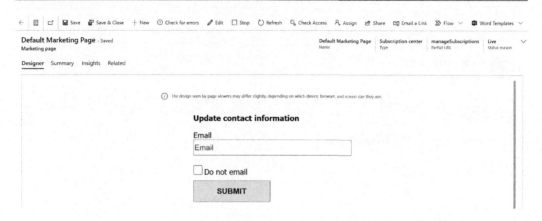

Figure 3.30: Marketing page subscription

Your subscriptions are now ready to be used in emails. You can do this more easily by adding your subscription center to your content settings, as you can see marked in red in *Figure 3.31*. Remember that you must have gone live with your form, your marketing page, and your content settings to be able to utilize them:

Figure 3.31: Default content settings

Now, we've gone through the subscription centers and how lists in Dynamics 365 Marketing are used. If you're familiar with Dynamics 365 Sales or Customer Service, you might be familiar with marketing lists. These aren't used much in Dynamics 365 Marketing, but you can add them in, for example, Dynamics 365 Sales and utilize them in a segment.

Marketing lists

These lists have some similarities to segments but can't be used in customer journeys (except for subscription lists) and don't run on marketing insights services. You can create a static marketing list in sales, where your salespeople add their contacts to the list and use that as an inclusion list in a segment. You might not want the salespeople to have access to Dynamics 365 Marketing, but you still want them to be able to add people to the Christmas presents list. You would then create a marketing list in Dynamics 365 Sales and use that list as an inclusion in your Christmas card segment.

Summary

In this chapter, you've learned that there are several ways of grouping your contacts.

With segments, you can group based on queries. Queries can use information based on a contact or any related table. Segments can query based on the interactions of a contact. Segments can also use a segment block and query based on other segments. You can also combine queries to include, exclude, or combine different blocks. These segments can be used in customer journeys or taking out lists.

You also have the very important subscription lists, which are where you can control all your newsletters and everything you send out from Dynamics 365 Marketing. We've gone through how subscription guests are connected to marketing forms and two marketing pages. We've also seen how important these subscription lists are for sending out emails in Dynamics 365 Marketing and for the general deliverability of emails, as well as GDPR. We've also gone through how you can add a subscription center to your content settings to make it easier to use this subscription center in your content. Subscription lists are a type of marketing list and are always static.

Last but not least, you have your marketing lists, which have been around in Dynamics 365 for several years already. Marketing lists (except for subscription lists) aren't used as much in Dynamics 365 Marketing as in other Dynamics 365 applications.

In Dynamics 365 Marketing, it's important to know what segments, subscription centers, and lists are and how you use them. If you don't set this up correctly, you might violate GDPR. For a lot of customers, it's important to group contacts together to know who your customers are, where your customers live, whether they open the emails you send, or whether they attend your events – or maybe you just have them in your system and never contact them at all, or you're allowed to contact them but you don't have control over that, thus not utilizing the full marketing potential of your contact.

In the next chapter, we're going to cover everything about marketing forms and pages. We've already talked a bit about it in this chapter, with adding subscription lists to subscription center forms and subscription center pages. In the next chapter, we're going to dig deeper into forms and pages and see what we can use them for and how you can make functional forms and pages.

Questions

The following are some questions that will help you gauge your understanding of the topics discussed in this chapter. The answers are available in the *Assessments* section at the end of the book.

1. What are the three different blocks you can use in segments?

   A. Demographic

   B. Query

   C. Segment

   D. Contact

   E. Behavior

2. Where do you add a subscription list?

   A. Marketing schema

   B. Marketing forms

   C. Marketing pages

   D. Marketing subscriptions

3. What are the three operators to combine several blocks in segments?

   A. include

   B. or

   C. but not

   D. exclude

   E. if else

   F. and also

4. Can marketing lists be used in customer journeys?

   A. Yes

   B. No

   C. Yes, but only subscription lists

Part 2 –
Core Features of
Dynamics 365 Marketing

This second part of the book gives you an in-depth walkthrough of the core functionalities of Dynamics 365 Marketing and gives you the dos and don'ts of the functionality. The following chapters are included in this part:

- *Chapter 4, Managing Marketing Forms, Pages, and Websites*
- *Chapter 5, Creating Marketing Emails*
- *Chapter 6, Outbound Customer Journeys*
- *Chapter 7, Real-Time Marketing Journeys*
- *Chapter 8, Managing Events*

4
Managing Marketing Forms, Pages, and Websites

We've gone through the fundamental aspects of **Dynamics 365 Marketing**, such as basic configuration in *Chapter 1, The Basic Configuration of Dynamics 365 Marketing*, and core tables in *Chapter 2, Managing Leads, Accounts, and Contacts*. In the next chapters, we're going to dig deeper into the core marketing functionalities.

In this chapter, we're going to start by going through and learning what **marketing forms**, **marketing pages**, and **marketing websites** are and why it's so important to go through **analytics** and constantly improve your forms and pages. We're also going to look at the different types of forms and pages you can create, and some use cases for each of them.

We'll cover the following topics in this chapter:

- Understanding and managing marketing forms
- Understanding and managing marketing pages
- Understanding and managing marketing websites
- Analytics

Understanding and managing marketing forms

Most companies that work with customers want, at some point, to gather information from their customers. In Dynamics 365 Marketing, the easiest way of gathering information from your customers or potential customers is to create a marketing form. Let's go through the different types of marketing forms you can create, see how you can create and edit them, examine the different relevant settings, and discover how you can incorporate your **customizations** into marketing forms.

Types of marketing forms

When we start creating a marketing form, the first thing we need to know is what type of form we need to create. There are four different types of marketing forms that you can create, as seen in the following list:

- The landing page form
- The subscription form
- The forward-to-a-friend form
- The event registration form

The event registration form is not one of the standard ones but has to be activated in the settings if your company is going to use events. Let's start with the most used form, the landing page form.

The landing page form

The landing page form is the type of form you will use most often. This form covers all kinds of information you might want to collect from your customers or potential customers. A lot of companies use a landing page form as their *Contact us* form on their website. Other companies use it so customers can update their personal information so that they always have the correct information about their customers.

The subscription form

The subscription form is where your customers register their email information and other contact details for the purposes of subscriptions; there may also be information on all the subscriptions your company offers and how they can be added and removed. A subscription form can only be used to make changes to existing contacts; it can never create new contacts.

The forward-to-a-friend form

The forward-to-a-friend form is mostly used for analytics. Most people, if they want to forward an email to a colleague, will click the **Forward** button. When the **Forward** button is clicked, the connection to Dynamics 365 Marketing or other marketing applications is maintained, including all analytics and other information. If you add a forward-to-a-friend form to an email and your customer clicks the **Forward** button and registers information about the new recipient, the receiver will get a new clean email without any connections to the other person.

If one person forwards an email to five other colleagues, and all five colleagues open that email, then it will register as though the original receiver of the email opened their email six times (once for the email they opened and once for each of the colleagues they forwarded it to), as shown in *Figure 4.1*:

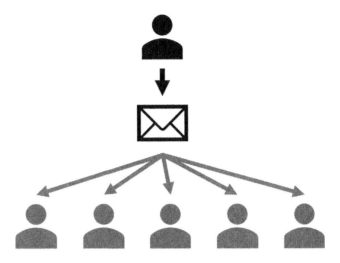

Figure 4.1 – Forward one email to multiple receivers

If the receiver used forward-to-a-friend functionality and registered the names and email addresses of their five colleagues, then those colleagues would each get a new email and each would be registered in the system as a single recipient. The data would show that the email was opened by six different customers, as shown in *Figure 4.2*:

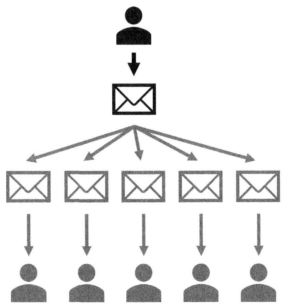

Figure 4.2 – Forward-to-a-friend, creating copy of the email and sending to receiver

This is the only use for the forward-to-a-friend form.

The event registration form

This is an option that you need to go into the settings to activate. We went through the event registration form activation in *Chapter 1, The Basic Configuration of Dynamics 365 Marketing*. The basic configuration of Dynamics 365 Marketing is in the feature switch section in the **Settings** area of Dynamics 365 Marketing. You do not need to use event registration forms if you do not use Dynamics 365 Marketing for events. Event registration forms are used where your customers or potential customers have already registered for the events you offer.

Before we go into how we create marketing forms, there's something you need to have first – marketing form fields.

Marketing form fields

If you are going to use a field in any form and collect data in Dataverse, it must be an active **marketing form field**.

In the **Marketing templates** area, you can find **Form fields**, as shown in *Figure 4.3*:

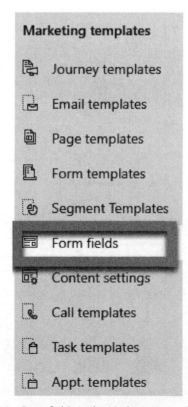

Figure 4.3 – Form fields in the Marketing templates area

If you open any of the existing form fields in your system, as shown in *Figure 4.4*, you can see that they all have a name, field type, and format, and they have **Contact mapping** and/or **Lead mapping** options:

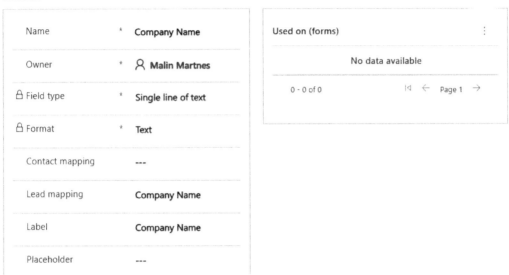

Figure 4.4 – Form fields

As you can tell from *Figure 4.4*, you can also see which form fields are used on which forms. You cannot delete an active form field that is used on a form.

If you do not connect **Marketing form field** to a column in Dataverse, you cannot store any data from a marketing form in this column.

Now that we've gone through how you can create marketing form fields, we're ready to start creating marketing forms.

Creating marketing forms

To create marketing forms, you need to go to **Outbound marketing** and find **Internet marketing**. Here, you will find **Marketing forms**, as shown in *Figure 4.5*:

Figure 4.5 – Internet marketing | Marketing forms

We'll execute the following steps to create marketing forms:

1. In the menu at the top, you will see the + **New** button, which you can use to create any of the four marketing forms.

    You should also see a + **Capture form** button; this is where you can connect your existing forms on your website to Dynamics 365 Marketing. We will get back to the **capture form** later in this chapter.

2. The first thing that happens when you click + **New** on the **Marketing forms** page is you get a new window where you can select your **marketing form templates**. If you did a good job before you started to use the system, you will have your own company templates. You can select one of the marketing form templates to get a flying start or you can skip and start from scratch with your own marketing forms.

3. If you choose to skip the templates, you will need to select a form type before you can do any editing on the form. You do that by clicking the arrow in the top-right corner of your new marketing form, clicking on the **Form type** field, and selecting the desired form type, as shown in *Figure 4.6*:

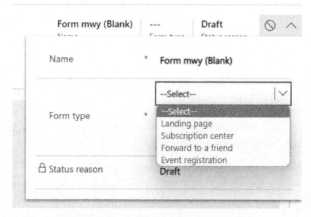

Figure 4.6 – Setting the Form type field

4. When you have chosen the form type, the form will consist of some fields. All the form types will have a **Submit** button but will have different fields:

   - - The landing page; email.

   - - Subscription form; email, do-not email box.

   - - Forward-to-a-friend; name, email.

   - - Event registration only has the submit button.

5. As you can see from *Figure 4.6*, this settings area also contains the name of the form and the status reason. When you select a form type, on certain forms, you can choose whether you want to update contacts and/or leads.

Now that we've created a marketing form, let's go through all the features and functionalities you have at your disposal to create beautiful marketing forms.

Layout designer

The first thing you need to think about is what kind of layout you want on your form. We have five different layout types, as shown in *Figure 4.7*:

Figure 4.7 – Layout designer

The different layouts are as follows:

- One column

- Two columns

- Three columns

- Two columns, where the one on the left is bigger than the other

- Two columns, where the one on the right is bigger than the other

You can see how these look in a form in *Figure 4.8*:

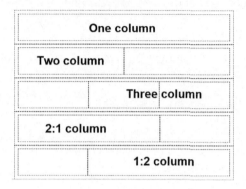

Figure 4.8 – Layout designer form options visualized

You can use one of these layout types or combine them to create the form you are looking for.

Basic elements

The next thing to do is add the basic elements, as shown in *Figure 4.9*:

Figure 4.9 – Basic elements

The basic elements are as follows:

- **Text**: The **Text** element is where you enter the information you want your customers to read. It can be any kind of text, such as information about the form, information about the competition the customer is about to enter, or information about your company.

- **Image**: The **Image** element is where most companies add their company logo. You can also add other images to help make your form look better. To add images, they need to be in the system. You can upload pictures beforehand or you can add new pictures when you need them.

- **Divider**: The **Divider** element is a means of separating other elements; for example, if you have lots of **Text** elements, it might be easier for the reader if you divide and add some space between them. A divider can be made bigger and can be presented in different colors. You can also set it to be transparent so that it appears as a blank space.

- **Button**: Using the **Button** element, you can add links to things; this could be a link to an external web page, a white paper of your choice, or some other external URL. A basic **Button** element cannot be used to submit a form; you can only add links to buttons.

- **Content block**: If you want to make things easier for your company, you should create some content blocks before you start using the system. These content blocks are the elements that you and your company use most often. Most of the companies I have worked with have created a content block to use as a header, containing their company logo and some general text about the company. They also have created a footer content block. These are reusable elements that make it easy to create new forms while still following company design guidelines. It's very important to know that if you update a content block, the emails and forms that are using this content block will not update. They will only be changed for new emails and forms.

  You can also lock a content block so that nobody can change the look of the block after it's been added to an email or form. This way, you can make sure that your header is always the same and that nobody has changed it.

In a marketing form, the basic elements appear as shown in the following screenshot:

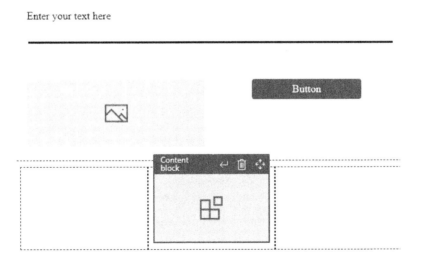

Figure 4.10 – The different basic elements of a form

Now we will go a bit further into what you can do with each of the basic elements.

Advanced elements

The next set of elements you can add to your marketing form is the advanced elements. These are **Reset button**, **Captcha**, and **Submit button**, as seen in *Figure 4.11*:

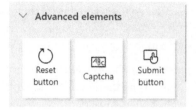

Figure 4.11 – Advanced elements

Their out-of-the-box versions are as follows:

Figure 4.12 – Advanced elements in a form

Let's look at each advanced element next.

Reset button

The **Reset** button does as its name suggests: it resets the form and deletes everything that has been put in the form, making it blank again.

Captcha

You probably know that a CAPTCHA is used to separate robots from humans. It shows you a set of characters that you need to type into a field before you can submit a form. A CAPTCHA can give you a new set of characters or you can play the audio of it if you're having difficulty reading the CAPTCHA.

Submit button

The **submit** button is used to submit a form. This will send the information from the form into your Dynamics 365 Marketing solution. Out of the box, you can change the name of the button from **Submit** to, for example, **Send in** or **Participate**. You can also make changes to the padding of the button box if you want it to sit further to the right or the left or if you want more space above or below it. If you want to make other edits to the button, such as ones to do with color and font, you will have to do that in your HTML editor.

Fields

The **Fields** area is one of the most important areas of your form. This is where you add the fields that people filling out the form need to populate. If you want to know their first and last name, email, phone number, and company, these are all fields you need to add. You can also add special fields you have created for your solution, but you need to make sure that these are added as form fields first. In *Figure 4.13*, you can see the fields and a search bar where you can search for the fields you need:

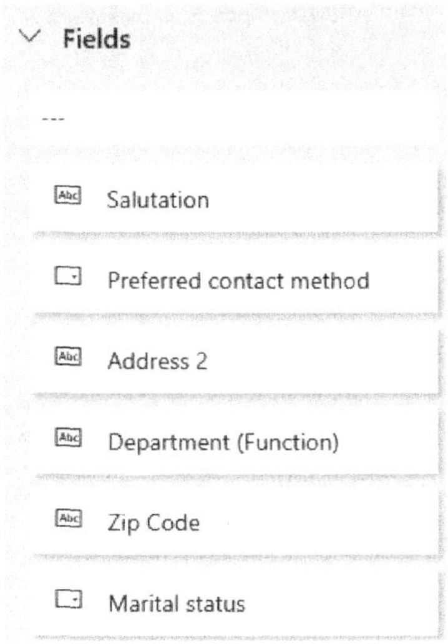

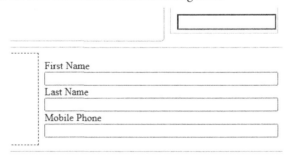

Figure 4.13 – Fields

In *Figure 4.14*, you can see how this looks in the marketing form:

First Name

Last Name

Mobile Phone

Figure 4.14 – Fields in the marketing form

In addition to this, you also have several field properties that you can change. As shown in *Figure 4.15*, you can change the label of the field, see what the field type is, and see the **Contact mapping** and **Lead mapping** properties.

You can add a placeholder, or ghost text, to each field. A placeholder is gray text in a box that disappears when you click on it. It's used so customers know what to put in each field.

A default value is something that is filled out for every customer that opens this form. Let's say you want to know the lead source. You can put `website` as the lead source in the **default value**, meaning that all forms that are filled out will be registered with a lead source of `website`. You can also say that a field is not shown on the actual form but is hidden from the customer. That way, you can get the information, but the customer doesn't have to see this field.

Figure 4.15 – Field properties (part one)

Continuing with the second part of **Field properties**, you can see in *Figure 4.16* that you have more options:

Figure 4.16 – Field properties (part two)

The other options in **Field properties** are as follows:

- You can set whether a field is required or not; if a field is required, the form cannot be submitted if that field is not filled out. If you have a field that is required and it's not filled out, the customer will get an error message, which you can add yourself in the **Required error message** field.

- **Label position** is where you want the label of the form to be shown. For example, do you want it to be at the top, to the left, or on the right? You can also set limitations on the characters.

- As we previously talked about in this chapter, if you want to register the lead source but you don't want to show the **lead source** field to the customer you can use the **Hide field** option, so you have information in the field, but the field isn't visible to your customers.

- You also have the option of using **Prefill** for your form. If you are dealing with a known customer in your system, they could have this specific field filled with their information in this form. **Prefill** works differently on the different types of forms. It's never available for Forward-to-a-friend form, it's always on for the subscription center form, and you can choose to turn it on or off for the landing page and event registration.

- The last thing you can do is add some spacing to your fields so that your form looks good.

You probably will not use all the options in every form you create. You will always use fields and the **Submit** button, but the rest is up to you and your company's needs.

The summary tab in forms

The **Summary** tab is an important tab and has a lot of information that you need to go through before you go live with your marketing form, as shown in *Figure 4.17*:

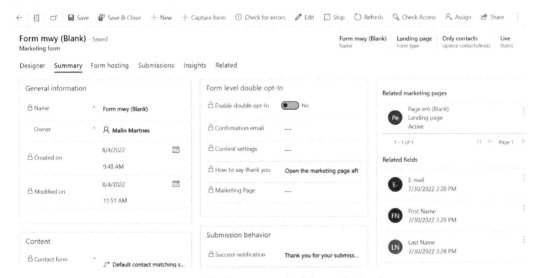

Figure 4.17 – The Summary tab of the marketing form

Next, let's look at the various sections of the **Summary** tab.

General information

In the **General information** section, as shown in *Figure 4.18*, you set the name of your form. This is a very important field because if your company has a lot of forms, the only way to differentiate between all your forms is by name. Give your forms good names, and make sure you have a proper naming convention in your company. The **General information** section also contains who the owner is. This is the user who created this form. You can also see when the form was created and when it last was modified:

General information

Name	*	**Form mwy (Blank)**
Owner	*	☐ **Malin Martnes**
☐ Created on		8/4/2022 ☐ 9:48 AM
☐ Modified on		8/4/2022 ☐ 9:48 AM

Figure 4.18 – General information in the Summary tab

This is how we create forms in Dynamics 365 Marketing, but some people might have forms that are already created that they wish to connect to their systems.

Content

In the **Content** section of the **Summary** tab, as shown in *Figure 4.19*, you add how to match the contacts or leads from this form to your system. You can also say whether you want to generate leads without matching so that every lead that registers on this form will always be created as a new lead in your system.

Content

Contact form matching *	↱ **Default contact matching strategy**
Lead form matching	---
Generate leads without matching	**No**
Purpose	---
Visual style	---
Prefill fields	**No**

Figure 4.19 – The Content section in the Summary tab

You can also add the purpose and set the visual style of the form.

The prefilled fields are important. If you want your customers to come to a form that is prefilled with their information, you can either set specific fields or set the whole form to be prefilled.

Form-level double opt-in

In *Chapter 1, The Basic Configuration of Dynamics 365 Marketing*, we talked a bit about **double opt-in**. There is a section on the **Summary** tab dedicated to form-level double opt-in, as shown in *Figure 4.20*:

Figure 4.20 – The Form level double opt-in section of the Summary tab

If you have a form where your customer needs to sign up for something that will cost them money, I highly recommend using double opt-in for that specific form. You need to enable it and configure a confirmation email, content settings, a thank you, and a marketing page.

Submission behavior

What should happen when a customer submits a form? You can set this behavior in the **Submission behavior** section of the **Summary** tab, as you can see in *Figure 4.21*:

Content

Contact form matching	*	↗ **Default contact matching strategy**
Lead form matching	---	
Generate leads without matching	**No**	
Purpose	---	
Visual style	---	
Prefill fields	**No**	

Figure 4.21 – The Submission behavior section of the Summary tab

All of the following fields will let you decide what happens when a customer submits a form:

- **Success notification** and **Success image URL** are where you set what will be shown when the customer successfully sends the form.

- **Error notification** and **Error image URL** are where you set what will be shown if the customer can't send in the form or if something happens and it's not sent in.

- **Limit exceeded notification** is where you set what is shown if the customer has sent the form too many times.

- **Redirect URL** is used if you want the customer to be sent to another URL upon completing the form.

- **Store form submission** is a **Yes/No** field asking whether you want to store the submissions your customers complete in the form. The subscription center and forward to a friend do not store form submissions under the **form submissions** tab. You will find the information for subscription centers under the **insights** tab. If you want to update and resubmit form submissions, **Store form submission** needs to be set to **Yes**. If it's set to **No**, then the submissions will still be stored, but you cannot make any changes to them. If it's set to **No**, then only the pending and failed submissions will be in the **Form submissions** tab.

Related marketing pages, Related fields, and Timeline

On the right side of the **Summary** tab, you can find three different sections, shown in *Figure 4.22*:

Figure 4.22 – Related marketing pages, Related fields, and Timeline in the Summary section

The top section is **Related marketing pages**. This is where you find the pages where your marketing forms are used. You then have **Related fields**, which contains the fields you have in your form. Lastly, you have **Timeline**. This is the same type of timeline we talked about in *Chapter 2, Managing Leads, Accounts, and Contacts*. If you communicate with your colleagues or external partners about your form, you can save that information to Dynamics 365 Marketing and it will be shown in the timeline.

Using marketing forms

The first thing you need to do before you can start using your marketing forms is check for errors and then go live. You cannot use your marketing forms anywhere if they are still in draft status. You can easily click on **Check for errors** at any time to make sure the form doesn't have any errors. You can also click **Go live** in the header, as when you click **Go live**, it will check for errors at the same time, as you can see in *Figure 4.23*:

Figure 4.23 – The Check for errors and Go live buttons

As soon as your marketing form has gone live, you get a new tab on the form called **Form hosting**, as shown in *Figure 4.24*:

Figure 4.24 – The Form hosting tab

On the **Form hosting** tab, you have **Related marketing form pages** and **Available domains for form hosting**. Your form can either be used on marketing pages (which we are going to go through later in this chapter) or, if you have your own website and you have your domain connected to Dynamics 365 Marketing, you can use your marketing forms on your website.

Capturing forms

Imagine that your company has spent a lot of money creating forms on its website. If you tell them they need to create the forms again from scratch, they will probably not be very happy. With Dynamics 365 Marketing, you can create **capture forms** to take forms that you already have elsewhere and get that data into your system. Let's look at how this is done.

In the same area as where you create new marketing forms, click on the + **Capture form** button; you will then get the popup shown in *Figure 4.25*:

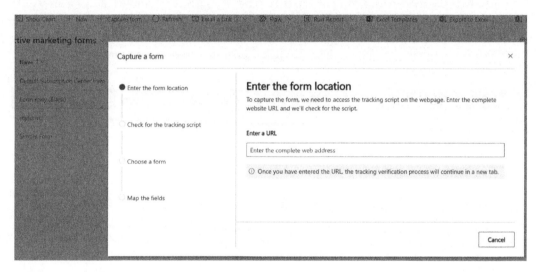

Figure 4.25 – Capture a form

To create the capture form, you need to follow these steps:

1. The first thing we need to do is enter the URL where your form is stored. If this URL does not contain the tracking script from Dynamics 365 Marketing, you will not have access to the form. We go through how you generate and use the tracking script in the *Understanding and managing marketing websites* section.

2. If you've added the tracking script to your web address, the next step is for the system to check for the tracking script.

3. If your tracking script is on your page and you have multiple forms on that page, you will then have to choose the form you want to create the capture form for.

4. The last thing you need to do is to map the fields. Remember that all the fields you want to map will need to have already been created as form fields in your system. The type of field will need to match Dynamics 365 Marketing and the form fields from your website.

When this is done, your form is ready to send data to Dynamics 365 Marketing.

Now we've seen how we can connect forms from our own website and how we can create marketing forms and use them on our existing websites, let's look at how we can create marketing pages to use our marketing forms.

Understanding and managing marketing pages

We've now gone through our marketing forms and seen how they are created. Now, let's embed them in marketing pages. To use marketing pages built in the marketing page designer in Dynamics 365 Marketing, you need **Power Pages**. You can create pages on your own **CMS** and track the information in Dynamics 365 Marketing. The subscription center is the only type of marketing page that is always available even if you do not connect your system to Power Pages. Be aware that using Power Pages will also trigger Power Pages licensing. We'll go through Power Pages and how you use it in *Chapter 10*, *Power Platform*.

There are a lot of similarities between marketing pages and marketing forms when it comes to creation. Because there are so many similarities, we are only going to go through the differences between the two and not dig deep into the parts that are common to both.

Types of marketing pages

As you have seen in marketing forms, you have three different types of marketing pages: landing page forms, subscription page forms, and forward-to-a-friend forms. You can only embed marketing forms in marketing pages of the same type. A landing-page-type marketing form can only be embedded in a landing-page-type marketing page, subscription forms can be used only on subscription marketing pages, and the forward-to-a-friend form can be used on forward-to-a-friend marketing pages.

Let's look at how to create our different marketing pages.

Creating marketing pages

Creating marketing pages has the same look and feel as creating marketing forms. You start by selecting the marketing page template that you used previously. If you do not select a marketing page template, you will have to select a type of marketing page before you start creating the page.

On the right side of the page, you have **Sections**, **Basic elements**, and **Design elements**, as shown in *Figure 4.26*:

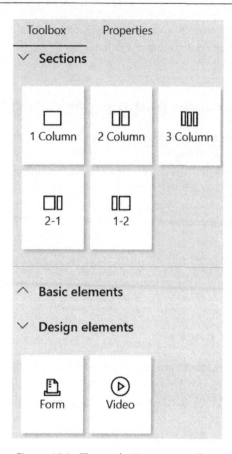

Figure 4.26 – The marketing page toolbox

Sections

The sections are the same as those of the layout designer for marketing forms. You can select **1 Column**, **2 Column**, **3 Column**, **2-1**, or **1-2**. These behave in the exact same way as they do in marketing forms.

Basic elements

The basic elements of marketing pages are the same as you have in marketing forms. These are as follows:

- Text
- Image
- Divider
- Button
- Content block

Design elements

Design elements is where a marketing page differs the most from a marketing form. You can add two types of design elements – a marketing form or you can add a video.

The marketing form

To add a marketing form to your marketing page, both must be of the same type. You can't have a forward-to-a-friend form on a landing page. The form also needs to have a status of live. If you cannot find your marketing form, make sure it is of the same type as the marketing page and that the form is live.

When you have added your form to your marketing page, you can edit some of the properties, such as the submission behavior, as shown in *Figure 4.27*:

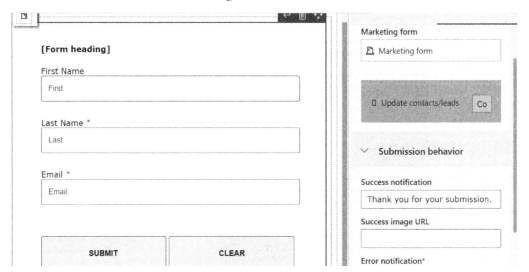

Figure 4.27 – Marketing form added to the marketing page

Video

In addition to embedding your marketing forms in your marketing page, you can also embed videos. Be aware that you can only upload videos from the outbound marketing library. This means that videos cannot be uploaded to Dynamics 365 Marketing but need to be hosted somewhere else. The videos you upload to the asset library in the real-time marketing area are not available for your marketing page.

The Summary tab for marketing pages

On the **Summary** tab, as shown in *Figure 4.28*, you can find information about the marketing page, such as who the owner is, when it was published, and whether it's connected to a marketing website (which we will explore in the next section of this chapter):

Figure 4.28 – The Summary tab for a marketing page

It's also important to notice from *Figure 4.28* that when you go live with your page, you get a full page URL. This is the URL of your marketing page and can be used wherever you desire.

Understanding and managing marketing websites

Your marketing website is used to connect your own CMS to Dynamics 365 Marketing. In order to capture information from your website, you need to create a new marketing website. As you can see in *Figure 4.29*, you need to register the URL of your website, give it a name, and save the record. Once you have saved the record, you will get some lines of JavaScript code and some lines of form capture code. This code has to be embedded in your CMS.

Figure 4.29 – Marketing website record

When your tracking script is embedded into your CMS, you will start getting insights and analytics from your website. Let's go through how analytics works for marketing forms, pages, and websites.

Analytics for marketing forms, pages, and websites

There's always room for improvement. This also applies to your marketing forms, pages, and websites. So, how do we improve? By going through our **analytics** and **insights**, and seeing how people are using our forms, pages, and websites.

Marketing forms

The different types of marketing forms will give you different kinds of data and insights. In *Figure 4.30*, you can see that this form has had **496** submissions and **353** unique submissions between **01/01/2022** and **08/08/2022**. Be aware that you can change the date to see the data on each of your forms.

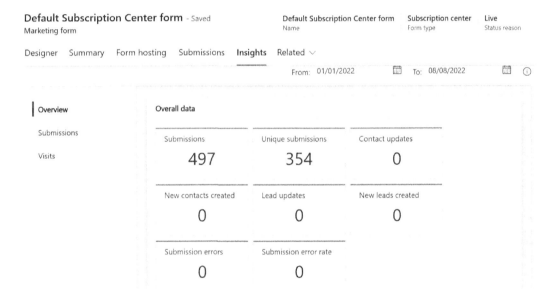

Figure 4.30 – An overview of the Insights section for a marketing form

You can also see all the visits to a form in the **Visits** area of **Insights**, as you can see in *Figure 4.31*:

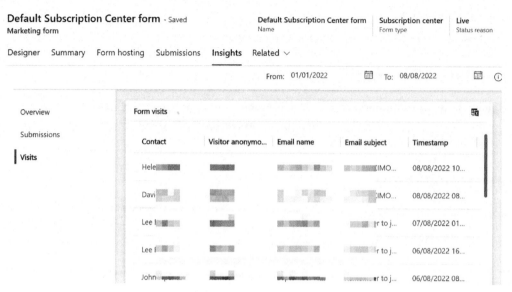

Figure 4.31 – Visits to a marketing form

This marketing form is used on a default marketing page; let's see what insights look like on a marketing page.

Marketing pages

On your marketing page, you also have an overview of insights, as shown in *Figure 4.32*:

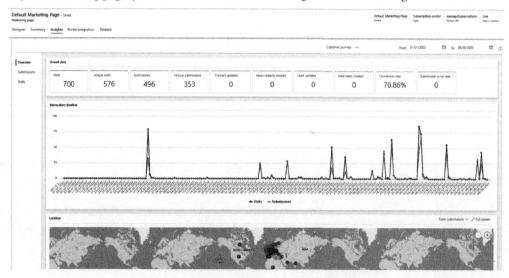

Figure 4.32 – An overview of a marketing page

In this overview, you can see the number of visits and unique visits your page has had, submissions and unique submissions, and the all-important conversion rate. Your conversion rate is how many visits your page has had and how many people have filled in the form. If you have a low conversion rate, you might want to go back to your form and see if it can be improved. You also want to have a low submission error rate; when this number is 0, nobody has had any issues submitting your form. In the interactions timeline, you can see when people visited and submitted your form. Under **Location**, you can also see where the people who have visited your marketing page are based.

In your **Submissions** and your **Visits** tabs, you will see the contacts and anonymous visitors who have visited your marketing page, what email address they used, and a timestamp.

Marketing websites

Once you have added your script to your marketing page, you will see some statistics coming back into Dynamics 365 Marketing. In the overview, you can see your top 10 pages and the location of your visitors, as shown in *Figure 4.33*:

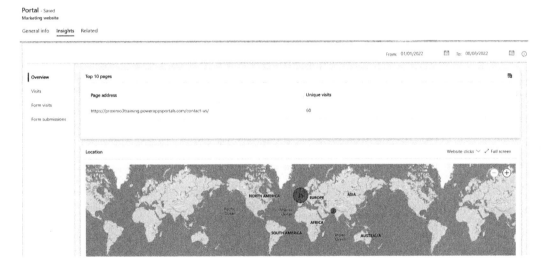

Figure 4.33 – Overview of insights for a marketing website

On the **Visits** tab, you can see who has visited, whether they're known contacts or anonymous, what address they visited, the referrer URL, how long they visited for, and the timestamp of the visit, as shown in *Figure 4.34*:

Figure 4.34 – The Visits tab under Insights

If there are any forms on your website and you have a capture form set up, you will also see the **Form visits** and **Form submissions** for your website.

All the insights and statistics for all forms, pages, and websites can be exported to Excel and Azure Blob Storage.

We've now gone through analytics for your forms, pages, and websites. Let's summarize this chapter's coverage.

Summary

In this chapter, we have gone through how we understand and manage marketing forms, marketing pages, and marketing websites.

We've looked at the different types of marketing forms and pages and when to use which. We now know that we can use landing pages to get contact information into our system and that subscription centers can be managed through subscription center forms and subscription center pages. We have also learned the benefits of using forward to a friend.

We've gone through how to design and style your own forms and pages and looked at the analytics of forms and pages and how you can better understand your customers use of your forms and pages by using analytics.

We've also seen how to connect your existing websites to Dynamics 365 Marketing to get analytics and improve your websites.

In the next chapter, we are going to see how to create and use marketing emails.

Questions

The following are some questions that will help you gauge your understanding of the topics discussed in this chapter. The answers are available in the *Assessments* section at the end of the book.

1. What are the three standard marketing forms?

    A. A landing page form

    B. A subscription form

    C. A contact information form

    D. An event registration form

    E. A forward-to-a-friend form

2. Why are marketing form fields important?

    A. You need them to create your fields in a marketing form

    B. You need them to connect the fields in a form to your data in Dataverse

    C. They are the fields shown on your marketing form

3. Where do videos in a marketing page need to come from?

    A. A real-time marketing asset library

    B. An outbound marketing library

4. What are marketing websites used for?

    A. Creating new websites

    B. Connecting Power Pages to Dynamics 365 Marketing

    C. Connecting websites to Dynamics 365 Marketing

    D. Connecting marketing pages to websites

5
Creating Marketing Emails

For a lot of companies, using marketing solutions and marketing emails are key features in their marketing efforts. **Dynamics 365 Marketing** has also put a lot of effort into marketing emails.

In this chapter, we're going to learn how we can use different marketing emails to send to our customers. We're going to take a look at the differences between Real-time marketing emails and Outbound marketing emails. We're also going to look at creating email templates and how we can send our marketing emails from Dynamics 365 Marketing. Finally, we're going to go through our analytics so that we know how we can improve the performance of our emails.

In this chapter, we're going to go through the following:

- Creating marketing emails
- Email templates
- Sending emails
- Analytics

Creating marketing emails

According to Litmus (`https://www.litmus.com/resources/email-marketing-roi/`), an email drives more ROI than any other marketing channel – $36 for every dollar spent. No wonder most companies prefer to use emails in their marketing strategy. Sending emails and creating good emails are important features of any marketing automation system. Before you can start sending your emails, you will first have to create your emails. In this section, we're going to go through everything we need to know to create high-performing emails.

Getting started with emails in Dynamics 365 Marketing

Because there are two different marketing areas, there are two different ways of creating your marketing emails:

- If you are using **Real-time marketing**, you will find your emails under **Channels** as shown in *Figure 5.1*:

Figure 5.1 – Emails under Channels in Real-time marketing

- If you are using **Outbound marketing**, you will find marketing emails under **Marketing execution** as shown in *Figure 5.2*:

Figure 5.2 – Marketing emails under Marketing execution in Outbound marketing

Let's look at the necessary steps for getting started with emails in the outbound area of Dynamics 365 Marketing:

1. To create and start designing new emails, you have to create a new email. That's done in the action bar, at the top. You will find **+ New** as shown in *Figure 5.3*:

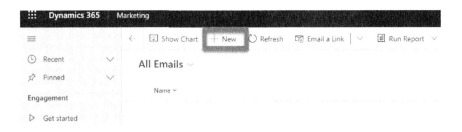

Figure 5.3 – The + New button in the action bar for creating a new email

2. Click + **New** and a new popup will appear where you can select email templates as shown in *Figure 5.4*:

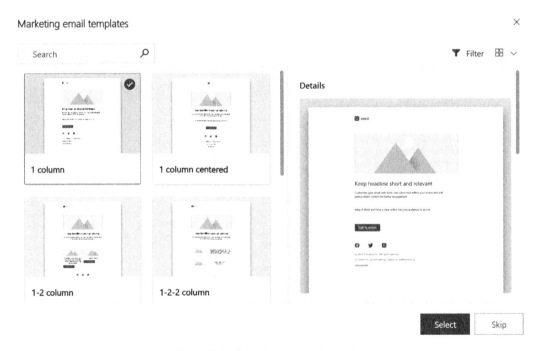

Figure 5.4 – Selecting an email template

3. If you do not select any templates, you will start with a blank canvas and can start creating your own marketing emails.

4. Now, you need to define the settings. You can find the settings as shown in *Figure 5.5*:

Figure 5.5 – Settings area of email

5.   Here, you set the subject of the email and the **Send settings** options as shown in *Figure 5.6*:

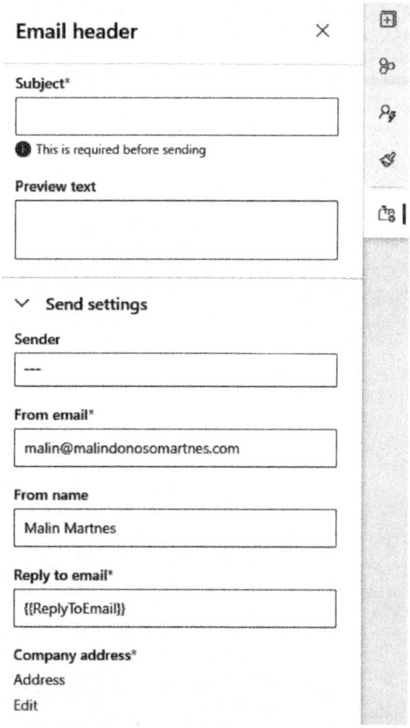

Figure 5.6 – Settings of the email

You can also edit the base email settings, such as the template, compliance, email content type, and language. More importantly, you can specify whether the message is a commercial or transactional email, as shown in *Figure 5.7*. A commercial email will need to follow the GDPR and privacy rules and can't be sent to recipients in Europe who haven't signed up for emails. Transactional emails can always be sent to customers. A transactional email can, for example, include customer receipts. You can also automatically generate plain text as shown in *Figure 5.7* or create your own plain text:

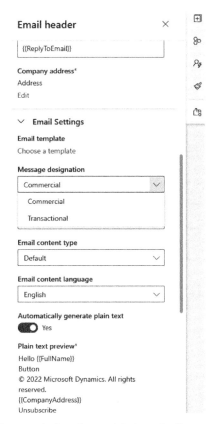

Figure 5.7 – Message designation and Automatically generate plain text

Now that we've gone through how you can create new emails, it's time to start adding content. Content is added to an email by using elements. Let's go through the different elements and how these are used.

Elements: creating content

The elements in marketing emails are almost the same as the ones we went through in the previous chapter on marketing forms. You can add four different types of elements in both marketing areas:

- Text
- Image
- Button
- Divider

In *Figure 5.8*, you can see how these different elements look in an email:

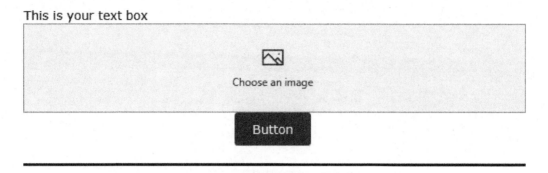

Figure 5.8 – Text, an image, a button, and a divider in a marketing email

Text

The text area is where you write the actual email. Everything you want your customers to know in the text should be in a text element. You can have several different textboxes or you can put everything in one textbox. You will most likely use text blocks in every email you send.

Images

Images can be a good way of creating beautiful emails. Most likely, you will always want to add your company's logo to your marketing email. If own a clothing shop and you want to show your clothes, for example, the use of images will also be very important here. You need to remember that to use an image, it will have to be in the system library; you can add it in advance or you can add it when you create your email. You can also reference an item that is stored in another public system with the use of the image URL.

Buttons

A lot of companies want to add a call-to-action in their email and a common way of doing that is to use a button. You can change the color text and visual style of a button. You can also specify where the clicks should lead, as shown in *Figure 5.09*:

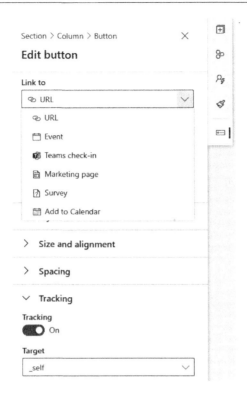

Figure 5.9 – Where the button should link to

You can add a link to the following:

- **URL**: The URL can be a link to any website.

- **Event**: The **Event** link connects to an event in Dynamics 365 Marketing.

- **Teams check-in**: If you have an online event that you are hosting in Microsoft Teams, you can use the **Teams check-in** option. When you select the **Teams check-in** option, you have to specify whether this is a check-in for the entire event or a session.

- **Marketing page**: Maybe you want to connect to one of the marketing pages we created in the previous chapter – this is also available as a link.

- **Survey**: You can link to a Dynamics 365 **Customer Voice** survey. We are going to go through Customer Voice in *Chapter 9, Dynamics 365 Customer Voice*.

- **Add to Calendar**: The **Add to Calendar** link is also connected to events. You can let your participants add the full event, the event and sessions they've registered for, or just the sessions they've registered for.

You can also set whether you want to enable tracking on the button to see whether your recipients have clicked on the button in the email.

Dividers

The divider in the email designer is a way to add more space to your email. It could be a solid line, a dotted line, or an invisible divider, just to make your email less compact and easier to consume for the reader.

QR codes

In *Chapter 8, Managing Events*, we're going to go through managing events, and QR codes can be a vital part of this. When you use Dynamics 365 Marketing for events, you can embed an event QR code into your marketing email. If you want to register the people that have arrived, you do this by scanning the QR codes. The QR codes must be connected to your event and each participant will have their own unique QR code.

Additional elements in outbound emails

In addition to these, in outbound marketing emails, you can also use these three elements:

- Videos
- Code

In *Figure 5.10*, you can see how these different elements are used in a marketing email:

Figure 5.10 – Videos, code, and QR codes in a marketing email

Videos

The video element is only available in **Outbound marketing** emails. This means you can only use the outbound library and cannot store the videos in your own system. You can add a video from your outbound library or you can add it from an external URL. You can also edit the size and alignment, style, and spacing of the video. Because the videos are not stored in the email as it is sent, it will not impact the size of the email.

Code

In the code section, you can add code elements. Maybe you have two different prices for your event – one early bird and one regular price. You want to send the email once but show the correct price depending on what day it is. You can then add some code that means before one date, it shows one price, and after it, it shows another, regular price. This way, you do not have to send out two different emails but can still show the correct price to your customers.

Layout section types

In marketing emails, you have similar layout types as you do for marketing forms and pages. You have six different layouts to choose from:

- 1 column
- 1:2 column
- 2 column
- 2:1 column
- 3 column
- Custom type with up to 8 columns

To find the layouts, you need to go to **Elements** and then **Layout section types** in the email. You can see the different layouts for an email in *Figure 5.11*:

Figure 5.11 – The different layouts for an email

Content blocks

We talked about content blocks in the previous chapter when learning about marketing forms. Content blocks are a good way of making sure your content follows company design guidelines. You probably have a header that you always want to use in every marketing email you send out. This header can contain your logo and some information about your company with links to your website. These content blocks should always look the same and should be included in every single email you send out. Creating these as content blocks will make the work easier for your users.

General styles

In the **General styles** tab, you can set the maximum width layout and choose the font family, body text size, text color, and email background, as shown in *Figure 5.12*:

Figure 5.12 – General styles for a marketing email

It's important to know here that you cannot add your own fonts to the general styles; you must use the HTML editor.

HTML editor

If your company has special requirements that you cannot fulfill using **General styles**, you can do so in the HTML editor. It is very important that you do not tamper with the HTML code if you do not know what you are doing. Tampering with the HTML code could destroy your entire email. Some marketers are used to using HTML code and will prefer this over the drag-and-drop editor. You can see the HTML editor in *Figure 5.13*:

```
HTML                                                                                                        ×

🖳 Command palette   ⌁ Format document                                                                      ▭ ∨   🌙
  1   ⦿!DOCTYPE html
  2        PUBLIC "-//W3C//DTD XHTML 1.0 Transitional//EN" "http://www.w3.org/TR/xhtml1/DTD/xhtml1-transitional.dtd" ▌
  3   <html>
  4
  5   <head>
  6       <meta http-equiv="Content-Type" content="text/html; charset=utf-8">
  7       <meta name="viewport" content="width=device-width, initial-scale=1.0">
  8       <title>My Email Subject</title>
  9       <meta name="referrer" content="never">
 10       <meta type="xrm/designer/setting" name="type" value="marketing-designer-content-editor-document">
 11       <meta type="xrm/designer/setting" name="layout-editable" value="marketing-designer-layout-editable">
 12       <meta type="xrm/designer/setting" name="layout-max-width" value="600px" datatype="text" label="Layout max width">
 13       <meta type="xrm/designer/setting" name="font-family" value="Verdana, Arial, sans-serif" datatype="font"
 14           label="Font Family">
 15       <meta type="xrm/designer/setting" name="body-text-size" value="14px" datatype="text" label="Body Font Size">
 16       <meta type="xrm/designer/setting" name="body-text-color" value="#000" datatype="color" label="Body Text Color">
 17       <meta type="xrm/designer/setting" name="outer-background" value="#FFFFFF" datatype="color" label="Email Background">
 18       <style>
 19           body,
 20           div {
 21               font-family:
 22                   /* @font-family */
 23                   Verdana,
 24                   /* @font-family */
 25                   Arial,
 26                   /* @font-family */
 27                   sans-serif
 28                   /* @font-family */
 29               ;
 30               font-size:
 31                   /* @body-text-size */
 32                   14px
 33                   /* @body-text-size */
 34               ;
 35               color:
 36                   /* @body-text-color */
 37                   #000
 38                   /* @body-text-color */
 39               ;
```

Figure 5.13 – The HTML editor

If you use a custom font in your design guides, you can change it in the HTML editor. You then need to remember to make those changes in every email you send out or add them to your email templates.

Additional features in real-time emails

Real-time marketing is the future. Moving forward, Microsoft is continuing to work with real-time marketing, and all new features will only be available in real-time marketing. Because of this, there are some differences when creating your marketing emails. Let us go through the additional features you get in **Real-time marketing** emails.

Personalized emails

In emails that you send to your company's customers, you might want to add the recipient's name to the email, or maybe the name of the salesperson responsible. These fields will differ from recipient to recipient:

1. To be able to do this in Dynamics 365 Marketing, you must click **Personalization** as shown in *Figure 5.14*:

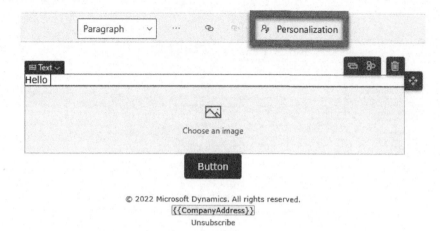

Figure 5.14 – Personalization in Real-time marketing

2.   After clicking on the **Personalization** button, I get a dropdown where I can see the dynamic text available to me, as shown in *Figure 5.15*, and I can add new dynamic text:

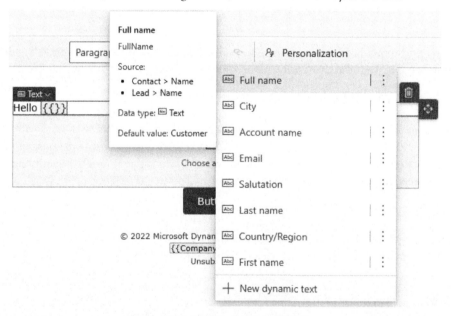

Figure 5.15 – Adding personalization

3.   When you click on the **Full name** field, you will see a new popup where you're asked whether your audience is **Contact** or **Lead** as shown in *Figure 5.16*:

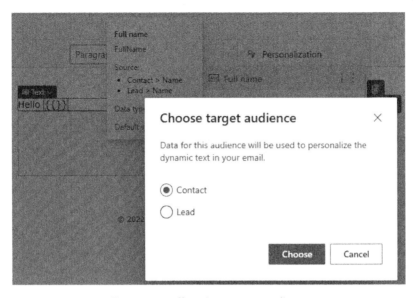

Figure 5.16 – Choosing a target audience

4. When you've chosen **Contact** or **Lead**, the personalization for **FullName** is added to your text area as shown in *Figure 5.17*:

Figure 5.17 – FullName in Personalization

When your email is sent, each contact will see their name after **Hello**. If for some reason, someone doesn't have their name registered, then they'll get **Hello Customer**.

Conditional content

I often get asked by customers to show different content to different users in the same email. One customer might be interested in product A and the other in product B. I do not want to send the same content to both, but I also don't want to create two emails. I can utilize conditional content to send customized content to both customers in one email.

When you add an element to the real-time email, you click on the **Enable conditional content button** as shown in *Figure 5.18*:

Figure 5.18 – Enabling conditional content on an image

On the right-hand side, a new pane will open where you can set your conditions. You can create a condition based on an attribute or segment membership (whether someone is or isn't part of one) as shown in *Figure 5.19*:

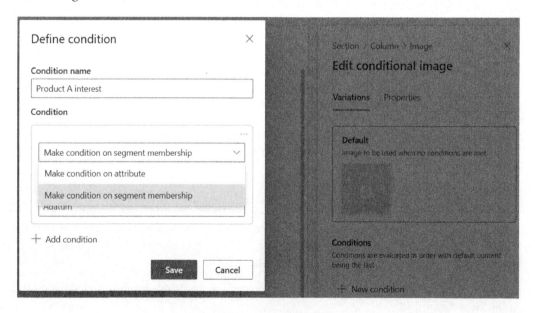

Figure 5.19 – Adding a condition to an image

When you've clicked **Save**, your condition will have been registered as shown in *Figure 5.20*:

Figure 5.20 – Conditions registered

As you can see, the image is still the same. You must go to the **Properties** tab and replace the picture with the alternative picture you want to show the customers that matches the conditions as shown in *Figure 5.21*:

Figure 5.21 – Changing the image for customers that met the condition

Once you've changed the image and gone back to **Variations**, you can see in *Figure 5.22* that your conditions image has been updated – customers that meet the criteria will see the image and the customers that don't meet the criteria will see the default image.

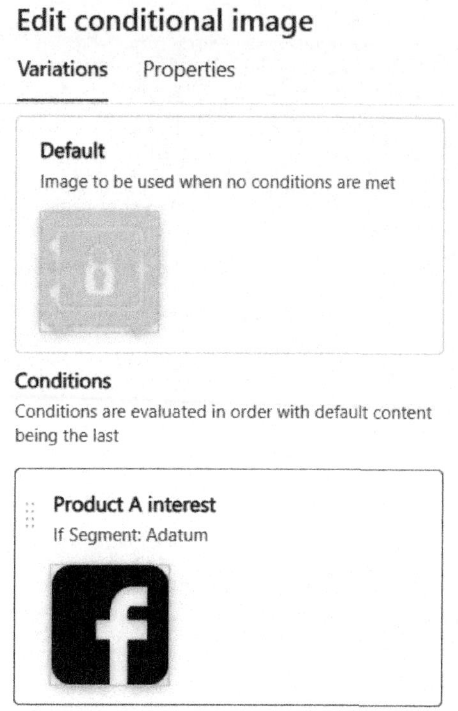

Figure 5.22 – Different picture for default customers and customers that match the condition

With this condition, you don't have to use code to show different users different content in your email. If you use advanced personalization, you must go into the HTML code to make the changes.

Brand profiles

Some customers have multiple brands they're managing in one environment. It's possible to define several brand profiles. In the brand profiles, you can add senders, where you define the sender and the reply email. You can add social media links to emails. You can easily change the brand profiles in the top-right corner as shown in *Figure 5.23*:

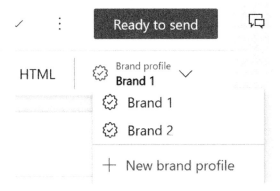

Figure 5.23 – Brand profile

Additional features in outbound emails

As of the wave 2 release, there is one feature that you can find in **Outbound marketing** emails and not in **Real-time marketing** emails. In **Real-time marketing**, you do A/B testing through the marketing journey, not the email. Let's go through how you can do A/B testing in an **Outbound marketing** email.

A/B testing

On the right-hand side, you can find A/B testing as shown in *Figure 5.24*:

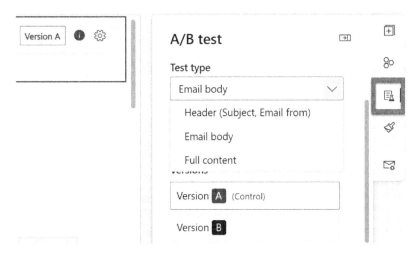

Figure 5.24 – A/B testing in an outbound email

In an A/B test, you define what you want to test:

- **Header (Subject, Email from)**
- **Email body**
- **Full content**

Depending on which test type you choose, you can make small changes to the email, or create two completely different emails to see which performs best.

To send the email and select the best option, you add the email to your outbound customer journey and enable A/B testing as shown in *Figure 5.25*:

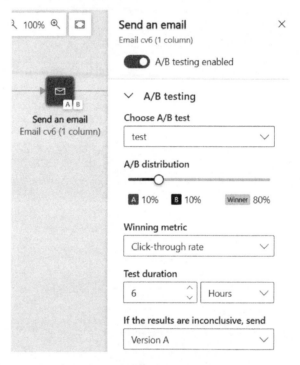

Figure 5.25 – A/B testing from an outbound customer journey

As you can see in *Figure 5.25*, you can say how you want to distribute the email and what the winning metric should be – either **Click-through rate** or **Open rate**.

Now that we've gone through the unique features in both **Outbound marketing** and **Real-time marketing**, let's see how we can make sure our email looks good and will be received in our customers' inboxes.

In addition to A/B testing, you must do the personalization a bit differently in **Outbound marketing**. Let's go through how this works in **Outbound marketing**.

Personalized emails

To make the same personalization as we went through for **Real-time marketing**, we have to go through some more steps in **Outbound marketing**.

We click on the same **Personalization** button in the email, but we get a different window with different options as you can see in *Figure 5.26*:

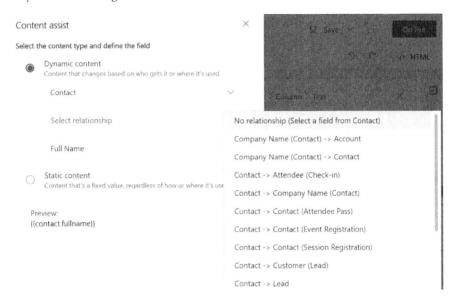

Figure 5.26 – Adding personalization to an outbound email

There are three steps to add the **Full name** details as a personalization:

1. You select the table and the required **Contact**.

2. Choose **Select relationship**. Here, you have to know your data to understand where you can find the different information. We want the full name from the contact table, so we select **No relationship (Select a field from Contact)**.

3. The last step is to find the column we want to add as the personalization. Here, we selected **Full Name**.

The **Full Name** column is now added as a personalization as shown in *Figure 5.27*:

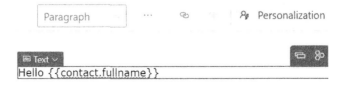

Figure 5.27 – The personalization for Full Name – contact.fullname is added

Checking the content

Before you start looking at your email to see whether it's acceptable to send to customers, you need to check your content. You do that by clicking on **Check content** in your ribbon as shown in *Figure 5.28*:

Figure 5.28 – Check content

If everything is in order, your email will pass the check. If not, you'll get a notification saying you have this many notifications and to view the errors as shown in *Figure 5.29*:

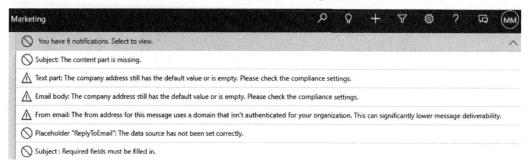

Figure 5.29 – Notifications after content is checked

When everything you have been notified about is fixed, then it's time to check your accessibility.

Accessibility checker

Every email you send should be accessible to everyone. You never know whether the recipient has any kind of disability that makes reading your email harder for them. To check accessibility, click on the arrow next to **Check content** and select **Accessibility checker** as shown in *Figure 5.30*:

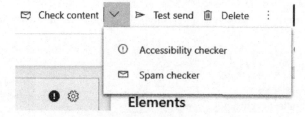

Figure 5.30 – Accessibility checker

When you've clicked on **Accessibility checker**, you will see a side panel that will show you the issues you have in your email as shown in *Figure 5.31*:

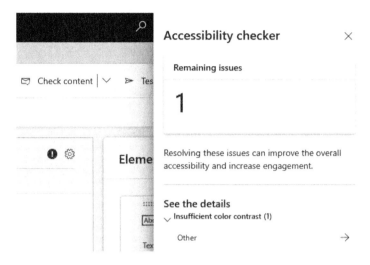

Figure 5.31 – Accessibility checker issues

You can fix any accessibility issues from within the checker. You click on the issue and it will tell you exactly how to fix the problem as shown in *Figure 5.32*:

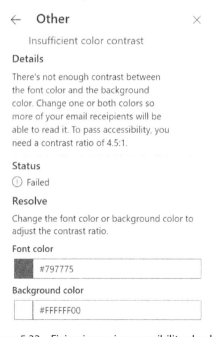

Figure 5.32 – Fixing issues in accessibility checker

When you are done with **Accessibility checker** and have fixed all the issues in your email, it's time to see what your spam score will be like.

Spam checker

We've all gotten them – spam emails. Make sure your recipient's email servers don't see you as a spammer and run **Spam checker** as shown in *Figure 5.33*:

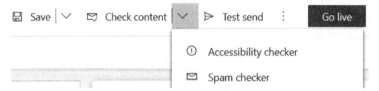

Figure 5.33 – Running Spam checker

Spam checker will now run through your email and show you how much of a risk it is that email servers will tag the email as spam as shown in *Figure 5.34*:

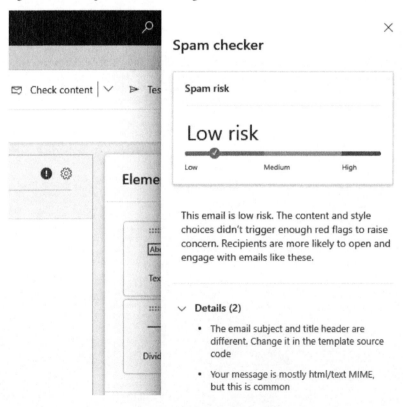

Figure 5.34 – Spam checker results

Low risk is what you want as a result. If you do get a medium or high chance of spam, you will get suggestions on how you can fix it, and you should go through the details and try to get as low a score as possible.

Now that you've gone through **Accessibility checker** and **Spam checker**, you know that your email is ready to be previewed and tested.

Preview and test

Before you go live with your marketing email, you need to make sure it will look good to your recipients. You must preview your email to make sure it looks good. When you click on the **Preview and test** tab, you'll see a preview of your email as shown in *Figure 5.35*:

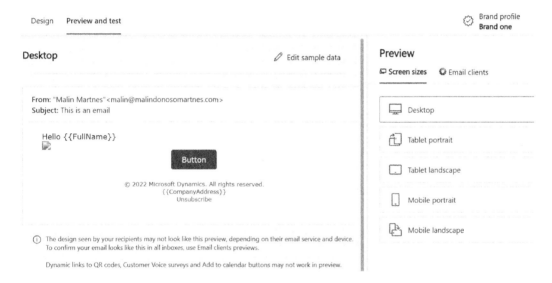

Figure 5.35 – The Preview and test tab for the email

In this email, we've used the customer's full name as a personalization, by clicking **Edit sample data**, highlighted in *Figure 5.36*:

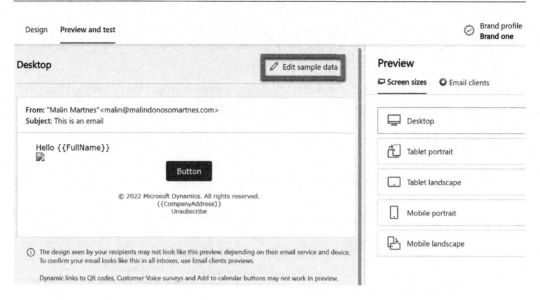

Figure 5.36 – Edit sample data

By doing this, a new section will open on the right-hand side, where I can edit the sample data and add the test data I want for this email, as shown in *Figure 5.37*:

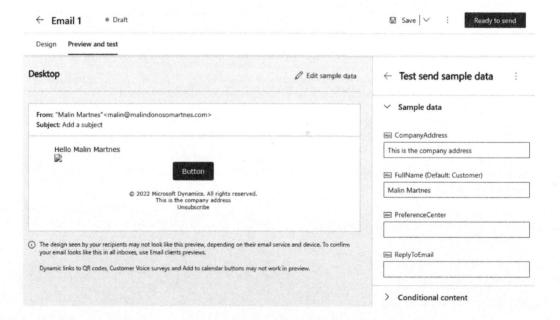

Figure 5.37 – Edited sample data

This way, I can test different types of data and make sure everything looks good when it's sent. For example, I can test that even the longest or shortest names will not look bad in an email.

In addition to testing the sample data, you can also preview the different screen sizes as shown in *Figure 5.38*:

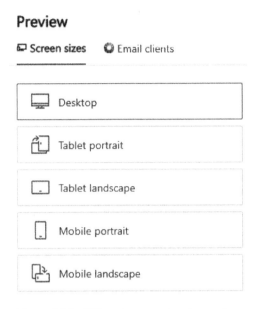

Figure 5.38 – Different screen sizes to preview

Be aware that this preview just shows you how the email will look in your system. It does not preview how it will look in the different email services and devices. For that type of preview, you use the Litmus preview.

Litmus preview

If you have worked with marketing emails previously, you know how difficult it is to find out how your email looks in your customer's inbox. I remember creating marketing emails and wondering how they would look for each email service. We would test send the email to all our own accounts and try them out on different applications.

Even doing that, we always had some email services or devices that we could not test out our email on. If you are looking at an email in the Outlook app on your laptop, it will look different than if you look at the email on Outlook on your Android phone. If your customers are using old legacy systems or are using other email providers, you want your email to look good in every inbox.

Litmus integration will make your life much easier. You will have to enable the integration in your **Default settings** area, as shown in *Figure 5.39*, before you can use it:

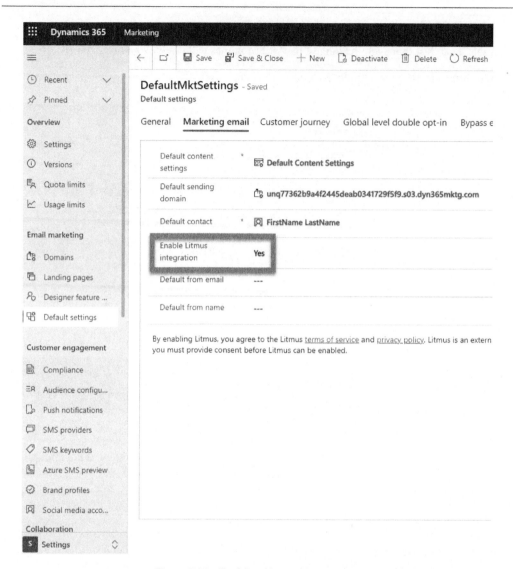

Figure 5.39 – Enabling Litmus integration

Once enabled, you will have a fixed number of previews per tenant per month, defined by your license. You can always see how many you have and how many you've used in the **Settings** | **Default settings** | **Quota limits** options. If you want to add more inbox previews, you can buy these directly from the Litmus web page (find pricing information here: `https://www.litmus.com/pricing/`).

Now, we've created functional and hopefully pretty emails from blank forms. Your company probably has certain ways they want the emails to look. One of the easiest ways of doing that is by using email templates. Let's take a look at how we can create them.

Email templates

Before a user starts creating their own emails, they should create company design guidelines as a template. You design the emails the same way as you've learned in this chapter, but let us see where we can create these in **Real-time marketing**.

Creating Real-time marketing templates

You can create your **Real-time marketing** templates under **Assets | Templates** and by clicking **+New** on the ribbon, as you can see in *Figure 5.40*:

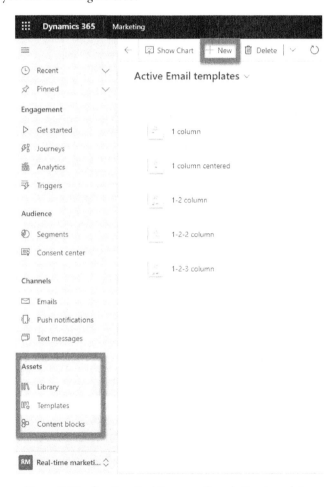

Figure 5.40 – Creating Real-time email marketing templates

The emails will then have to be created the same way as we've already gone through in this chapter.

Now, let's see where we can create an **Outbound marketing** email template.

Creating outbound marketing templates

You'll find the email templates under **Marketing templates** in **Outbound marketing**, as shown in *Figure 5.41*:

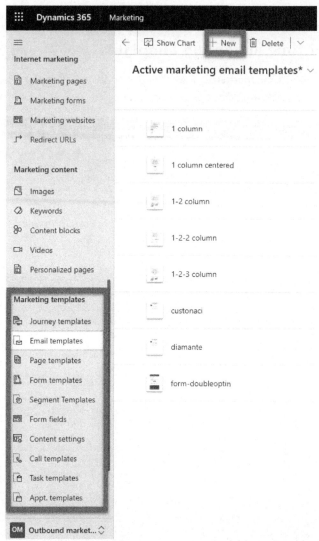

Figure 5.41 – Outbound marketing email template

In **Outbound marketing** as well as **Real-time marketing**, you can create your templates the same way you create your regular emails. Remember that the **Outbound marketing** and **Real-time marketing** areas are different, so you cannot use a template from one area in the other area. If you're using one of the areas and want to move to the other, you must create new templates.

Now, you've created your template and your users are ready to start creating and sending marketing emails.

Sending emails

In order to send any emails from Dynamics 365 Marketing, you must set emails to **Ready to send**. When you click on **Ready to send** in **Real-time marketing**, as shown in *Figure 5.42*, the email is uploaded to your cloud and can be accessed by the marketing recipients:

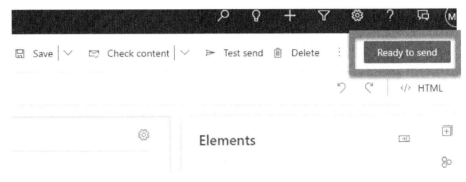

Figure 5.42 – Setting a Real-time marketing email (Ready to send)

In **Outbound marketing**, you click **Go live** as shown in *Figure 5.43*:

Figure 5.43 – Go live with an Outbound marketing email

Now that you've got your email ready and live, you can start using the email to send it to recipients.

Send now

In **Outbound marketing**, you have the option to send the email immediately.

> **Important note**
> Be aware that you can only send the email to 30 recipients and there is no guarantee that QR codes, Customer Voice surveys, or the **Add to calendar** button will work.

To use the **Send now** feature, click on the three dots next to **Go live** and then click **Send now**, as shown in *Figure 5.44*:

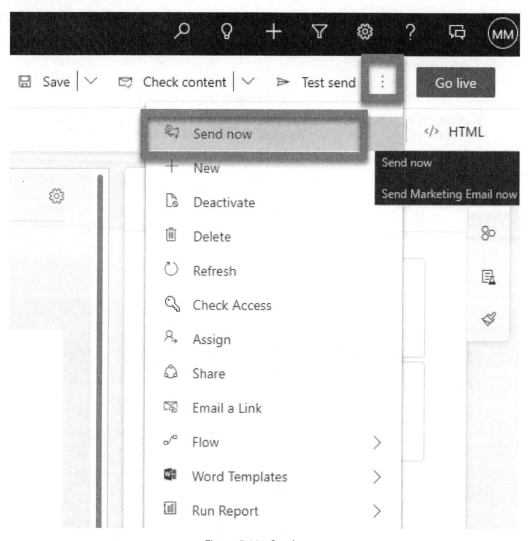

Figure 5.44 – Send now

When you've clicked that, a new popup opens, and you can select the recipients you want, as you can see in *Figure 5.45*:

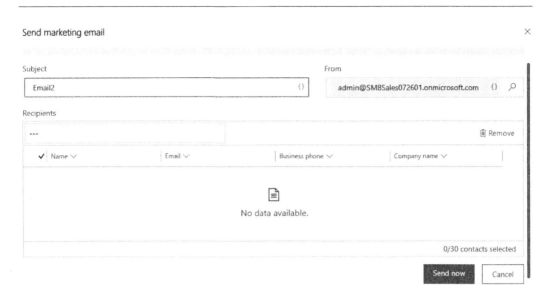

Figure 5.45 – Selecting a maximum of 30 contacts to send the email to

When you send the email to the recipients, a customer journey will be created in the background of the system.

Customer journeys

Customer journeys are where most of your emails will be sent from. In the next two chapters, we will go through all the features of customer journeys. To send an email from a customer journey, you will first have to create the customer journey and then add the marketing email, add your recipients, and go live with the customer journey.

Double opt-in confirmation

Another way to use emails is to use them to confirm double opt-in. You can have one confirmation email for all double opt-ins or multiple emails for each of your forms using double opt-ins.

Now we've seen some ways of sending the emails you've created, let's see what kind of analytics you can get.

Analytics

It's always important to analyze what you do. How can you know whether you created a good email if you don't look at the analytics? You need to see whether your recipients read the email and click on the links you send them. How many bounces you have will tell you a bit about the quality of your data. If you have a lot of bounces, your email might get flagged as spam by more email servers. If you send too many emails, your customers might not be happy with you.

There is a difference between what you'll see in **Outbound marketing** and **Real-time marketing** when it comes to analytics. Let's start with how this looks in the **Outbound marketing** area.

Outbound analytics

In the out-of-the-box dashboard, as you can see in *Figure 5.46*, you can see an overview of your emails. You can see statistics and analytics of the emails in your system:

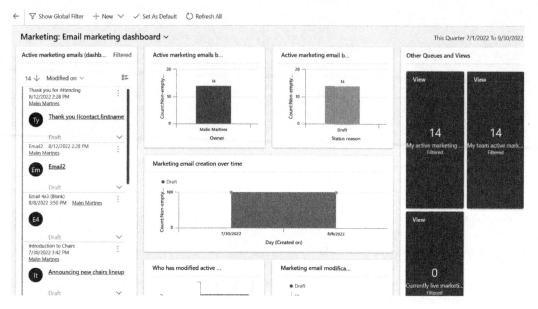

Figure 5.46 – Out-of-the-box email dashboard

For each email, you can see different statistics, as shown in *Figure 5.47*. You can see how many were delivered and opened and can also see other important statistics for a single email:

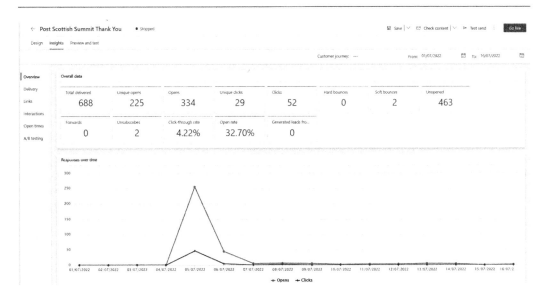

Figure 5.47 – Overview of one specific email

There is a lot of relevant analytics you can go through for a specific email, all emails your company has sent, or how one specific customer behaves with email interactions. Now, let's go through how **Real-time marketing** uses analytics.

Real-time marketing analytics

In **Real-time marketing**, you can see a lot of the same information as you can in **Outbound marketing**.

As soon as you open an email that is live and has been sent, you will see email analytics on the right-hand side of the screen, as shown in *Figure 5.48*:

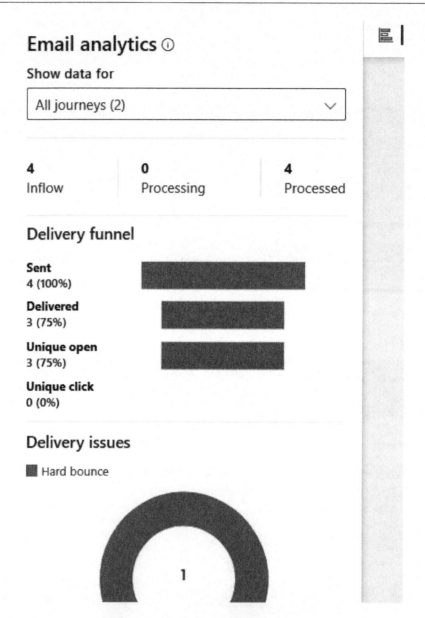

Figure 5.48 – Email analytics for a sent email

In the **Reports** section for the email, you will see a Power BI report showing the email's delivery trends as shown in *Figure 5.49*:

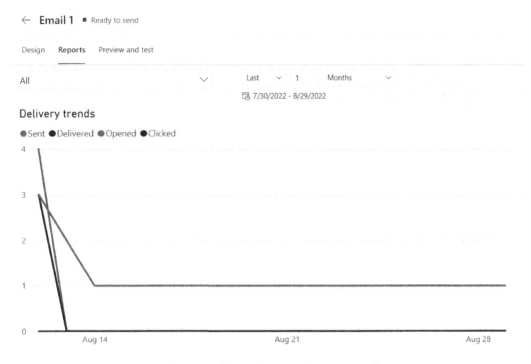

Figure 5.49 – Power BI report for a sent email

Summary

Email is a very important feature for a lot of companies that work with marketing. We've gone through how you can create emails. We've seen different elements and how you can create pretty emails. We've seen the differences between **Outbound marketing** emails and **Real-time marketing** emails.

We've also seen the importance of previewing and testing and have seen that the Litmus preview functionality is amazing and will help your company a lot. We've also talked a bit about the importance of creating marketing templates.

We've seen how you can send your emails, which we are also going to talk about in the next chapter. We finished this chapter by talking about analytics and how important analytics are to improving your company's email marketing.

Questions

The following are some questions that will help you gauge your understanding of the topics discussed in this chapter. The answers are available in the Assessments section at the end of the book.

1. To start using Litmus integration, you first must do what?

    (a) Sign in to Litmus

    (b) Create a Litmus account

    (c) Activate Litmus integration in the settings

    (d) Activate Litmus integration in the settings and on the Litmus page

2. Which two elements are only available in **Outbound marketing**?

    (a) Text

    (b) Images

    (c) Personalization

    (d) Videos

    (e) Dividers

    (f) Code

    (g) QR codes

3. In **Send now**, you can send an email to a maximum of how many people?

    (a) 10

    (b) 20

    (c) 30

    (d) 40

    (e) 50

4. Can a marketing form be embedded into a marketing email?

    (a) Yes

    (b) No

6
Outbound Customer Journeys

Customer journeys write the story of how your customers interact with your company. It is how you wish to guide them and give them information. A customer journey could be signing up for a **newsletter** and receiving that newsletter by **email**. A customer journey could also be a complete route for an event participant, such as registering, getting a reminder email with the **event QR code**, and **evaluating** the event through **Customer Voice**. As of August 2022, there are two areas where you can create and manage customer journeys: **Outbound marketing** and **Real-time marketing**. In this chapter, we are going to go through outbound customer journeys. We're going to see how they work and what options you have.

We're going to go through the following topics:

- Outbound customer journeys
- Analytics
- Checking your knowledge

We will begin with how you create and understand outbound customer journeys.

Creating and understanding outbound customer journeys

Outbound customer journeys were the first customer journey to come to Dynamics 365 Marketing. Outbound customer journeys are connected to the **marketing emails** that you can find in the Outbound marketing area. This means that if you create a marketing email in Real-time marketing, you cannot use it in an outbound customer journey. If you want to use an email you have created in Real-time marketing, you need to use a Real-time marketing journey. In outbound customer journeys, you set up the route the customer should take when interacting with your company. This could be when they register for an event and what emails you want to send to them. A new potential customer that downloads a whitepaper should be contacted by the sales department. In other words, every way of communicating with your customer or potential customer is via a customer journey.

Now, let's go through how we create an outbound customer journey.

Creating an outbound customer journey

To create an **outbound customer journey,** you must first make sure you are in the **Outbound marketing** area:

1. You can find the **Customer journeys** option in the **Marketing execution** section, as shown in *Figure 6.1*:

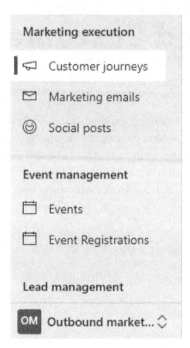

Figure 6.1 – Customer journeys under Marketing execution in Outbound marketing

2. Once you've clicked on **Customer journeys**, you will see a list of all the active customer journeys. In this area, you can click on the + **New** button to create a new customer journey, as shown in *Figure 6.2*:

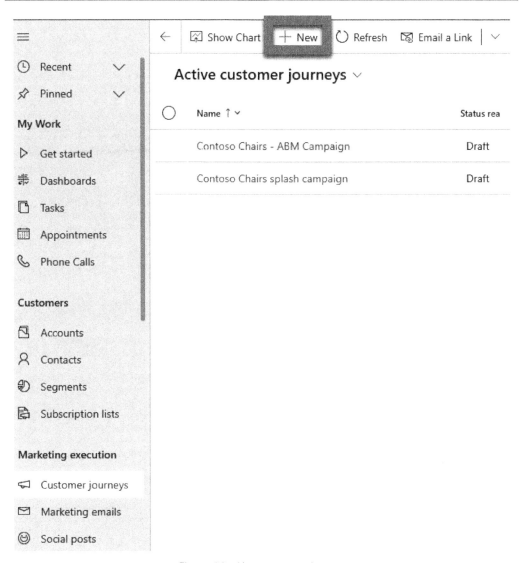

Figure 6.2 – New customer journey

3.   You then get asked whether you want to select a customer journey template, as shown in *Figure 6.3*:

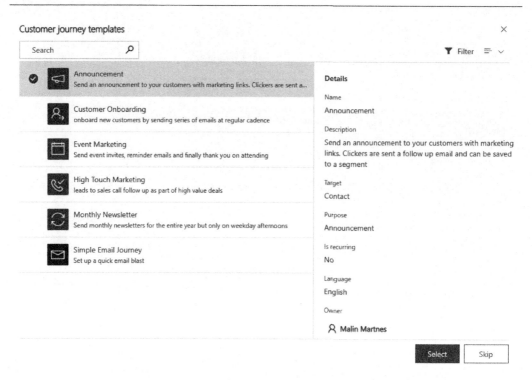

Figure 6.3 – Choosing a customer journey template

4. If you repeat the same **customer journey** often or use the same steps in a lot of your customer journeys, you should create them as customer journey templates.

    If you do not select a template, a blank customer journey is created for you, as shown in *Figure 6.4*:

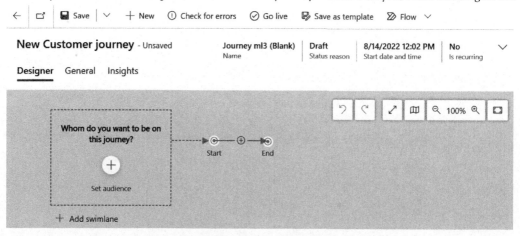

Figure 6.4 – Blank customer journey

5. You can now start filling it with information to guide your customers through the best customer journey possible.

Now that you know how to create a journey, it's time to fill the journey with what you want your customers to do. You can do this in the **Designer** tab.

Using the designer

The **designer** is where you create the customer magic. This is where you specify who your customers are and how they're going to **interact** with your company. You have two important areas in the designer: choosing the audience and adding tiles. Let's start by looking at the audience (who you want to communicate with) before moving on to adding tiles (what you want to do with the audience).

Audience

The **audience** is the start of your customer journey. These are the people that enter your customer journey. Click **+ Set audience** and select which audience you're targeting, as shown in *Figure 6.5*:

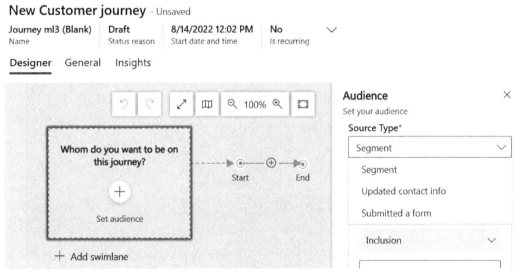

Figure 6.5 – Selecting a source type for your audience

Your audience can come from the following places:

- A segment

- Contacts updating their contact information

- Contacts that have submitted a form

Let's go through each of the audience options.

Segment

In *Chapter 3, What Are Segments and Lists?*, we went through what a **segment** is and how to create one. Now, you can use these segments as a starting point for a customer journey. These are the customers you want to talk to. For example, in a **dynamic segment**, when a new contact meets the criteria of the segment and is added to the segment, they will also start the customer journey. You can say the segment is either a regular **Segment** or a **Subscription List** option, as shown in *Figure 6.6*:

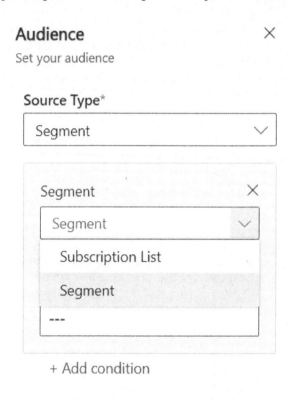

Figure 6.6 – Segment or Subscription List

You can select one segment, add conditions, create segments from the journey, add customers from several segments, or exclude customers from certain segments, as you can see in *Figure 6.7*:

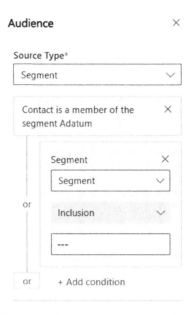

Figure 6.7 – Adding a condition to a segment – exclusion or inclusion

If you cannot find a segment, make sure the segment is published.

When the condition uses **or**, which you can see on the left-hand side in *Figure 6.7*, you are saying "this segment OR this segment." When you click on **or**, it changes to **and**, as shown in *Figure 6.8*:

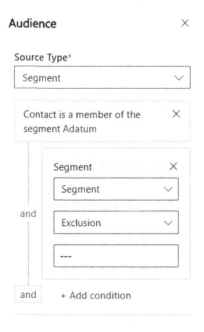

Figure 6.8 – Condition with and instead of or

When you have **and** in your **condition**, you can select whether you want to include or exclude the segment. Maybe you want to start the journey for all customers in this segment, but not those that already have bought the product and are in another segment as well. Then, you can use the **Exclusion** element, as shown in *Figure 6.8*.

Be aware that if you choose **Subscription List** as the audience and the contact is removed from that list or **unsubscribes**, they will continue all active journeys until completion.

Updated contact info

To be able to use **updated contact information**, you will have to go through several selections. First, you must find the entity name of the table you want to use. In *Figure 6.9*, I've selected **Contact** because I want to use a change of contact information to trigger this customer journey:

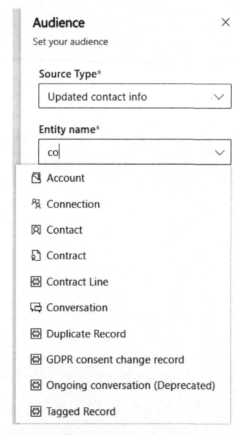

Figure 6.9 – Selecting an entity

Then, you need to select the contact field name. This is the unique identifier of the table you chose. As you can see in *Figure 6.10*, I've selected **Master ID (masterid)**:

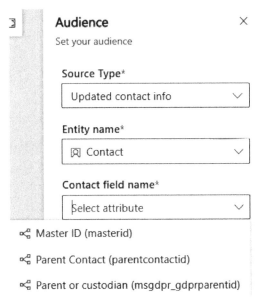

Figure 6.10 – Selecting the contact field name

Trigger Event is the next field. Here, I can select whether the record should trigger when it's created, deleted, or updated, as shown in *Figure 6.11*:

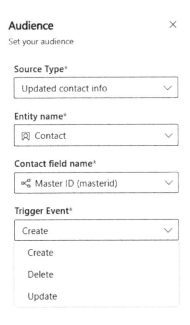

Figure 6.11 – Selecting the trigger event

Now, we select the column or field that we want to trigger the customer journey. As you can see in *Figure 6.12*, this is the **trigger name**, and I've selected the email column:

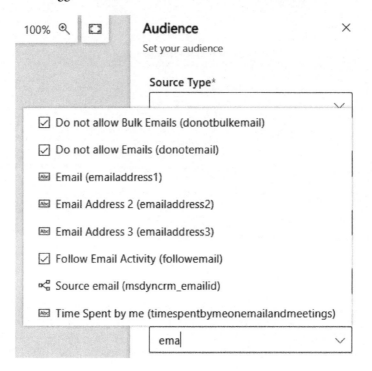

Figure 6.12 – Trigger name

Now, every time a contact updates their email address, it will trigger this customer journey. You can choose to trigger the customer journey from any column from any table related to the contact.

Let's see how a submitted form is going to trigger a customer journey:

1. **Submitted a form**

    When **Submitted a form** is selected as the source type, you need to select the form, as shown in *Figure 6.13*:

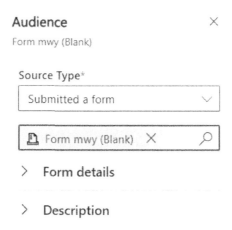

Figure 6.13 – Submitted a form as the source type

2. **Add tiles**

Now that you've gone through who your audience is, you need to define what you want your audience to do. You can add tiles by clicking +, as shown in *Figure 6.14*:

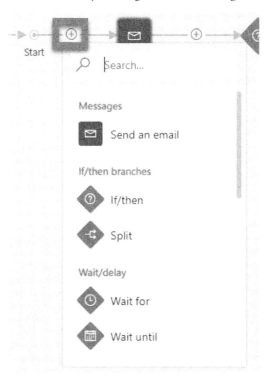

Figure 6.14 – Clicking + in the customer journey

When you click to add a tile, you get a lot of options regarding the type of tile you want to add. You can add these tiles:

- **Messages**
- **If/then branches**
- **Wait/Delay**
- **Actions**
- **Sales activities**
- **Custom tiles**
- **Legacy tiles**

Let's go through all the different types of tiles you can add:

- **Messages**: **Messages** is probably the most commonly used tile in a customer journey, as these are our emails. Click on **Send an email** and then choose the email you want to send to your customers, as shown in *Figure 6.15*:

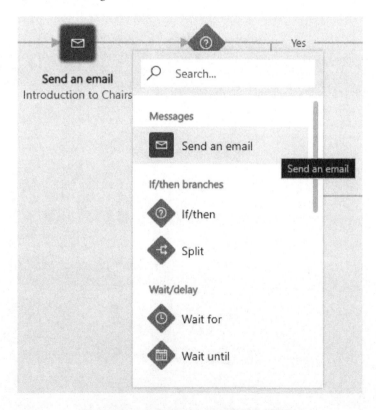

Figure 6.15 – Selecting the send an email tile

If you cannot find an email in the list, to add the email, make sure the email has gone live. If you're adding an email with links to an event, page form, or Customer Voice survey, you also must add the elements under email elements to make sure the recipients get the correct information in the email.

- **If/then branches**: In the **If/then** branches, a tile can either use **If/then** or **Split**.

The other option is to create an **If/then** tile, as shown in *Figure 6.16*:

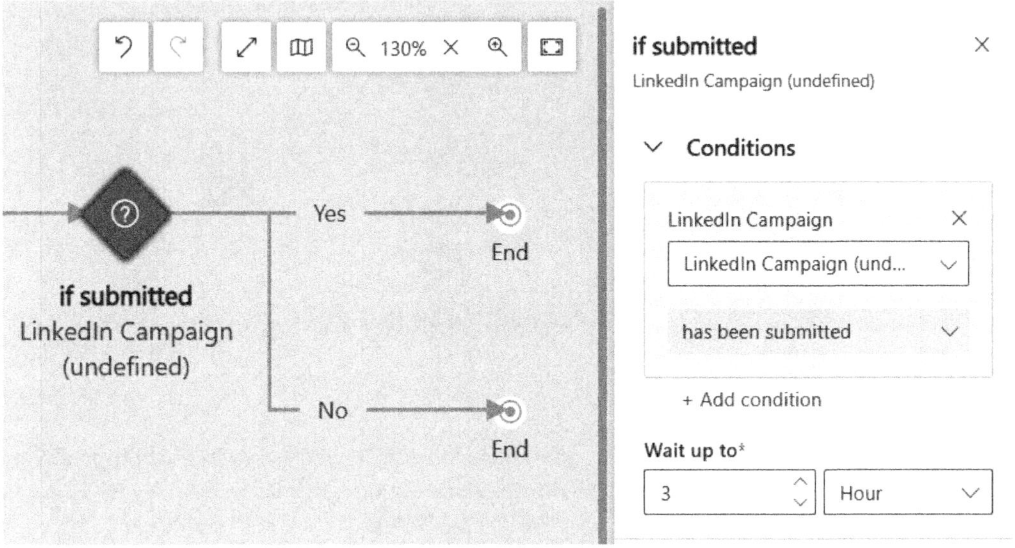

Figure 6.16 – If/then condition

In this tile, you will have to set some conditions. Based on your previous tiles, you can add your conditions. You can also have multiple conditions. You then select the waiting time, which can be hours or days. After the selected waiting time, your audience will go down the path for the condition they want to fulfill.

When using **Split**, you divide your audience into two or more paths. By default, it is split by percentage, and the two paths receive 50% each, as you can see in *Figure 6.17*:

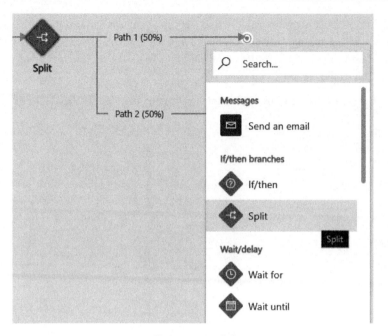

Figure 6.17 – Split

You can also add as many paths as you want and select the percentage you want to send down each path. You can even use the **Distribute evenly** option, as you can see in *Figure 6.18*:

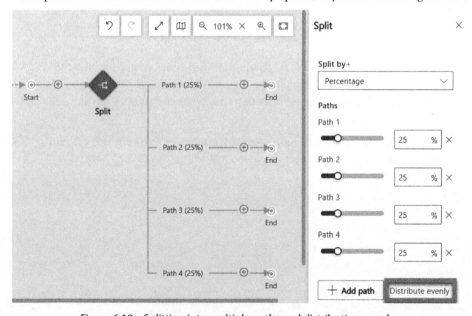

Figure 6.18 – Splitting into multiple paths and distributing evenly

After you have defined your splits, you will also need to add tiles to each path.

- **Wait/Delay**: In **Wait for** tiles, you can specify the amount of time you should wait for. You can set that duration to a number of hours, days, weeks, or months. Your audience will move on to the next title after that amount of time, as shown in *Figure 6.19*:

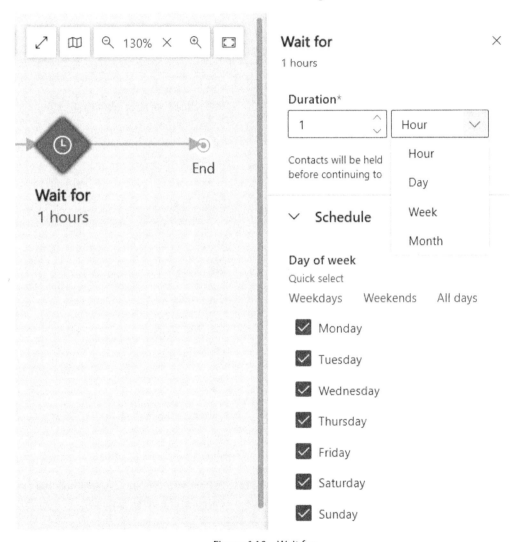

Figure 6.19 – Wait for

The other waiting tile is a **Wait until** tile. Here, you will need to specify a date and time, as shown in *Figure 6.20*:

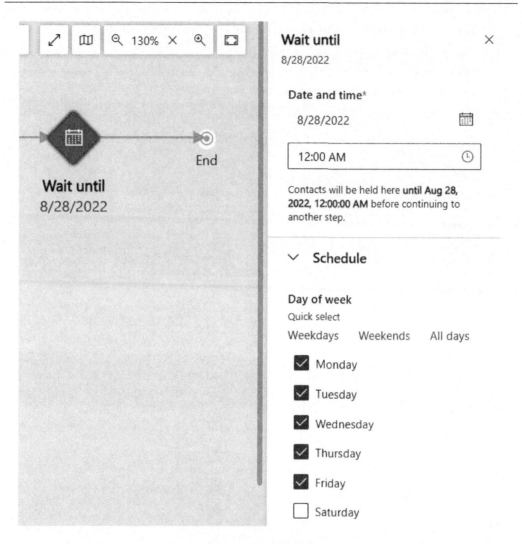

Figure 6.20 – Wait until

In both waiting tiles, you can set up a **schedule**, where you can specify whether the email should be sent on a specific date of the week or at a specific time of day, as shown in *Figure 6.21*:

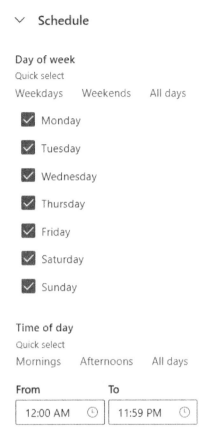

Figure 6.21 – Schedule in a waiting tile

- **Actions**: You have three different action tiles:

  - **Create lead**: This will create a lead based on the information from the contact doing the previous steps

  - **Choose a campaign**: This tile links the contact to a specific LinkedIn campaign

  - **Choose a workflow**: A classic workflow allows you to make certain actions within Dataverse

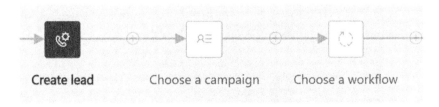

Figure 6.22 – Action tiles

- **Sales activities**: In sales activities, you can create an appointment, phone call, or task tile, as shown in *Figure 6.23*:

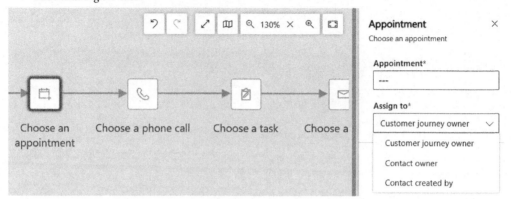

Figure 6.23 – Sales activities

To be able to create any of these activities, you will first need to create them as marketing templates, and then you can choose them in the tile. The next step is to decide who to assign the activity to, as shown in *Figure 6.23*.

- **Custom tiles**: In custom tiles, you can add a custom channel, as shown in *Figure 6.24*:

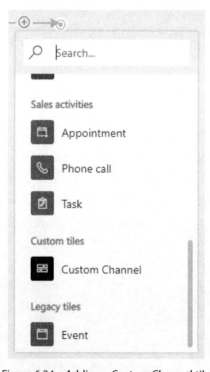

Figure 6.24 – Adding a Custom Channel tile

To add a custom channel, you will first have to create it and then connect the customer journey to it. A custom channel could be SMS, social media, or another channel that you wish to use in your customer journey. Custom channels contain custom tables, workflows, or plug-ins with your developer's logic.

- **Legacy tiles**: The **Event** tile is the only legacy tile. Here, you can connect your outbound customer journey to an event and use that information in another tile. In *Figure 6.25*, I've selected an event for that tile:

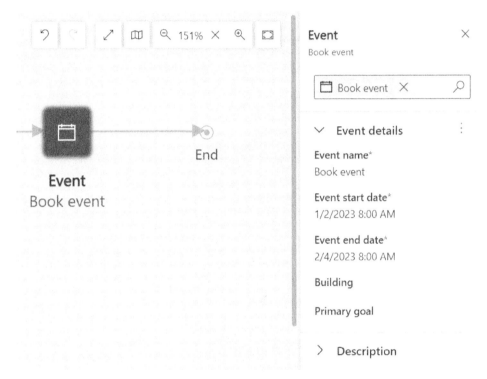

Figure 6.25 – Event tile

Now, you're familiar with all the tiles and can build your outbound customer journey. Before you start using it, let's go through some general settings first.

General settings

In the **General** tab of the customer journey, as you can see in *Figure 6.26*, you can find important information, such as the **Name**, **Owner**, and **Status** details of the customer journey:

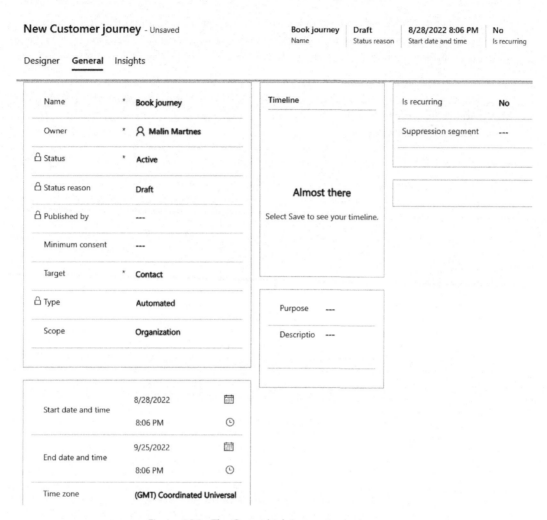

Figure 6.26 – The General tab in a customer journey

Let's go through some of the most important information in the **General** tab.

Minimum consent

In the **Minimum consent** field, you can set which consent level your contacts need to be part of this customer journey. As you can see in *Figure 6.27*, a drop-down menu appears, from which you can select five different consent levels:

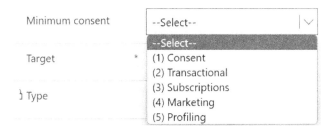

Figure 6.27 – Minimum consent

There are different rules and legislation you need to follow depending on where you and your customers live. If your customer journey sends marketing information, then you need to be allowed to send your contacts marketing information and should select **(4) Marketing**. If your customer journey is to send a receipt to your customer, then the **(2) Transactional** option is what you want to use. When you send out your newsletters, you can select the **(3) Subscriptions** option.

Target

The **Target** field is where you select your **target audience** for this customer journey. As you can see in *Figure 6.28*, you can select either contact or an account:

Figure 6.28 – Target audience

Your customer journey will always be sent to contacts, no matter what you choose in this column. If you choose contacts in this column, then every contact is treated as an individual with no consideration of the account they are connected to in Dataverse. If your target audience is **Account**, the journey can group all your contacts by account, and show your contacts' movement through the tiles on the account timeline.

Recurring

By default, your customer journey will only process each contact once. If you want a contact to go through the same customer journey more than once, you must add it as a **recurring customer journey**. To set a customer journey as recurring, you set the **Is recurring** field to **Yes**. You then get two new fields, as shown in *Figure 6.29*:

Figure 6.29 – Recurring customer journey

The **Recurrence count** setting is how many times a contact can go through the customer journey. The **Recurrence interval (days)** setting is how many days each recurrence interval should be – that is, how long it should be before a contact can go through the same customer journey again.

Suppression segment

If you have some customers to whom you should never send any messages, you can add them to a **suppression segment**. Some of you might be wondering about the difference between a suppression segment and specifying an exclusion segment in the audience style. They both do the same thing but work slightly differently. In the exclusion segment of the audience, you exclude contacts from starting the customer journey. If a contact is added to the exclusion segment after they have started the journey, they will still continue the journey until the end. If you use a suppression segment, these contacts will be blocked from continuing the customer journey. You can use a suppression segment by going to the **General** tab and finding the segment you want to exclude, as shown in *Figure 6.30*:

Figure 6.30 – Suppression segment

Last but not least, let's take a look at how we can use content settings.

Content settings

As shown in *Figure 6.31*, you can connect your **content settings** to your customer journey. This way, all your content will be linked to the correct content settings, and we'll fill out some information from the content settings:

Content settings   🖥 **Default Content Settings**

Figure 6.31 – Content settings

Now, we've gone through how you create and what you can do with an outbound customer journey, but we also want to get better at what we do, so let's look at analytics and how they work.

Analytics

Scottish Summit (https://scottishsummit.com/) is one of the biggest community events in the Microsoft world. Scottish Summit uses Dynamics 365 Marketing to keep track of its events and communication with contacts. The analytics we can see in *Figure 6.32* are an email blast that was sent to previous attendees of Scottish Summit:

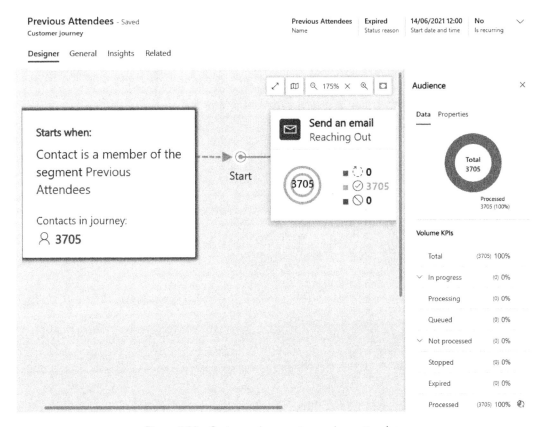

Figure 6.32 – Customer journey to previous attendees

If I click on the **Audience** tile in a customer journey that has run, I will see some data end statistics about the audience.

If I click on the **Send an email** tile, I will get a different set of statistics, as shown in *Figure 6.33*:

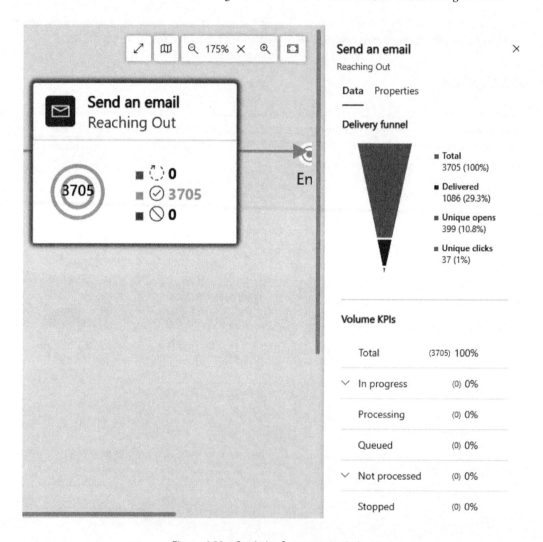

Figure 6.33 – Statistics from an email tile

All the different tiles you are using will show you different statistics based on how your contact has interacted with that specific tile.

When you've selected an email tile and see the delivery KPIs, you can click on **View details**, as shown in *Figure 6.34*, to get more information about email statistics:

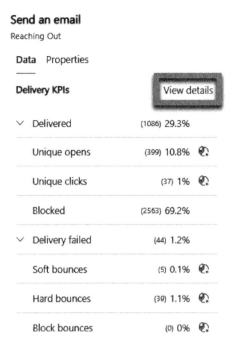

Figure 6.34 – Viewing the details of delivery KPIs

You can then get more statistics about the email connected to the customer journey and can see how people have interacted with the email as shown in *Figure 6.35*:

Figure 6.35 – Email statistics of a customer journey

In the **Insights** area, you can see some statistics as shown in *Figure 6.36*:

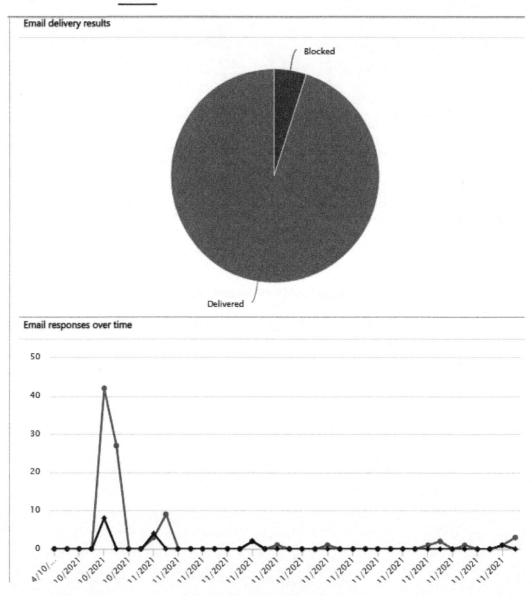

Figure 6.36 – Insights statistics

You can see a **pie chart** of the **email delivery results**. The green is **Delivered** and the red is **Blocked**. You can also see the **email responses** over time, showing who has clicked on the links and who has opened the email.

You can also see **incomplete journeys**, as shown in *Figure 6.37*:

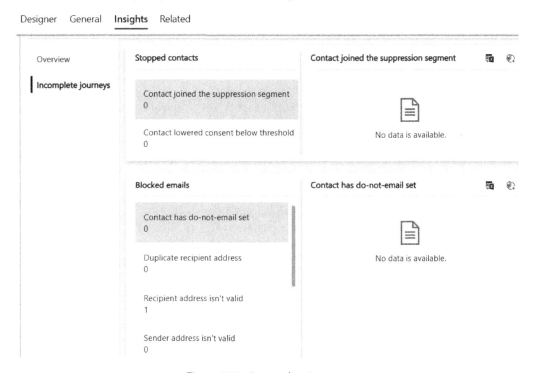

Figure 6.37 – Incomplete journeys

Here, you can go through all the **stopped contacts**. Maybe they have joined a suppression segment, or they don't have the correct consent.

You can also see the ones that have **blocked emails** for any number of reasons. This list should be looked after by your users and cleaned up so that you have good data quality.

Summary

In this chapter, we have gone through most of the things you need to know about creating an outbound customer journey. We've seen how you can create an outbound customer journey. We've gone through all the tiles you can use when creating one and how they can help you. We've gone through the important settings and how they can affect your contacts and your customer journeys. We finished by looking at the analytics to find out how they can help us get even better and create more amazing outbound customer journeys for our contacts.

In the next chapter, we are going to see how we create our customer journeys in Real-time marketing. There are several similarities between outbound customer journeys and Real-time marketing journeys. Which one is most suited for your company's needs will become clearer when we go through *Chapter 7, Real-Time Marketing Journeys*.

Questions

The following are some questions that will help you gauge your understanding of the topics discussed in this chapter. The answers are available in the *Assessments* section at the end of the book.

1.   How can you use outbound customer journeys?

   (a) To send emails to customers

   (b) To reply to your customers

   (c) To say how you interact with customers

2.   How many times will a contact go through a customer journey by default?

   (a) 1

   (b) 10

   (c) Unlimited

3.   You can use either a suppression segment or an excluding segment audience; they both do the same thing.

   (a) True

   (b) False

4.   In the Send an email tile, you can make changes to what?

   (a) The design of the email

   (b) The send time of the email

   (c) The content settings of the email

   (d) The expiration of the email

5.   What always needs to be done before you can start using the customer journey?

   (a) Saving

   (b) Publishing

   (c) Going live

Real-Time Marketing Journeys

In the previous chapter, we went through what customer journeys are – how you interact with your audience. Outbound customer journeys was the first way of doing this. Real-time marketing journeys are the new preferred way of doing this. Microsoft is focusing on developing real-time marketing journeys, so this is where all the new and helpful tools will be.

In this chapter, we are going to go through real-time marketing triggers and journeys, how you can create them, and what you can do with them.

We're going to cover the following topics:

- Real-time marketing triggers
- Creating and understanding real-time marketing journeys
- Analytics

We're going to start by looking at how you create and understand real-time marketing journeys. We're going to see how you can use them and how you can utilize the real-time marketing triggers to create marketing journeys for your customers in real time. By the end of the chapter, you will be able to create and use triggers and real-time marketing journeys.

Real-time marketing triggers

One of the biggest differences between outbound marketing and real-time marketing in Dynamics 365 marketing is the triggers. There are several triggers set up out of the box, but you can also set up your own triggers. Let's say you want to send an email to everyone that has abandoned their cart on your website; this can be done with triggers. You can find and create triggers from the **Real-time marketing** area, under **Engagement** and **Triggers**, as shown in *Figure 7.1*:

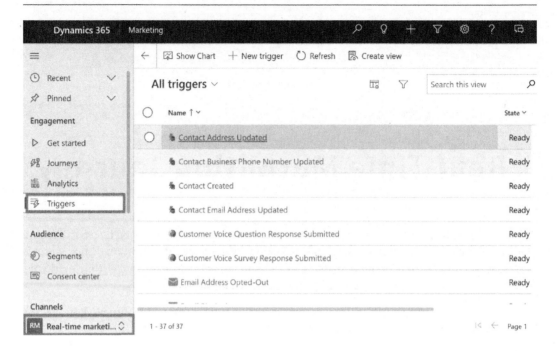

Figure 7.1 – Out-of-the-box Real-time marketing triggers

As you can see in *Figure 7.1*, there are several triggers ready for you to use, such as when a contact updated their email address or responded to a Customer Voice Survey. Let's go through some of the out-of-the-box triggers.

Out-of-the-box triggers

There are several out-of-the-box triggers already set up in Dynamics 365 Marketing. If you want to start a journey if the contact address is updated, or if there are any issues with the email, SMS, or push notification, all these triggers are already set up in the system:

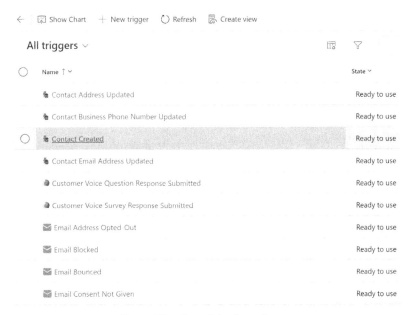

Figure 7.2 – Out-of-the-box triggers

Now that we've looked at the out-of-the-box triggers, let's take a look at how we can create our own custom triggers.

Creating custom triggers

At times, it's not enough to use the out-of-the-box triggers – you want to create your own triggers. Let's see how we can create custom triggers. When you click on **+ New trigger**, you can create a new custom trigger, as shown in *Figure 7.3*:

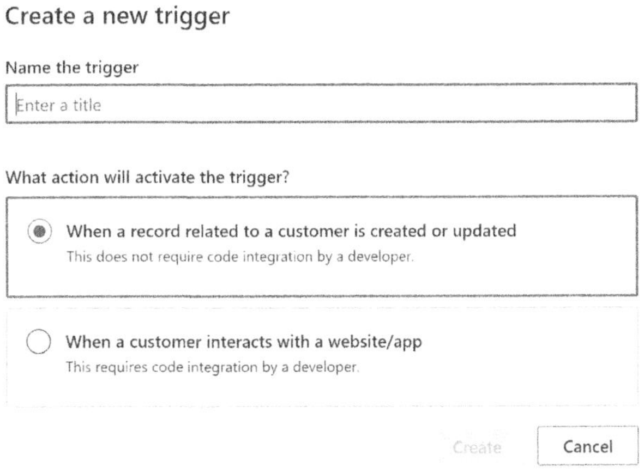

Create a new trigger

Name the trigger

Enter a title

What action will activate the trigger?

⦿ When a record related to a customer is created or updated
This does not require code integration by a developer.

◯ When a customer interacts with a website/app
This requires code integration by a developer.

Create   Cancel

Figure 7.3 – Creating a custom trigger

First, you need to give the trigger a name. You then select the action that will activate this trigger. You can select **When a record related to a customer is created or updated**, where you don't need to integrate the code with anything, or you can select **When a customer interacts with a website/app**, where you need to integrate the code to a website or an app. Let's start with going through how you can activate the trigger when a record related to a customer is created or updated.

When a record related to a customer is created or updated

When you select **When a record related to a customer is created or updated**, there are several choices you need to make to create the trigger. Let's go through all of them and see what they all mean:

1. **In which table is the record created or updated?** is the first dropdown you get. This is where you choose the table that the contact created or updated, as shown in *Figure 7.4*:

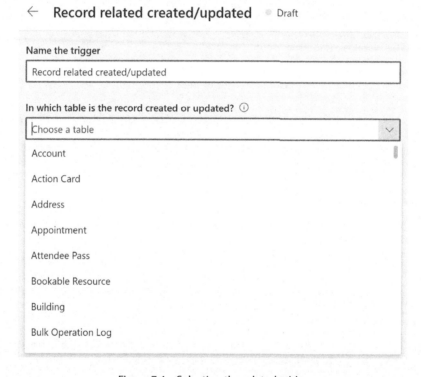

Figure 7.4 – Selecting the related table

2. The next step is **Who is the audience for this trigger?**. Here, you can select **Contact (via attribute Primary Contact)** or **Lead (via attribute Originating Lead)**, as shown in *Figure 7.5*:

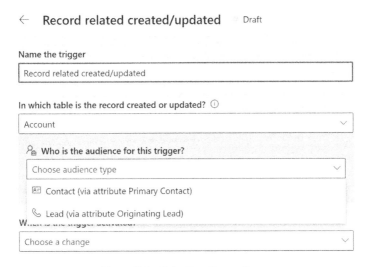

Figure 7.5 – Selecting the audience

When you select the audience, these are the rows that will trigger the journey. It will only trigger for the one person who is the primary contact for the account, or for the originating lead that created the account.

3. You can then select an option for **When is the trigger activated?**. Here, you can decide whether it should trigger when a new record is created, when an existing record is updated, or when any of the two happen, as shown in *Figure 7.6*:

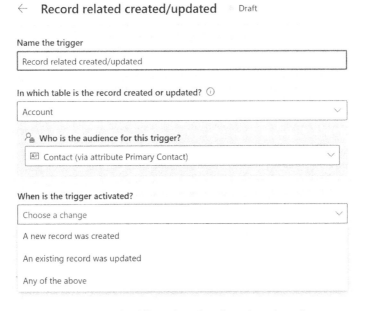

Figure 7.6 – Deciding when the trigger is activated

4. The last step is to select which attribute updates should activate the trigger. In this step, you can select any of the columns that are on the related record that should activate the trigger, as shown in *Figure 7.7*:

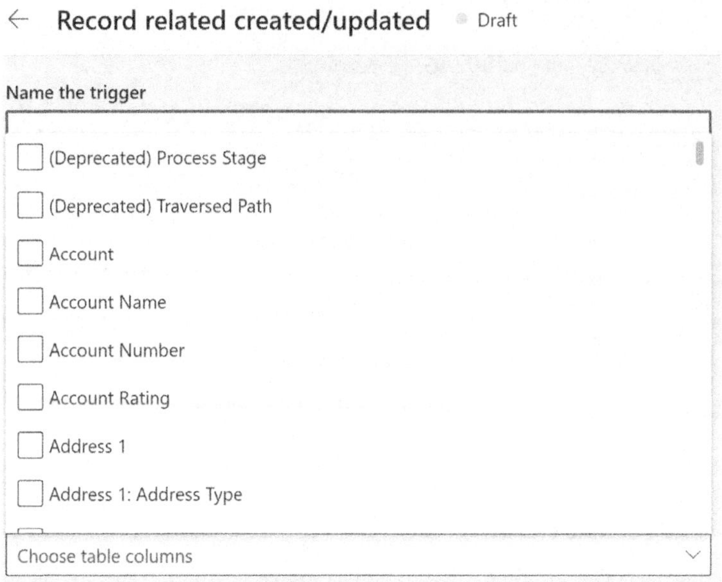

Record related created/updated
Draft
Name the trigger
(Deprecated) Process Stage
(Deprecated) Traversed Path
Account
Account Name
Account Number
Account Rating
Address 1
Address 1: Address Type
Choose table columns

Figure 7.7 – Attribute updates that should activate the trigger

For example, if you select **Email**, then this trigger will activate for the contact or lead every time the **Email** column is changed on the related table.

5. When all these steps are completed, you can use the trigger in a journey after you've set it as ready to use. The **Ready to use** button will appear when you've completed all the previous steps, as shown in *Figure 7.8*:

Record related created/updated
Draft
Ready to use
Name the trigger
Record related created/updated

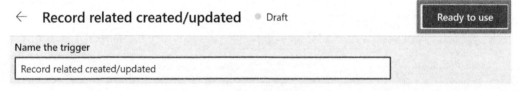

Figure 7.8 – Ready to use

Now, your new custom trigger that activates when a related record is created or updated is ready to use.

If you want to activate the trigger based on contact information changing, you do the following steps:

1. Select **Contact** as the table.

2.   Select **Contact (via self)** as the audience.

3.   Select when the trigger is activated.

4.   Select the attributes that should activate the trigger.

When you do this, you get the setup shown in *Figure 7.9*:

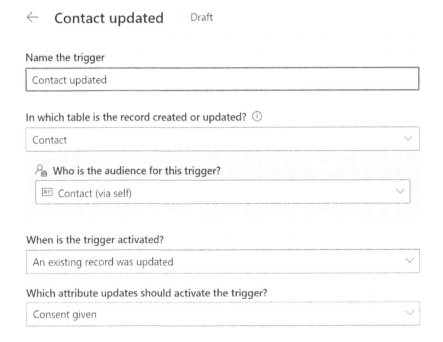

Figure 7.9 – Contact updated

Creating a trigger as we have done in these examples is a no-code version of setting up triggers. Let's see how you can create a trigger and integrate it with some help from a developer.

When a customer interacts with a website/app

The other way of creating a custom trigger is to select **When a customer interacts with a website/app**. This has different steps and will most often require help from a developer to use:

1.   The first step is the actual setup of the trigger. As shown in *Figure 7.10*, the first action is to select the data type – do you want this trigger to contain information about the lead or the contact?

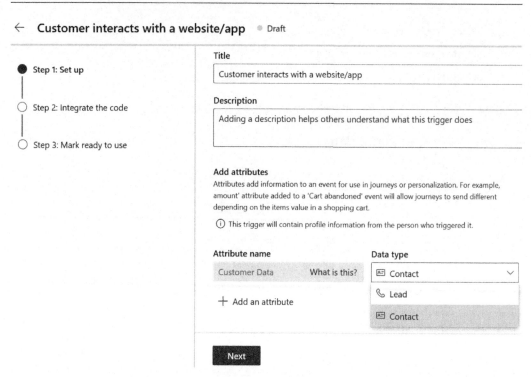

Figure 7.10 – Selecting the data type

2. The next step is to add the attributes; these are the pieces of information you want to use further in your journey. In my example, I've added **First name**, which is a **Text** data type, and **Is working in IT**, which is a **True or false** data type, as shown in *Figure 7.11*:

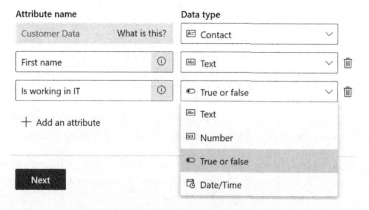

Figure 7.11 – Selecting attributes and data types

You can add as many attributes as you want to in this step; you'll map them when you add them to a journey.

3.   After you click **Next**, it's time to integrate the code where you want to use it. You can either download the file or copy the code snippet link, as shown in *Figure 7.12*:

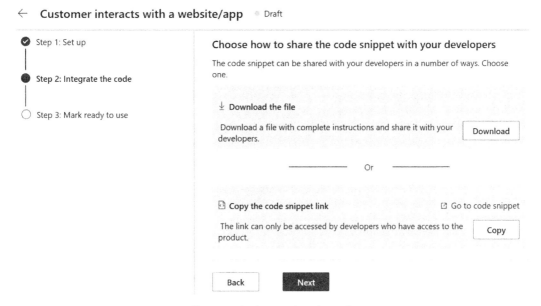

Figure 7.12 – Integrating the code

4.   If you click on **Go to code snippet**, you can select which code language you want to copy the code in:

- JavaScript

- C#

- iOS/macOS (Objective-C)

- Python

- Android

Your developer will be able to tell you which language they want the code in. Once you've copied the code, you can move on to the next stage.

5.   The last stage is **Mark it ready to use**. You can use the trigger once it's been set as ready to use, but it will not do anything until it's integrated where you are getting the information – for example, your website or Power Automate. You can see from *Figure 7.13* that it can be used to build customer journeys, but it can't be triggered until it's integrated:

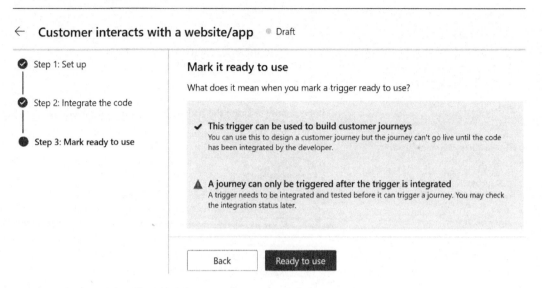

Figure 7.13 – Marking the trigger ready to use

When you click **Ready to use**, you will see a message saying the trigger is getting ready to use. It will start working as soon as you've integrated the trigger code, as you can see in *Figure 7.14*:

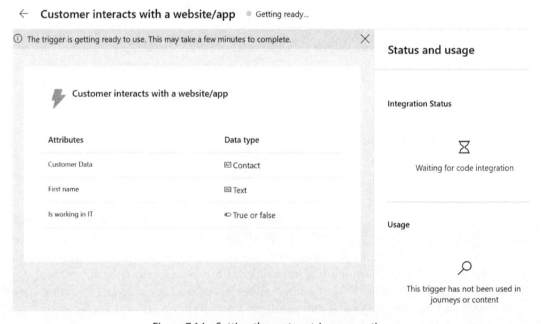

Figure 7.14 – Setting the custom trigger as active

Now, it's time to start using the triggers in a real-time marketing journey. Let's look at how you create and understand real-time marketing journeys.

Creating and understanding real-time marketing journeys

Real-time marketing journeys are how you will interact with your customers. They are the interactions your customers will have with you. This is where you define what kind of information the different people should get. Let's see how we can create and use real-time marketing journeys.

Creating a real-time marketing journey

The first thing you need to do when creating a real-time marketing journey is to give the journey a name. You should give the journey a name that describes what this journey does so that it is easy to find that journey later.

The next thing to do is to choose the type of journey: should this journey be trigger-based or segment-based? To determine that, let us dig deeper into these two different types of journeys.

Trigger-based journey

To start a journey that is trigger-based, you select the **Trigger-based** tile. You can then choose the trigger; this trigger must already be in the system and set to ready to use. Once you've created your trigger, you can also add conditions. Perhaps you don't want to run this journey on everyone it triggers for; maybe you just want to run this for your Gold customers. You specify the trigger you want to use to define your audience, as shown in *Figure 7.15*:

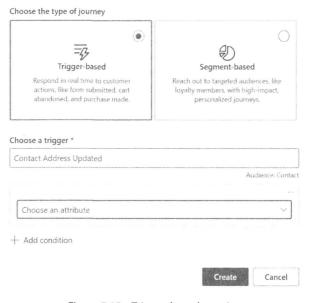

Figure 7.15 – Trigger-based creation

After you've chosen the trigger, you can choose an attribute from that trigger to activate the journey. In *Figure 7.16*, you can see that I've chosen the custom trigger that we created earlier in the chapter and decided that it should trigger every time the customer is working in IT. This makes sure that none of the people that *don't* work in IT activate this trigger and start this journey:

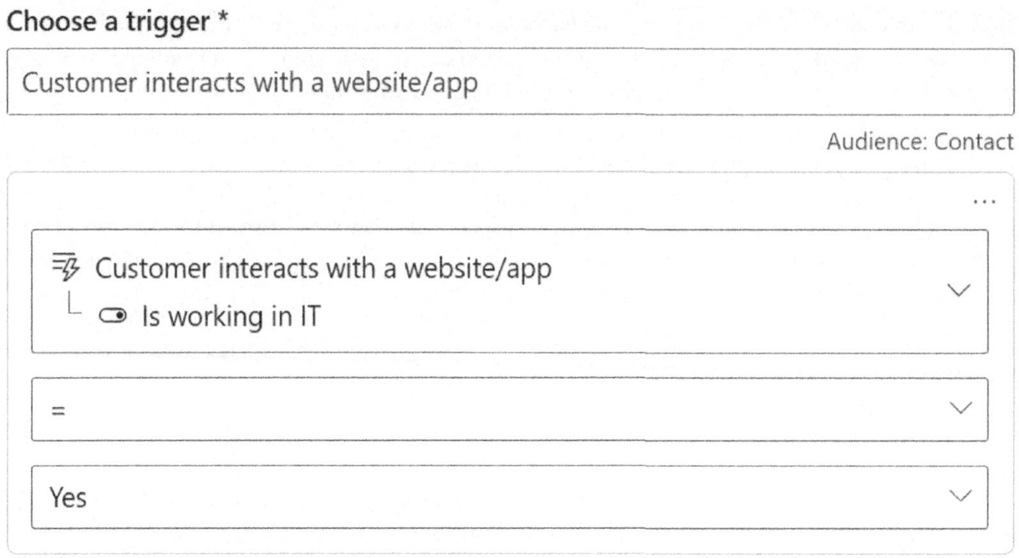

Choose a trigger *

> Customer interacts with a website/app

Audience: Contact

> ...
>
> ⇶ Customer interacts with a website/app
>   ∟ ⊙ Is working in IT   ⌄
>
> =   ⌄
>
> Yes   ⌄

Figure 7.16 – Selecting an attribute from the trigger

Now, we've gone through how you start a journey by using a trigger. This can be any of the out-of-the-box triggers, or you can use custom triggers to get the journey to trigger based on anything you want.

We can now look at how we create the other type of journey: segment-based.

Segment-based journey

As you do in outbound customer journeys, you can select to start a journey by choosing a segment. There are some steps you must complete before you can create your journey:

1. Click on **Segment-based** and select a segment, as shown in *Figure 7.17*:

Create a new journey

Name the journey

Journey 1

Choose the type of journey

○	◉
⚡ **Trigger-based** Respond in real time to customer actions, like form submitted, cart abandoned, and purchase made.	◑ **Segment-based** Reach out to targeted audiences, like loyalty members, with high-impact, personalized journeys.

Select a segment *

Adatum

Audience: Contact

Figure 7.17 – Selecting a segment

2. The next thing to do is select the frequency of this journey, as shown in *Figure 7.18*:

Figure 7.18 – Selecting the frequency

Let's look at the frequency options:

- **A one-time journey with a static audience**: This will only trigger the journey once with the audience you set and will not be triggered again, even if contacts are added to the segment.

- **A one-time journey where newly added audience members can start anytime**: This will allow contacts to go through the journey one time and never again. New contacts will also be added to the journey.

- **A repeating journey is where all audience members repeat the journey every** X **days, weeks**, or **months**: With this option, the contacts can go through the same journey several times – how often is defined by the time restriction you set.

3. The time zone that is set in your system is automatically set as default, but this can be changed, as shown in *Figure 7.19*:

Figure 7.19 – Time zone

4. Select a start date and time, as shown in *Figure 7.20*:

Start *

Select a date	📅		12:00 AM ⌄

Figure 7.20 – Start date

5. Now, you can click **Create**, and a new canvas will open where you can create your customer journey, as shown in *Figure 7.21*:

Figure 7.21 – A blank canvas for the journey

Now we have the canvas where we can create our journey, but first, let's go through the journey settings.

Journey settings

When you first set up your journey, you will see **Journey settings** on the right-hand side, as shown in *Figure 7.22*:

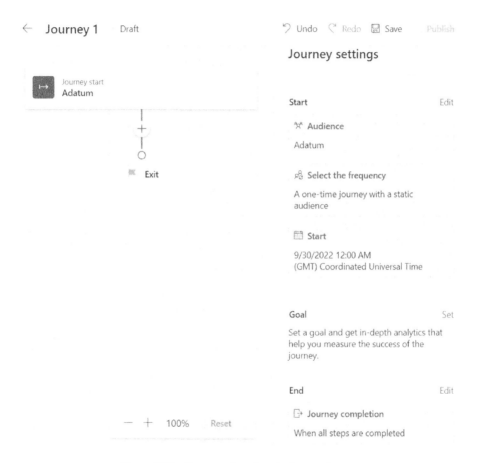

Figure 7.22 – Start, goal, and end of a new journey

Here, you can make some changes to the setup that you used when creating this journey. You can change the start date/time, set a goal, and set an end for when the journey is completed. Let's take a closer look at the changes you can make in the settings area.

Start

In the **Start** section, you can change the very same things that you selected when you set up the journey. If you chose a trigger-based journey, you can now change the trigger, add or change conditions, exclude contacts from certain segments, and decide whether the contact should repeat the journey, as shown in *Figure 7.23*:

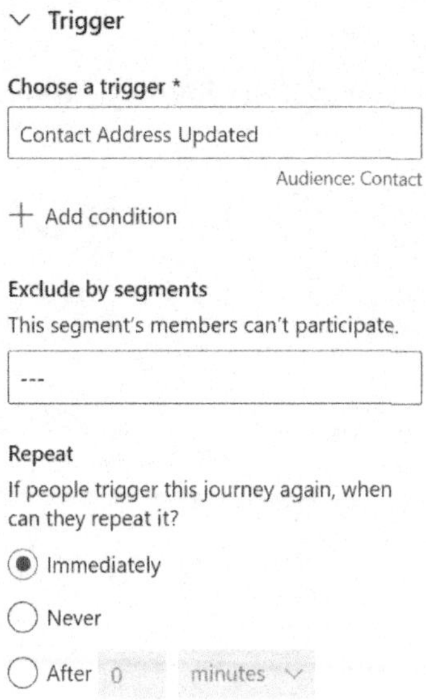

Figure 7.23 – Changing the trigger

If you chose a segment-based journey, you can set the segment that triggers the journey, select the frequency (who the journey should trigger for and how often), and exclude people in certain segments, as shown in *Figure 7.24*:

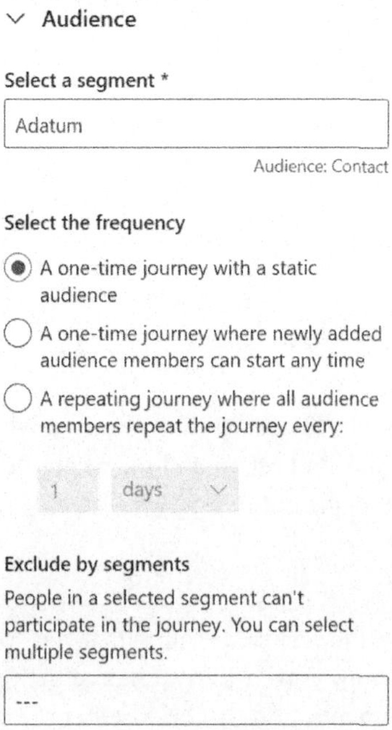

Figure 7.24 – Changing the segment, selecting the frequency, and excluding by segment

Goal

In the **Goal** section, you can set what the goal of the journey is, when the goal is met, and how many people are needed to achieve this goal. As you can see in *Figure 7.25*, you have a standard set of goals, but you can also create your custom goal. You can define that a goal is met when it has triggered one of your marketing event triggers:

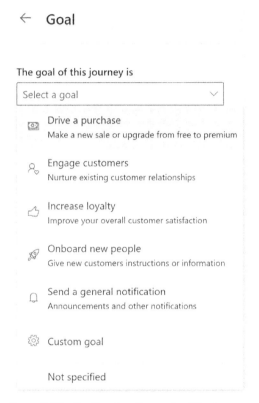

Figure 7.25 – Configuring the goals of the journey

Now, let's go through how we can set an end to the journey.

End

In the **End** section, you can set when a journey is completed. By default, when a contact has completed all the steps in the path, then the journey is set as **Completed**. You can also set up other exit routes, such as when a trigger occurs or when a contact is put in a segment. Maybe you've put up a sales journey to get customers to buy your new solution; if they do buy this solution, then you don't want them to continue to get notifications and emails about that solution. Even though they still haven't completed all the steps in your journey, you want them to exit this part because they are now in the segment of customers who have bought this solution.

Now that we've seen how we can set our goals and make changes to the settings, let's start going through how we can make changes to the journey.

Adding actions or other elements

The first step in creating a journey for the customer is to create actions and other elements. These are all the steps that your journey will go through. Let's go through what you can create with actions and other elements.

Action

Adding an action to a journey is what you will do most in any journey. This is where you can add the ability to send an email, text message, or push notification. To select an action, you click on the blue + button in your canvas, as shown in *Figure 7.26*:

Figure 7.26 – Adding an action to the journey

When you click on the blue + button, a new window will open where you can select **Send an email**, **Send a text message**, or **Send a push notification**, as shown in *Figure 7.27*:

Actions

📧 Send an email

📱 Send a text message

🔔 Send a push notification

Figure 7.27 – Adding actions

Send an email

To send an email through the real-time customer journey, select the **Send an email** tile. A panel on the right-hand side will appear where you can select the email and select where you want to send that email, as shown in *Figure 7.28*:

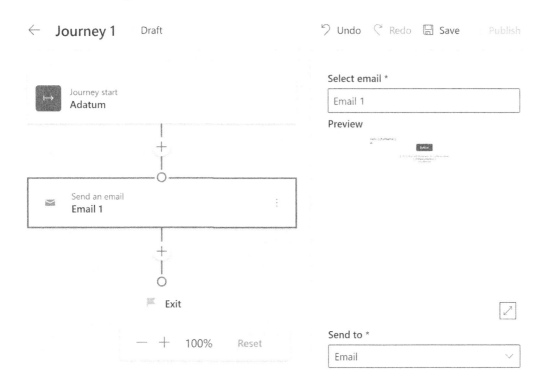

Figure 7.28 – Send an email

To connect your journey to an email, you must have created the email previously. You can also create an email from the journey window; this will automatically add the email. Let's see how we can send a text message.

Send a text message

To send a text message, select the **Send a text message** tile. As you can see in *Figure 7.29*, this opens a panel on the right in which you have to choose the text message you want to send, choose a text message sender, and choose to whom you want to send the text message:

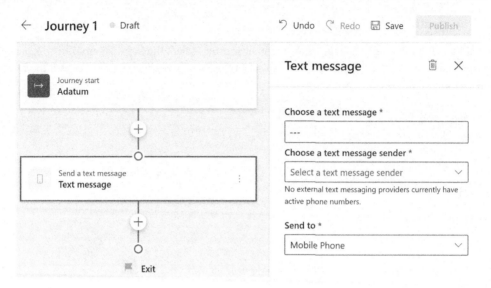

Figure 7.29 – Send a text message

As with sending an email, you must have created the text message and the text message sender before you can send the text message. As with the email, you can create the text message from this window and have it connected with the journey. Let's look at the last action tile, sending a push notification.

Send a push notification

To send a push notification, you select the **Send a push notification** tile. This will open the same type of panel as you saw with email and text. Here, you need to select a mobile application and the actual push notification you want to push, as shown in *Figure 7.30*:

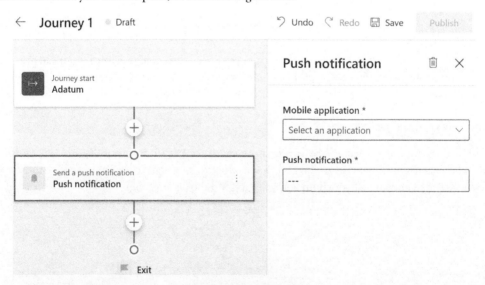

Figure 7.30 – Push notification

The push notification and mobile application must be set up before you can do this. As with emails and text messages, you can set up the push notification from this window.

These are the action tiles, and they are the ones you will use the most. Other elements will help you create a better journey for your audience. Let's get to know the other elements better.

Other elements

As well as sending emails, text messages, and push notifications on the journey, you can also act on how the customer reacts. Other elements that you can add are shown in *Figure 7.31*:

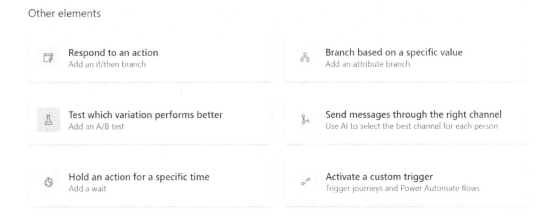

Other elements

Respond to an action Add an if/then branch	**Branch based on a specific value** Add an attribute branch
Test which variation performs better Add an A/B test	**Send messages through the right channel** Use AI to select the best channel for each person
Hold an action for a specific time Add a wait	**Activate a custom trigger** Trigger journeys and Power Automate flows

Figure 7.31 – Adding other elements

Let's go through these elements and see how they can help you create a better journey for your customers.

Respond to an action

When you select **Respond to an action**, you get an **If/then branch** option. You can send the customer down a positive or negative branch, as shown in *Figure 7.32*:

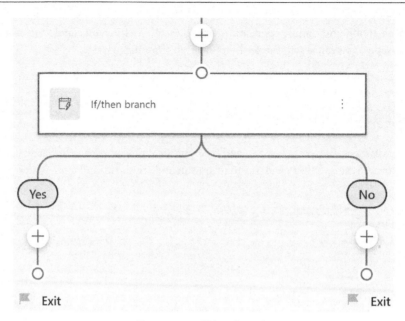

Figure 7.32 – If/then branch

You first choose the branch condition type. This is where you can choose the email, text, or push notification we sent to the customer in a previous step, as shown in *Figure 7.33*:

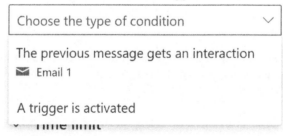

Figure 7.33 – Choosing the interaction point for the if/then branch

You should also define the time limit, where you can specify when the customer has to have performed the trigger to go down the positive (**Yes**) branch. If they do not perform the trigger within the set time, then they'll go down the negative (**No**) branch.

After you've set what interaction element your branches are based on, you can set what type of interaction trigger you want to use, as shown in *Figure 7.34*:

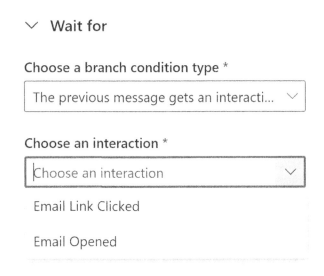

Figure 7.34 – Choosing an interaction point

When you're using email, you can either select when the email link is clicked or when the email is opened as the interaction point. You want to see whether a customer has opened the first email you sent before you send another email. You don't want to send the email to the customer if they haven't opened the first email, or you might want to send a follow-up email if they haven't clicked on a link to sign up for something.

The next thing you do is select the actions you want in both branches, as shown in *Figure 7.35*. If you want one of the paths not to do anything, then you can leave it blank:

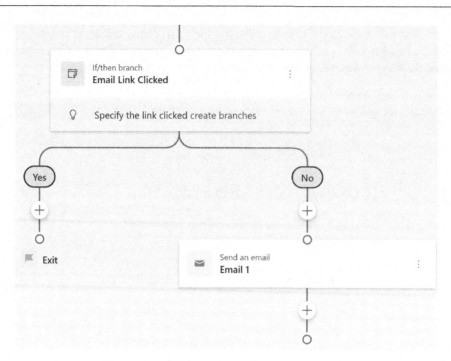

Figure 7.35 – Adding a step to the negative branch

Now, you can continue to build your customers' paths until they have completed the steps. This type of branching is never combined again, so if you want to combine the branches or have a need to branch based on a specific value, then you shouldn't use this trigger, but use another element instead. Let's go through how you set up this element.

Branch based on a specific value

This element is a bit different from the previous element. When you add it, you get two branches as a start, but you can add multiple other branches. You must always have conditions in **Branch 1**, and customers that don't meet the conditions in **Branch 1** will move to the **Other** branch. These branches merge back together again, and you can continue the path as one journey. You can see this behavior in *Figure 7.36*:

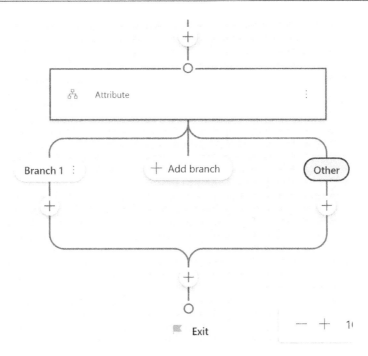

Figure 7.36 – Branch based on a specific value

To select who goes down the different branches, you can add conditions to each branch, as shown in *Figure 7.37*:

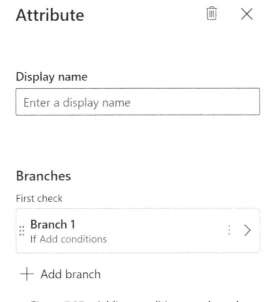

Figure 7.37 – Adding conditions to a branch

When you click on **Add conditions**, you can choose to make the condition on an attribute or a segment membership, as shown in *Figure 7.38*:

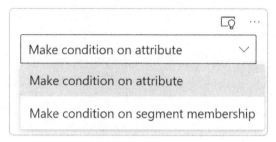

Figure 7.38 – Make condition on attribute or segment membership

When you select **Make condition on attribute**, you can choose columns from the **Contact** table, as shown in *Figure 7.39*:

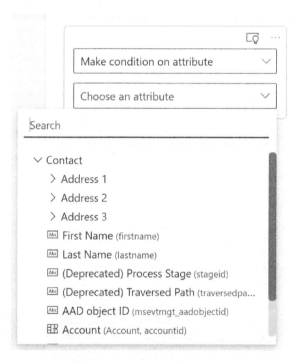

Figure 7.39 – Choosing an attribute

When you select **Make condition by segment membership**, you can choose the segment that you want to include or exclude contacts from going down a specific branch, as shown in *Figure 7.40*:

Figure 7.40 – Condition in a branch

Everyone else (not included in this branch) will go down the other path. After the contacts have progressed through the branch, they consolidate and continue the path forward as one group again.

Now, let's look at how we can do A/B testing in a journey.

Test which variation performs better

The **Test which variation performs better** tile is for A/B testing. You're testing whether **Version A** or **Version B** performs best, as you can see in *Figure 7.41*:

Figure 7.41 – Adding an A/B test

You can select an email, text message, or push notification for versions A and B; this means that you can compare an email against another email or test any of the different channels against each other to see which performs best.

After you've selected what you're going to send, an option set will appear on the right where you select the email, push notification, or text message that you want to send to your customers. You also decide what proportion of the total audience should receive each test version, as shown in *Figure 7.42*:

Figure 7.42 – Selecting versions and audience

The next step is **Test completion**. Here, you set the winning metric (which defines which version is the winner). You can select from the following options:

- **Clickthrough rate**
- **Open rate**
- **Based on the journey goal**

The test will also end on either a specific date and time or automatically on statistical significance. Statistical significance is when one of the journeys are the clear winner over the other.

The last thing is to set the default version; if there is no clear winner, then this is the version that will be sent to new people. All of this is shown in *Figure 7.43*:

Test completion

Set the winning criteria and test duration.

Winning metric

| Clickthrough rate | ⌄ |

This test ends ⓘ

| Automatically (on statistical significa... | ⌄ |

Default version

| Version A | ⌄ |

If there's no clear winner when the test ends or is stopped,
this version will be sent to new people added to the audience.

Figure 7.43 – Test completion

You can create up to five tests per journey in real-time marketing. This way, you can create multiple different tests and check which performs best. Now, let's go through another element: a smarter way of selecting the right channel.

Send messages through the right channel

In the **Send messages through the right channel** tile, you use AI to send the message to each person via the right channel based on their previous behavior. If you prefer emails, then that's what you'll get, but if you prefer text messages, then that's the channel through which you'll receive the information. You need to select at least two channels to start with, as shown in *Figure 7.44*:

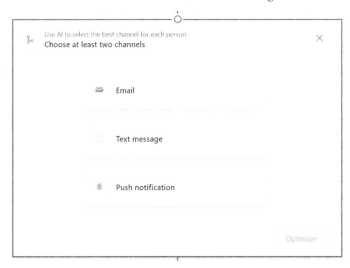

Figure 7.44 – Use AI to select the best channel for each person

You can select the content for at least two channels and set the default channel, as shown in *Figure 7.45*:

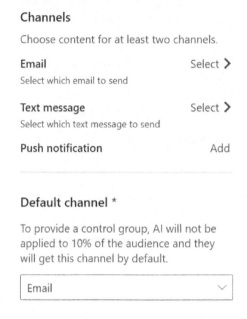

Channels

Choose content for at least two channels.

Email Select which email to send	Select **>**
Text message Select which text message to send	Select **>**
Push notification	Add

Default channel *

To provide a control group, AI will not be applied to 10% of the audience and they will get this channel by default.

| Email | ∨ |

Figure 7.45 – Selecting the content and default channel

Once this is done, then based on the preference of each person, the best channel will be sent to the right people. Remember that you need to have used the channels before setting this up; otherwise, you won't have any statistics on what your customer prefers.

Even though we would like to think otherwise, most of our customers aren't waiting for emails from us and clicking on our content the second they get it. Because our customers aren't waiting for the email, let's see how we can add waiting criteria to our journey.

Hold an action for a specific time

The **Hold an action for a specific time** tile allows you to wait for your customers. You can wait for a set amount of time, until a specific date and time, or until a time specified by a trigger. This way, you can send an email and not continue down a path until the customer has had the chance to read the email. You should wait for longer than an hour before moving on to the next tile in your journey, as the data from the Microsoft servers needs to update and send the data back to your system, and this can sometimes take over an hour.

Activate a custom trigger

The final tile is **Activate a custom trigger**. Here, we can use the custom trigger we created earlier. We can also trigger a Power Automate flow, as shown in *Figure 7.46*:

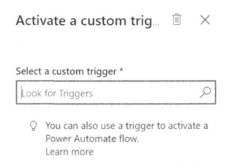

Figure 7.46 – Select a custom trigger

If you select the trigger we previously created, you must map the attributes we created in the trigger to the audience or another trigger, as shown in *Figure 7.47*:

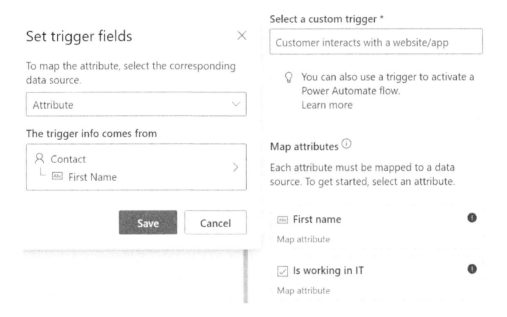

Figure 7.47 – Map attributes

Now, we've gone through all the different tiles we can create in a real-time marketing journey. Remember that Microsoft comes out with new features every month, so make sure you're up to date on what is coming.

After we've created our journeys, it's time to start using them and, hopefully, improve the journey. How do we best improve the journeys? We look at the analytics and see how the journey has performed and how we can make it even better.

Analytics

We all know analytics is how we can get better. Let's go through how we can look at analytics in a real-time marketing journey.

Once the journey is activated and the audience has gone through all the steps, the journey is set to **Read-only** and **Completed**, as shown in *Figure 7.48*:

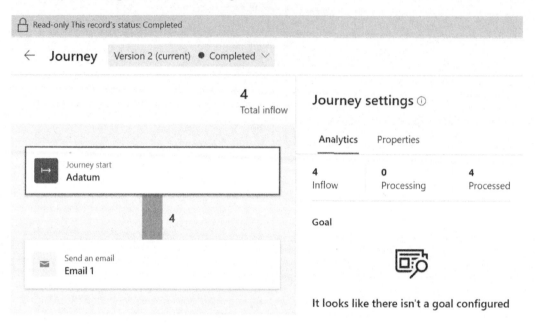

Figure 7.48 – The completed journey

You can see that four contacts have gone through this process and that all four have been processed. If you click on any of the tiles, a new tab on the right-hand side will open with tile-specific analytics. In *Figure 7.49*, you can see the analytics for the **Send an email** tile:

Figure 7.49 – Analytics for email

If you click on the link at the bottom of the right-hand tab (**Delivery and interaction details**), you can see more details, such as whether the email was delivered, blocked, or failed. In *Figure 7.50*, you can see that three out of the four emails were delivered, while one hard-bounced and wasn't delivered to the contact. If you have a lot of hard bounces, it can affect your spam score.

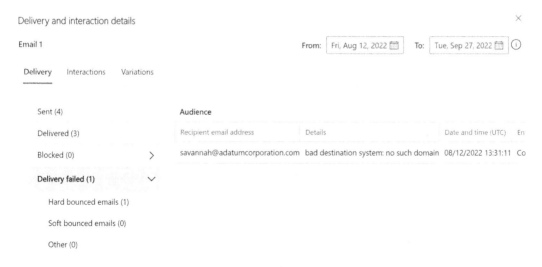

Figure 7.50 – Delivery and interaction details

In the **Interactions** tab, you can see the following:

- **Unique opens**
- **Unique clicks**
- **Marked as spam**
- **Unsubscribed**

With this, you have a good overview of how the steps in your journey have performed and how you can make your journey better.

In addition to having statistics for each journey, you also have a dashboard based on Power BI with full information on your journeys and channels. This dashboard, which you can see in *Figure 7.51*, shows a lot of information that will be important when you want to analyze and create better journeys:

Figure 7.51 – Analytics dashboard

In the analytics dashboard, we can see information about our journeys, including how long they've been active, how the emails, text messages, or push notifications have been engaged with, whether the journeys have reached the set goals, and why contacts have left the journeys.

We've now gone through the analytics and taken a quick view of some of the things you get in analytics. Remember, if you don't look at the analytics, you'll never create better journeys. It's time to wrap up this chapter with a summary.

Summary

In this chapter, we've gone through how you can use the out-of-the-box triggers and how you can create your own triggers. This way, you can trigger a journey any way you want to trigger it. We've seen how you can use these triggers to start a journey, but also how you can use the triggers in the middle of a journey. We've gone through the other option of starting a journey with the help of segments. With both of these options, you can use conditions to filter the audience of the journey to ensure that only the audience you want to target goes through the journey.

We've seen how you create and manage the journeys, and all the actions and elements you can use to create great journeys for your audience.

We concluded the chapter by discussing analytics, where we can discover how we can create better journeys through company communication with our audiences.

In the next chapter, we are going to learn about one of the features that sets Dynamics 365 Marketing apart from its competitors: the event module.

Questions

The following are some questions that will help you gauge your understanding of the topics discussed in this chapter. The answers are provided in the *Assessments* section at the end of the book.

1. When creating a custom trigger, it must be embedded as code on a website?

    A. Yes

    B. No

2. What two options are there to activating a journey?

    A. Audience

    B. Trigger

    C. Custom trigger

    D. Manually

    E. Segment

3. A goal for the journey is set out-of-the-box

    A. Yes

    B. No

4. You can always use AI to use the right channel to the audience?

    A. Yes

    B. No

8
Managing Events

The event module is one of the features that sets Dynamics 365 Marketing apart from all other marketing automation applications out there. You can run big events with thousands of people for several days, or you can run your breakfast meeting with 10 people attending for 2 hours. The event module is highly flexible and helps you to run any type of event you desire.

Throughout this chapter, we are going to look at how you can manage your events, and we are going to see how Scottish Summit event used the event module to run their previous two events. Because we are using a live, configured system, there might be some customizations you will not find in your system. These customizations might give you some ideas as to how you can customize your Dynamics 365 Marketing application to suit your needs best.

We are going to go through the basic setup of an event. Then, we are going to look at the in-person-specific setup before moving on to the webinar-specific setup. We will also go through how to use journeys to make sure our event participants get the information they need. Finally, we're going to look at the out-of-the-box event website that's based on Power Pages.

In this chapter, we will cover the following:

- Event management settings
- Creating and managing events
- Creating and managing in-person events
- Creating and managing webinars
- Event communication

Event management settings

Before we start working with events, we will go through our settings. We need to make sure all our settings are up to date and working as intended for our events. You can find the **Event management** settings in the **Settings** area as shown in *Figure 8.1*:

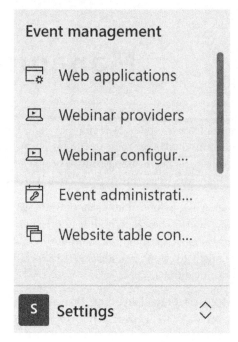

Figure 8.1 – Event management in Settings

Let's go through the settings and see what each of them does. We'll start with **Web applications**.

Web applications

Some companies have their own website from which they want to get all their event registrations. To connect external applications with Dynamics 365 Marketing, you must register a web application. Once you've registered the web application, you get a token and an endpoint, as shown in *Figure 8.2*, that your developers can use to connect to the event API:

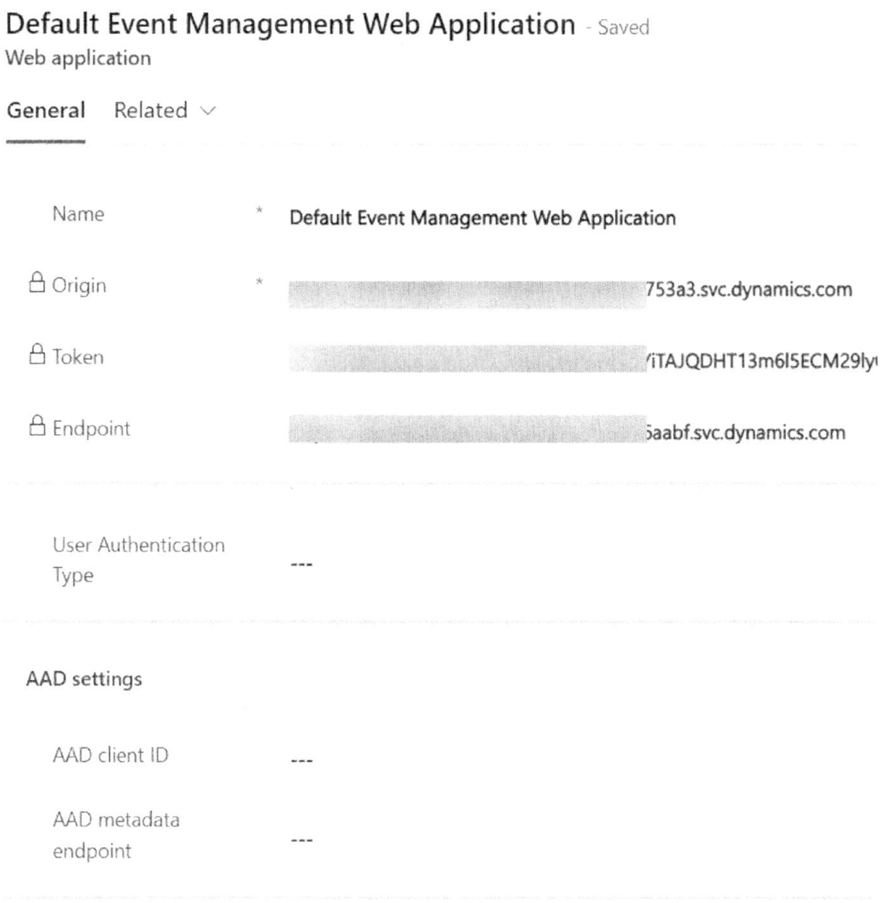

Default Event Management Web Application - Saved
Web application

General   Related ∨

Name	*	Default Event Management Web Application
🔒 Origin	*	753a3.svc.dynamics.com
🔒 Token		iTAJQDHT13m6I5ECM29ly
🔒 Endpoint		5aabf.svc.dynamics.com
User Authentication Type		---

AAD settings

AAD client ID	---
AAD metadata endpoint	---

Figure 8.2 – Web application

Once your web application is registered, it is time for your developer to do their magic. Looking at how to use the event APIs is out of the scope of this book. You can read more about using external websites here: `https://learn.microsoft.com/en-us/dynamics365/marketing/developer/event-management-web-application`.

Webinar providers

In the **Webinar providers** area, you can connect to a third-party company that hosts webinars. As of the wave 2 2022 release, the only vendor provider available out of the box in Dynamics 365 Marketing is On24. You can read more about On24 here: `https://www.on24.com/`. If want to use another provider, you need the help of a developer. The setup of On24 is configured as shown in *Figure 8.3*:

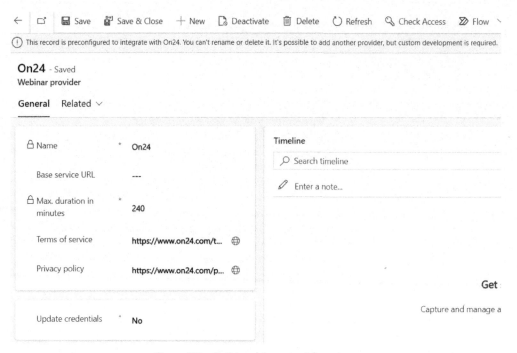

Figure 8.3 – On24 webinar provider setup

The actual connection with On24 isn't handled in the **Webinar providers** area but in the **Webinar configurations** area.

Webinar configurations

The **Webinar configurations** area is where you connect to your webinar providers. To create a new configuration, you must add a new configuration and register the client ID, access token key, and access token secret, as shown in *Figure 8.4*:

Figure 8.4 – Webinar configuration

Once the webinar configuration is set up and activated, you can use the provider chosen when you are running your event webinars.

Event administration

In the **Event administration** area, you can create settings for all your events. You can only have one event administration record active at a time, but you can have none active if you like. In *Figure 8.5*, you can see that you can give a record a name and set how to match the contact based on which fields, and enable demo payment confirmation if you want to:

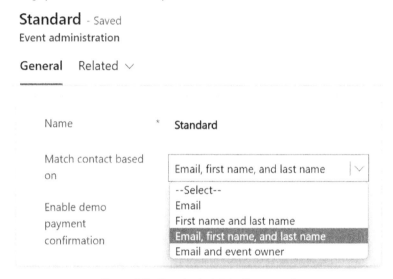

Figure 8.5 – Event administration record

If you choose to match contacts based on email, first name, and last name, then all those fields have to match. If you set your matching strategy to be based only on email, then every event registration connected to the email given will be automatically connected to the contact.

Enable demo payment confirmation should never be used in a production environment. This is only used to simulate payment on the event website for demo purposes. If you want to charge for your events and have your customers pay online, you need to partner with a third-party provider and develop a payment gateway.

Website table configurations

Most companies will require their own unique columns for their events. These custom columns are not exposed by the event API out of the box. To expose these fields in the event API, you create a website table configuration as shown in *Figure 8.6*:

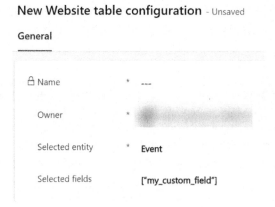

Figure 8.6 – Website table configuration

Now that we have gone through **Event management** in the **Settings** area and familiarized ourselves with the UI, we can start to set up our events.

Creating and managing events

Dynamics 365 Marketing has its own area for event planning. Here, you can administer every event and everything surrounding an event.

You can create an event from scratch or from a template. On the main event page, you can also create your event template. The **+ New**, **+ New from template**, and **+ Create template** options are shown in *Figure 8.7*:

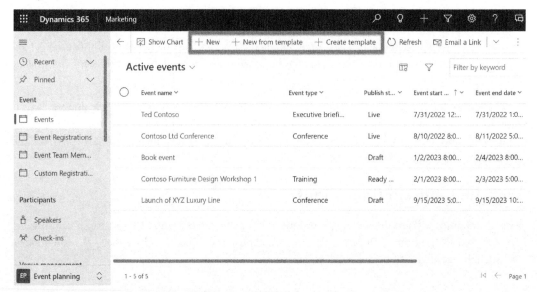

Figure 8.7 – Active events and event creation options

When you create a new event, a blank record is opened. The mandatory columns are **Event name**, **Event time zone**, **Event start date**, and **Event end date**, as shown in *Figure 8.8*:

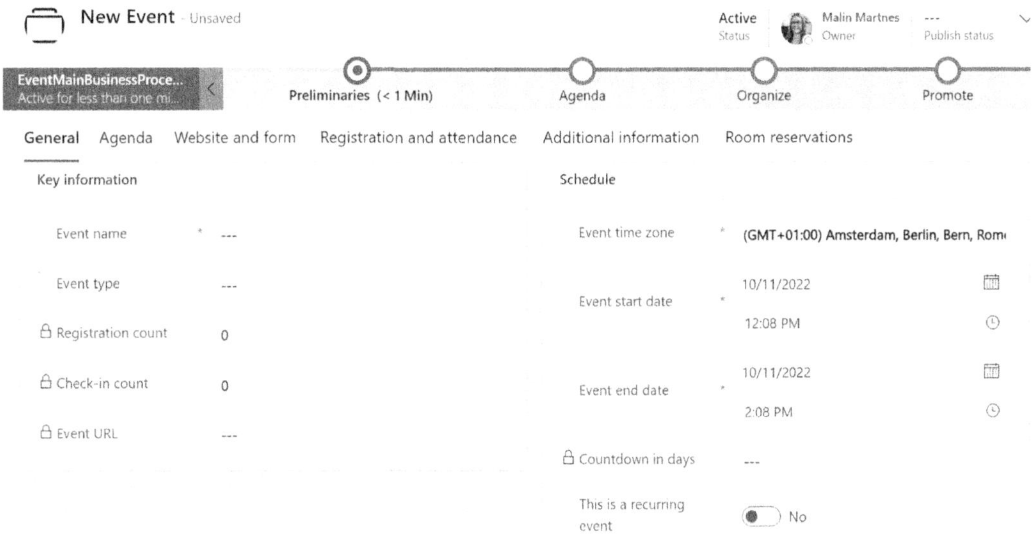

Figure 8.8 – Creating an event

If you don't fill out these columns, you cannot save your event. We will circle back to webinars and locations in later sections of this chapter.

If your event has a maximum capacity (whether it's an in-person event or a webinar), you can set **Maximum event capacity**. You can also turn on a waitlist for the event. When **Waitlist this event** is set to **Yes**, another section where you can add information about the waitlist appears. You can set the number of invitations per slot, which determines how many people should get the opportunity to register for each person that cancels. You can also set whether you want the contacts on the waiting list to be automatically registered. If you don't want the contacts to be automatically registered, you can set **Contacts can choose to be registered automatically** to **No**. This section is shown in *Figure 8.9*:

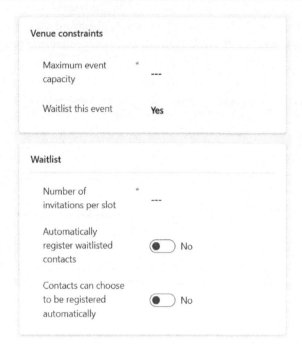

Figure 8.9 – Venue constraints and waitlist

At the top of the event form, you can see the **business process flow** (**BPF**) for your events. This BPF should be configured to suit the needs that you have for your events. This is where you can add reminders or other necessary information for all your events at certain stages.

Figure 8.10 – BPF for events

Now, let's go through the information you can find in the different tabs of an event record.

Tabs of an event record

We're going to go through the tabs of an event record that are relevant for every kind of event: **Agenda**, **Website and form**, **Registration and attendance**, and **Additional information**. We'll start by going through the **Agenda** tab.

Agenda

Using the **Agenda** tab, you can build your event's agenda. You can register the sessions, session tracks, speaker engagements, and sponsors, as you can see in *Figure 8.11*:

Figure 8.11 – The Agenda tab of an event record

Allow registrants to create their own agenda is a very important part of the tab. Out of the box, it is set to **No**. This means that attendees register for the full event rather than specific sessions or tracks. This column is automatically set to **No** and hidden if you create session passes because in that case, attendees sign up for the different sessions with the passes.

If this setting is set to **Yes**, then your attendees can sign up for one, some, or all of the sessions you have in your event. We'll go through the rest of these sections in more detail later in this chapter.

Website and form

On the **Website and form** tab, you connect your event to an event URL and set the registration information for the event. As you can see in *Figure 8.12*, Scottish Summit used a custom URL for their event:

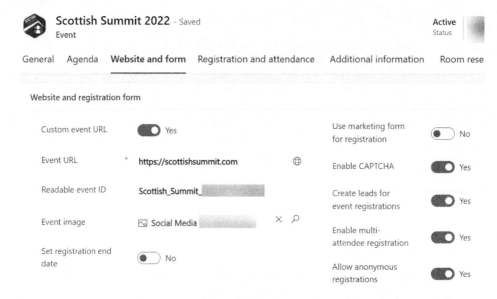

Figure 8.12 – The Website and form tab for Scottish Summit 2022

They are not using the out-of-the-box marketing form but a developed solution to register attendees. They have chosen **Enable CAPTCHA**, enabled **Create leads for event registrations** so that multiple attendees can register in one registration, and chosen **Enable anonymous registration**, meaning that people can join without letting them know who they are.

I highly recommend that you always set a registration end date; this makes sure that your attendees will get the information they need before the event starts.

Registration and attendance

In the **Registration and attendance** tab, as shown in *Figure 8.13*, you can do the following:

- See everyone that has registered or bought a ticket for your event
- Register new attendees
- See who has checked in
- See who is on the waiting list
- See contacts who have canceled

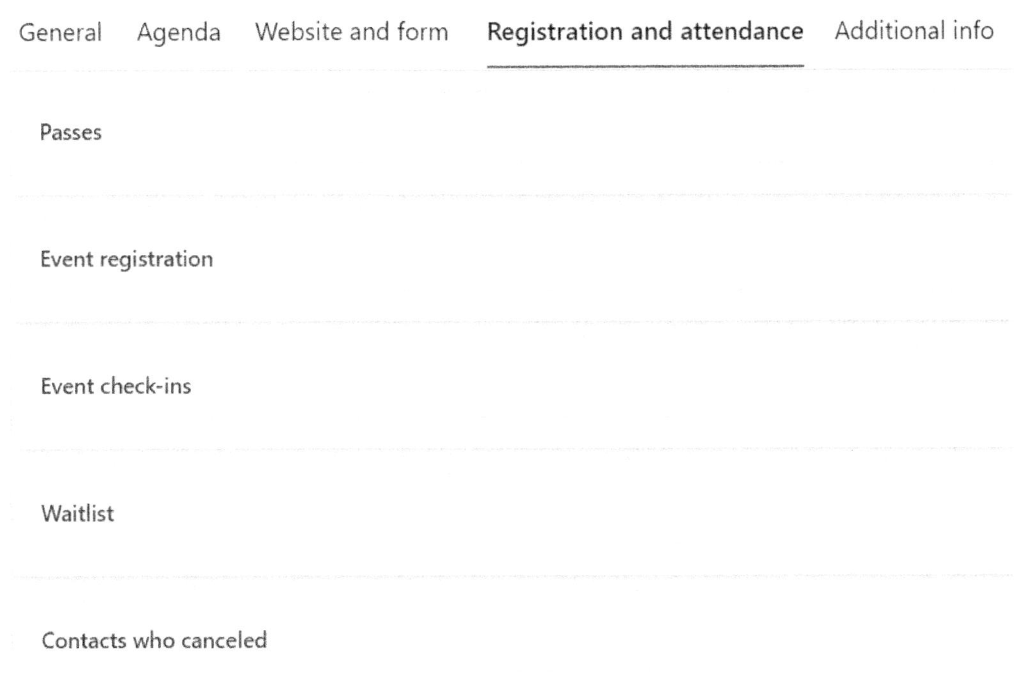

General   Agenda   Website and form   **Registration and attendance**   Additional info

Passes

Event registration

Event check-ins

Waitlist

Contacts who canceled

Figure 8.13 – The Registration and attendance tab

Attendees can cancel their tickets from the event website, or users can do it manually from the marketing application.

Additional information

In the **Additional information** tab, you can find a section for financial information. This is where you can do some budgeting for your event. Remember that Dynamics 365 Marketing is not an ERP system; all finances need to be handled somewhere else.

General   Agenda   Website and form   Registration and attendance   **Additional information**   Room reservation

Financials

Target revenue	---		Currency	🌐 Norwegian Krone
Total registration fee (package cost)	---		Budget allocated	---
Event venue cost	---		Cost of external members	---
Miscellaneous costs	---		Cost of event activities	---
Revenue from the event	---		Revenue from sponsorship	kr0.00

Figure 8.14 – Additional information – Financials

In the **Event team members** section, you can register everyone that is involved in your event. As you can see in *Figure 8.15*, Scottish Summit 2022 had four team members (in addition to the two main organizers). Each of these team members had a specific role. The clear roles made it easier for everyone involved in the event to have an overview of who was responsible for each task.

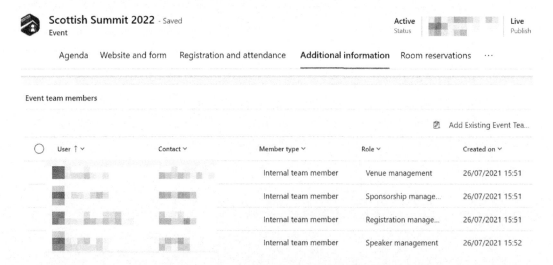

Figure 8.15 – Additional information – Event team members

Now, we've gone through the most important tabs for any event record, but there are some connected records that are extremely important for every event. Let's go through these connected records.

Speakers

At most events, you will have speakers. These are the people that are making presentations or delivering training. As you can see in *Figure 8.16*, you can register a lot of information about your speakers:

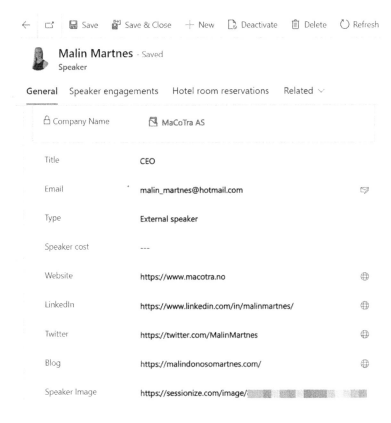

Figure 8.16 – Speaker record

This is a speaker record from Scottish Summit's Dynamics 365 Marketing solution. They integrated their system with other solutions, such as Sessionize, which updates this information. The speaker record is connected to the contact, and some of the information, such as the company name, is copied from the contact record.

In the **Speaker engagements** tab, you can see all the sessions this speaker is connected to, as shown in *Figure 8.17*:

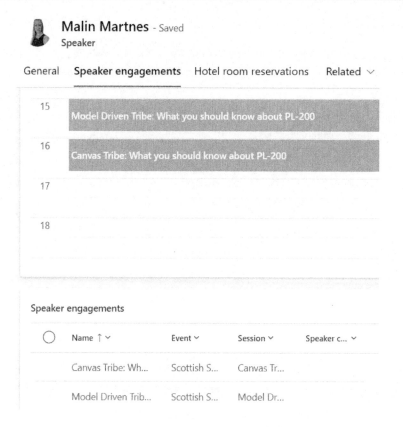

Figure 8.17 – Speaker engagements

Now, let's move on to the sessions that the speakers are connected to and see how they work.

Sessions

Sessions are the content of your event. They could include any presentations, training, or panel discussions you have at your event. Scottish Summit had all their sessions in Dynamics 365 Marketing from their 2020 to 2022 events. As you can see in *Figure 8.18*, they customized their marketing app to show all the sessions in one view:

Active sessions* ⌄

🖽 Edit columns

◯	Session title ↑ ⌄	Session t... ⌄	Start time ⌄	End time ⌄	Event ⌄	Audience type
	Driving Decisions with Data: Delight or Di...		10/06/2022 1...	10/06/2022 1...	Scottish Summit 2022	
	Dual Write VS Virtual Entities - Integrando...	General	27/02/2021 1...	27/02/2021 1...	Scottish Summit Virtual 2021	Level 300
	Dual-write and Power Platform: How do w...		11/06/2022 1...	11/06/2022 1...	Scottish Summit 2022	
	Dynamic 365 Certification	General	29/02/2020 1...	29/02/2020 1...	Scottish Summit 2020	Level 300
	Dynamics 365 & Power Platform Pub Quiz	General	27/02/2021 1...	27/02/2021 1...	Scottish Summit Virtual 2021	Level 300
	Dynamics 365 and Power Platform Certific...		10/06/2022 1...	10/06/2022 1...	Scottish Summit 2022	
	Dynamics 365 Implementation and One V...	General	27/02/2021 1...	27/02/2021 1...	Scottish Summit Virtual 2021	Level 300
	Dynamics 365 Marketing - the good, the ...	General	27/02/2021 1...	27/02/2021 1...	Scottish Summit Virtual 2021	Level 300
	Dynamics Field Service - Scheduling Auto...	General	27/02/2021 1...	27/02/2021 1...	Scottish Summit Virtual 2021	Level 300
	Dynamics Pub Quiz	General	29/02/2020 1...	29/02/2020 1...	Scottish Summit 2020	Level 300
	Effective Workshopping from a Customer'...		11/06/2022 1...	11/06/2022 1...	Scottish Summit 2022	
	Elevate your Personal Development/Brand...		11/06/2022 1...	11/06/2022 1...	Scottish Summit 2022	
	Elevate your PM skills by being an effectiv...		10/06/2022 1...	10/06/2022 1...	Scottish Summit 2022	

Figure 8.18 – Sessions for Scottish Summit

Every speaker is connected to their sessions through the speaker engagement record. This record connects the speaker to the session.

As you can see from *Figure 8.19*, you are given a calendar of the agenda of your event once you've connected all the sessions to your event:

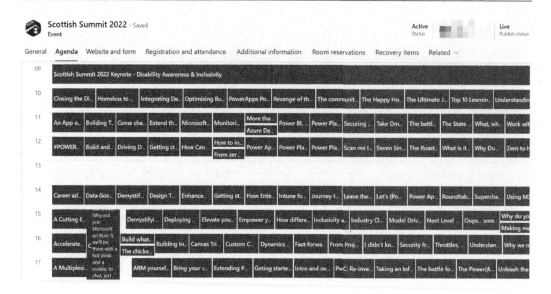

Figure 8.19 – Sessions of an event

To create a new session, go to the **Agenda** tab of your event and click on + **New Session** as shown in *Figure 8.20*:

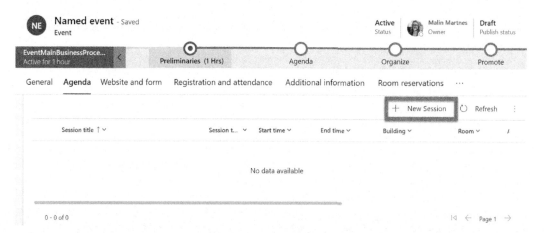

Figure 8.20 – Creating a new session

A new pane on the right side opens and you can register your new session as shown in *Figure 8.21*:

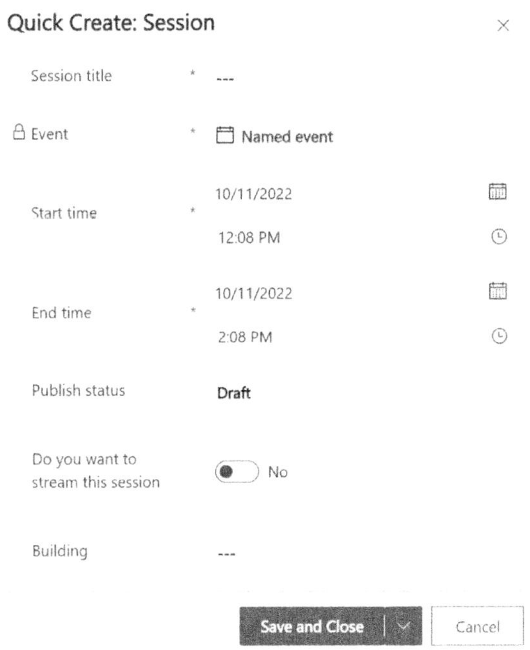

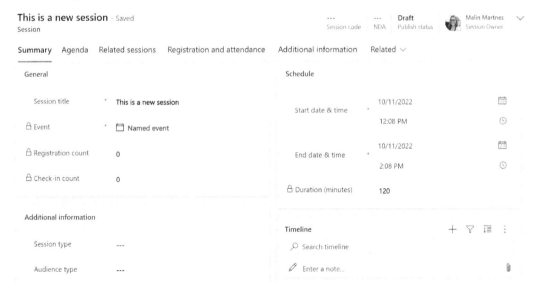

Figure 8.21 – Creating a new session (continued)

Once you've clicked **Save and Close**, you can open the new record and register more information as shown in *Figure 8.22*:

Figure 8.22 – New session to edit

The session is automatically created as a draft and must be published along with the event when it's time to go live.

Session tracks

Session tracks are a way of grouping your sessions. This can make it easier for attendees to know which sessions are relevant to them. You can create your session tracks by going to the **Agenda** tab of an event, finding **Session tracks**, and clicking on + **New Session Track**, as shown in *Figure 8.23*:

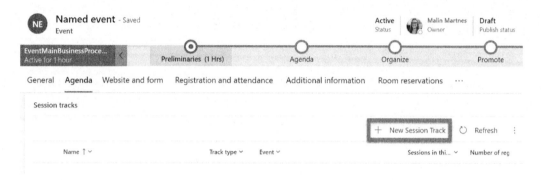

Figure 8.23 – Creating a new session track

A new pane on the right side will open and you can register information about your session track, as shown in *Figure 8.24*:

Figure 8.24 – New session track

Once this is done, you can connect all your sessions to your session tracks. I highly recommend starting with creating your session tracks before you create your sessions. This way, you can add your sessions to the track as you create the sessions and don't have to change this when all the sessions have been created.

Check-ins

You can manually check in attendees on the event record. When you send the registration email to your attendees, you can embed a QR code for check-ins. Dynamics 365 Marketing does not have any way of checking in registrations through QR codes. You can use the mobile version of Dynamics 365 Marketing to create a new event registration and use the camera on the phone to register the QR code. This means you must manually create it one at a time and then scan the QR code. The better solution is to develop a custom solution to automatically check in the attendees by scanning the QR code..

Sponsorships management

For free community events such as Scottish Summit, it is imperative to have sponsors. You also need to have an overview of what you are giving your sponsors and any monetary offerings they are giving you.

Scottish Summit had several sponsors and several sponsorable articles. Sponsorable articles are specific items that the sponsors can cover. In *Figure 8.25*, you can see the sponsorship record for one sponsor of Scottish Summit 2022. All the amounts from the sponsors are automatically connected to the event, and you can find the sum of the amounts in the **Financials** section of the **Additional information** tab for the event:

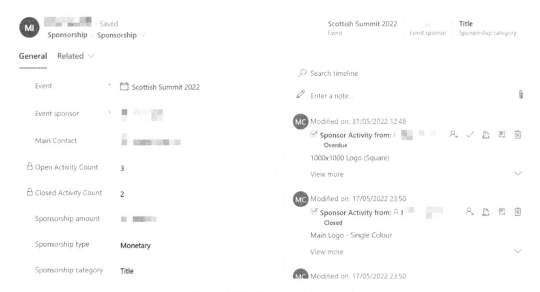

Figure 8.25 – Sponsorship record

We have gone through the parts of event management that are the same for both in-person events and webinars. Now, let's look at what in-person-event-specific options you have in Dynamics 365 Marketing.

Creating and managing in-person events

Managing an in-person event is quite different from managing an online event. You need to have control over all the buildings, rooms, event vendors, hotels, and even hotel room reservations. Let's go through the in-person event-specific things for an event record.

Room reservations

On an event record, the tab named **Room reservations** is where you can see the different rooms that you've reserved for the different sessions you have in your event. As you can see in *Figure 8.26*, Scottish Summit had several concurrent sessions held in different rooms. The calendar shows the different sessions that have been assigned rooms. This calendar is read-only and intended for informational purposes only:

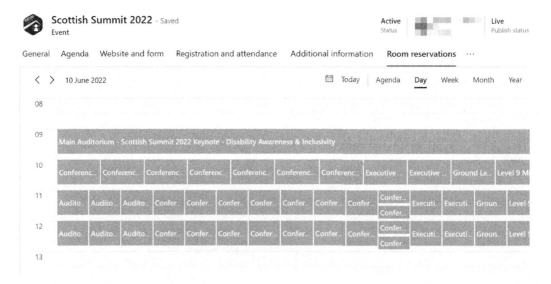

Figure 8.26 – Event room reservations

The next in-person-specific section you find in the event module is on the **Registration and attendance** tab, the section for event passes.

Event passes

Event passes are your attendees' tickets. You can choose not to use passes, or you can have multiple types of passes. If you want to use passes, you must create each of the passes you want to use before you can sell them to your attendees, as shown in *Figure 8.27*:

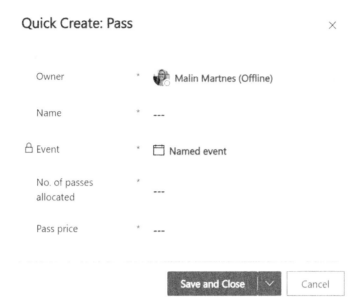

Figure 8.27 – Creating an event pass

Different passes can have different costs: they may be different types of attendees, different days of your conference, or early bird passes, for instance. You can use different prices and have different amounts of passes available. You can also see how many passes have been sold and how many passes are left. All this is shown in *Figure 8.28*:

| General | Agenda | Website and form | **Registration and attendance** | Additional information | Room reservations | ⋯ |

Passes

➕ New Pass   ↻ Refresh

◯	Name ↑ ˅	Pass price ˅	No. of passes allocated ˅	No. of passes sold ˅	No. of passes left ˅
	Early bird	kr11,500.00	100	0	100
	One day Thursday	kr8,500.00	400	0	400
	One day Wednesday	kr8,500.00	400	0	400
	Regular 2 day	kr15,500.00	500	0	500

Figure 8.28 – Different passes

Payment for passes is something you must develop yourself and is not included in Dynamics 365 Marketing.

Now, we've seen the tabs and sections that are relevant for in-person events. Let's dig deeper into the things that are specific only to in-person events.

Venue management

It doesn't matter whether you are hosting a big event with thousands of attendees or a small event for 20 people in your office: you need to have an overview of your venue. Let's go through **Venue management**, which consists of **Buildings**, **Rooms**, and **Layouts**, as shown in *Figure 8.29*:

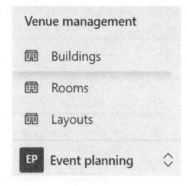

Figure 8.29 – Venue management

You can see from *Figure 8.30* that buildings, rooms, and layouts are all connected. One building can have several rooms, and each room can have different layouts and requirements:

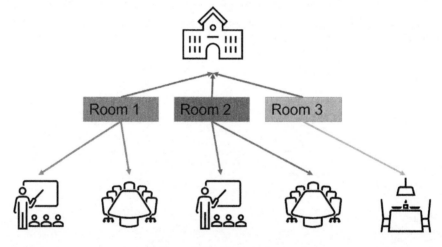

Figure 8.30 – Venue setup

Let's see how Scottish Summit configured its buildings, rooms, and layouts.

Buildings

Scottish Summit used the same building to host their event for 2020 and 2022. You can see the information registered for the building in *Figure 8.31*:

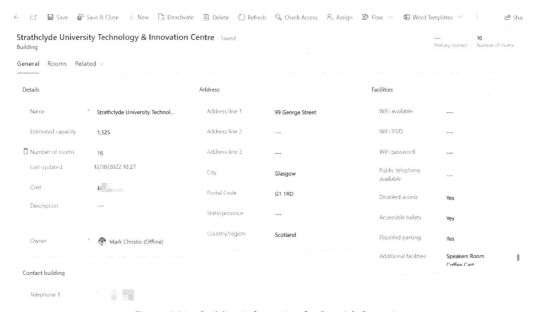

Figure 8.31 – Building information for Scottish Summit

As you can see, you can register a lot of information about the building, such as the following:

- **Estimated capacity**
- **Number of rooms**
- **Cost**
- **Address**
- **Facilities** (such as Wi-Fi and accessible facilities)
- **Contact information**

You also have all the rooms in a building registered. Let's look at how Scottish Summit administrated its rooms.

Rooms

As you can see in *Figure 8.31*, there were 16 rooms in the building for Scottish Summit. We can also see this in the **Rooms** view shown in *Figure 8.32*:

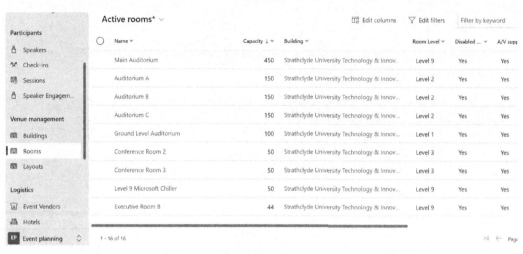

Figure 8.32 – View of all active rooms

If we click on one of the rooms, the room record opens and we can see more information and edit it, as shown in *Figure 8.33*:

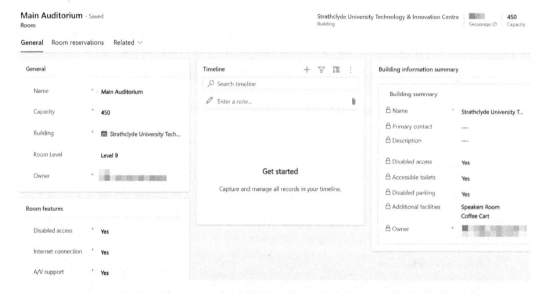

Figure 8.33 – Room record

As you can see in *Figure 8.33*, the room is connected to a building, and the building information is shown on the right-hand side of the form. If we click on the room reservations, we get the same calendar as we do for an event record, but we see all the sessions in the room.

We can also add the possible layouts of the rooms. Let's see how we can manage layouts.

Layouts

Each room can have several different layouts. Every layout is always connected to one room. One room can have different capacities using different layouts. A boardroom often has a big table and chairs around it, while a classroom needs desks and chairs and will have more space, while a theater just needs chairs and will have room for even more people. In *Figure 8.34*, you can see that **Conference Room 1** at Scottish Summit had five different layouts with different capacities.

Boardroom	Boardroom	Conference Room 1	20
Cabaret	Cabaret	Conference Room 1	24
Classroom	Classroom	Conference Room 1	24
Theater	Theater	Conference Room 1	42
U-shape	U-shape	Conference Room 1	20

Figure 8.34 – Layouts of Conference Room 1

Now, let's take a look at some of the things that surround the events: the logistics.

Logistics

To run in-person events, you often have a lot of logistics to consider. You might have different event vendors helping you with different things, as shown in *Figure 8.35*:

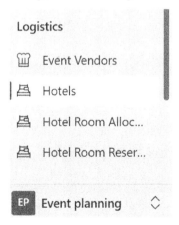

Figure 8.35 – Logistics of an event

You might have agreements with different food caterers, one or several hotels, and any other custom vendors that your event is using. Let's go through how Scottish Summit manages event vendors with Dynamics 365 Marketing.

Event vendors

Scottish Summit had several companies involved in running the event, as you can see from *Figure 8.36*. They had 10 different vendors registered and control over what they used the different vendors for. All vendors are connected to an account, and there you will find all the contact information:

Active event vendors* ∨

○	Name ↑ ∨	Account ∨	Type ∨
	DAS Signs	Das Signs	Clothing
	Dygate	Drygate Brewrey	Food caterer
	Eventicous	Eventicious	Mobile App
	Fiverr	Fiverr	Graphics
	General	Wordpress	Website
	House Of Tartan	House of Tartan	Clothing
	Ibis Styles	ibis	Hotel group
	Premier Inn	Premier Inn	Hotel group
	Strathclyde Uni	Strathclyde Uni	Venue
	The Card Network	The Card Network	Graphics

Figure 8.36 – Scottish Summit event vendors

You can see in *Figure 8.36* that Scottish Summit had the hotel group registered as vendors. In the next section, you'll see that the hotels are connected to a vendor hotel group.

Hotels

In the list of hotels in *Figure 8.37*, you can see that Scottish Summit has an agreement with three different hotels in two different hotel groups:

Active hotels ∨   🔲 Edit columns   ▽ Edit filters   Filter by key

○	Name ↑ ∨	Hotel group ∨	Address line 1 ∨	City ∨	Country/region
	Glasgow City Centre (George Square)	Premier Inn	187 George Street	Glasgow	Scotland
	Hotel ibis Styles Glasgow Centre George S...	Ibis Styles	Telfer House	Glasgow	Scotland
	Ibis Styles Central Hotel	Ibis Styles	Douglas House,	Glasgow	Scotland

Figure 8.37 – List of hotels used by Scottish Summit

In each of these records, we can see more information, such as the address, facilities, and primary contact. We can also see the hotel room allocations.

Hotel room allocations

Scottish Summit 2022 arranged for hotel rooms for all speakers that needed a room. To do that, they needed an agreement with each hotel and an agreement on how many hotel rooms would be available for them. As you can see in *Figure 8.38*, they had 81 rooms allocated in one hotel and 29 allocated in another hotel:

N... ↑ ∨	Room type ∨	Hotel/property ∨	Event ∨	Number of rooms allocated ∨	Number of rooms reserved ∨	Number of rooms left ∨
Hotel...	Single room	Hotel ibis Styles Glasgo...	Scottish Summit 2022	81	68	13
Ibis S...	Single room	Ibis Styles Central Hotel	Scottish Summit 2022	29	24	5

Figure 8.38 – Hotel room allocations

Out of these rooms, some were reserved, and you can see how many of the rooms were left. The hotel room allocations are tightly connected with the hotel room reservations.

Hotel room reservations

Scottish Summit had a complete overview of all the hotel room reservations for their speakers through Dynamics 365 Marketing. As you can see in *Figure 8.39*, all the speakers and their special requests, including the day they came and the day they left, were registered in the system:

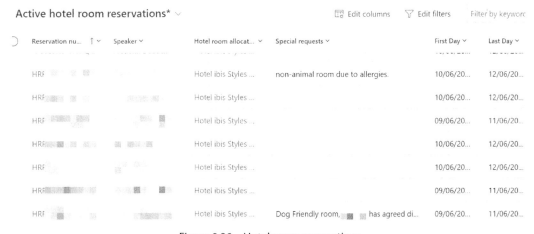

Reservation nu... ↑ ∨	Speaker ∨	Hotel room allocat... ∨	Special requests ∨	First Day ∨	Last Day ∨
HRF		Hotel ibis Styles ...	non-animal room due to allergies.	10/06/20...	12/06/20...
HRF		Hotel ibis Styles ...		10/06/20...	12/06/20...
HRF		Hotel ibis Styles ..		09/06/20...	11/06/20...
HRF		Hotel ibis Styles ...		10/06/20...	12/06/20...
HRF		Hotel ibis Styles ..		10/06/20...	12/06/20...
HRF		Hotel ibis Styles ...		09/06/20...	11/06/20...
HRF		Hotel ibis Styles ...	Dog Friendly room, ... has agreed di...	09/06/20...	11/06/20...

Figure 8.39 – Hotel room reservations

With all these reservations connected to the hotel room allocations, Scottish Summit had a complete overview of how many hotel rooms they needed to order and how many hotel rooms were left from their agreement with the hotels.

Now that we have been through what is unique to in-person events, let us go through how we can use Dynamics 365 Marketing to host webinars.

Creating and managing webinars

Webinars were never before as popular as they were during the COVID pandemic. To stream an event online, you need to set **Do you want to stream this event?** to **Yes** in the main event record, as shown in *Figure 8.40*:

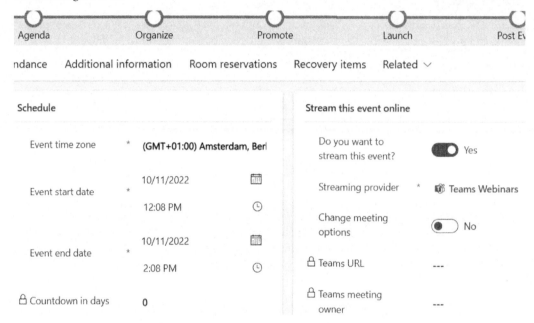

Figure 8.40 – Streaming an event using the main event record

A set of new columns will appear, and you can edit your online event. The **Streaming provider** option you choose should be one of the webinar providers you set in the **Settings** area, or you can choose Microsoft Teams. In this book, we're focusing on the out-of-the-box functionality with the use of **Teams Webinars**.

Teams

When you use Microsoft Teams for your webinars, you get different options depending on which Microsoft Teams license you have. You can create a Teams webinar, Teams meeting, or Teams Live event. Teams Live events do not allow attendees to share video, audio, or chat, apart from a Q&A feature. Teams Live events are best suited for a large audience with few presenters. After you save a record, when you've set it as a streaming event, Dynamics 365 Marketing will automatically create a Teams URL and the Teams meeting owner will automatically be whoever saved the event after it was set to stream; this can be someone other than the owner of the event record.

You can see this in *Figure 8.41*:

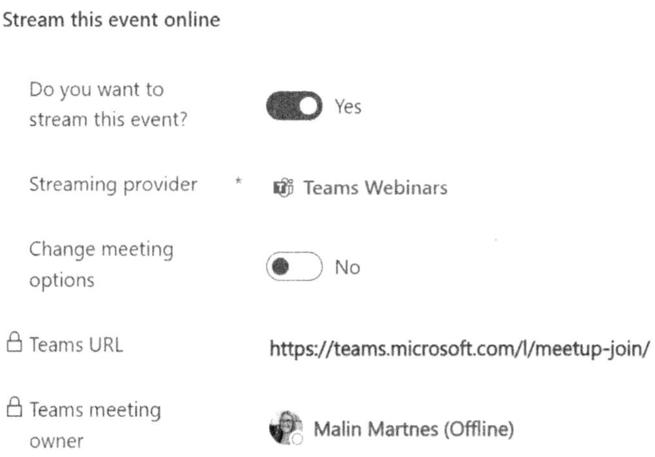

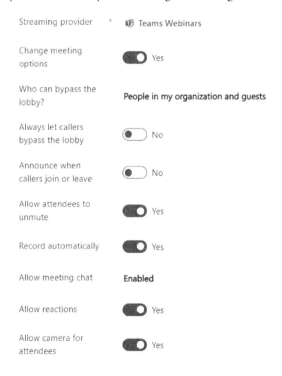

Figure 8.41 – Teams meeting options

If you set **Change meeting options** to **No**, the webinar or meeting will follow the policies that are set in your organization. If you set it to **Yes**, you can change the settings as shown in *Figure 8.42*:

Figure 8.42 – Change meeting options

It's important to know what each of these settings does:

- **Who can bypass the lobby?**

  This is for if you want certain people to be able to go right into the meeting and not have to be admitted in by the meeting organizer.

- **Always let callers bypass the lobby**

  This setting is used so that you don't have to admit attendees to the meeting; everyone comes straight into the meeting.

- **Announce when callers join or leave**

  Using this setting, you can set whether in the Teams chat for the meeting, there will be an announcement every time someone joins or leaves the meeting. This can be a disturbance otherwise; if there are many attendees, it can take focus away from the presenter.

- **Allow attendees to unmute**

  If you want your attendees to ask questions or take part in discussions, this must be set to **Yes**. If it is set to **No**, then no attendees can unmute.

- **Record automatically**

  I'm sure you've been in a meeting that was meant to be recorded but someone forgot to do so. With this setting, you don't have to remember to press the record button; the system does it for you. The attendees can watch the recording from the attendee URL given in the registration email.

- **Allow meeting chat**

  This can be enabled to activate the chat feature and disabled to remove it. It can also be set to an in-meeting-only setting, where chat is only available for the time you're attending the meeting and will be locked if you leave the meeting.

- **Allow reactions**

  If someone says something smart, we might want to send them a thumbs up – or send them a laughing emoji if they're being funny. This can be turned on or off in the settings.

- **Allow camera for attendees**

  For a lot of meetings, it's very nice to see other people in the audience so that it doesn't feel like we're talking to a black box. Other times, webcam images can take away focus. If there are many attendees, then the use of cameras can also use a lot of compute power and WiFi bandwidth.

In an event's record, on the **Additional information** tab, you can see **Calendar content** at the bottom of the form, as shown in *Figure 8.43*:

General   Agenda   Website and form   Registration and attendance   **Additional information**   Room reservations   Recovery items   Related

0 - 0 of 0

Calendar content

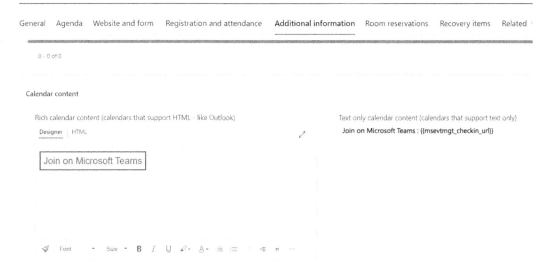

Figure 8.43 – Calendar content

The **Join on Microsoft Teams** button you see in *Figure 8.43* can be used to create an email to send to attendees. You can see the button and the **Link to** section in *Figure 8.44*:

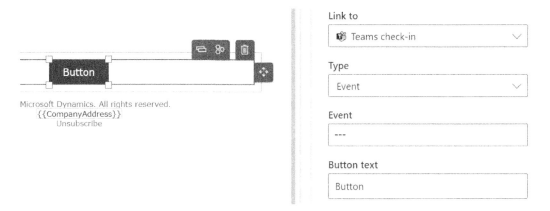

Figure 8.44 – Link to – Teams check-in

When your attendees join the meeting 30 minutes or less before the start, they will be created as a check-in record automatically. If they join more than 30 minutes before, a check-in record isn't created; this is to make sure that attendees testing the links won't be registered as checked-in. Be aware that every Teams check-in button is unique to each attendee; anyone attending through this button will be registered as a new check-in record attached to the original attendee.

Event communication

To communicate with attendees, you need to use journeys, either in Outbound marketing or Real-time marketing journeys, depending on your preferences. We went through how to create journeys in *Chapter 6, Outbound Customer Journeys*, and *Chapter 7, Real-Time Marketing Journeys*.

The attendees need to have somewhere to register, so you need to either create a custom form from your website or use the event registration marketing forms.

Once your attendees have registered, they also need to get emails throughout the journey. You need to create all the emails you're going to use in your journey, from registering for the event and canceling to reminders the day before the event and the thank-you and evaluation after the event.

Event website

Some companies running events have their own website for each event. Others put their registration forms on their regular website or in emails. Others still use Power Pages with the out-of-the-box template that is fully integrated with Dynamics 365 Marketing. Scottish Summit had its own event website and developed an integration with Eventbrite where all the attendees registered.

Power Pages

The Power Pages event template is a preconfigured website that gets all the information and graphics from your published event in Dynamics 365 Marketing. Your attendees can register, as well as see information about your events, speakers, sessions, sponsors, and any other information about your event. In *Figure 8.45*, you can see an event page that showcases the out-of-the-box features of this Power Pages template:

Figure 8.45 – Event website

On this page, you can create a payment gateway and use third-party payment providers to charge for your events. All the information for your events that has gone live is shown on the event portal automatically. We are going to go through how to create and manage Power Pages and other surrounding systems in *Chapter 10, Power Platform*.

Summary

In this chapter, we have gone through many features and functionalities of the event module in Dynamics 365 Marketing. The chapter has hopefully shown you why the event module is one of the things that separates Dynamics 365 Marketing from other marketing automation systems. You should have an idea of how you can utilize the event module to run your events. The event module can handle big events with many sessions and thousands of attendees. The module can also help you if you are just running a webinar for 10 people.

We've gone through the basic setup of events, including in-person-event-specific setup and webinar-specific setup. We've seen how we can organize and have full control over hotels, hotel allocation, hotel reservations, and other types of vendors. We've gone through how we can use Microsoft Teams as our webinar provider and the different settings you can configure for your webinars. With all that, we've learned about everything we need to know to be able to create and manage all our events.

We've seen how Scottish Summit used Dynamics 365 Marketing to run their events and the features they've used, as well as exploring some of the components they developed and configured.

A very big part of your work after each event is getting evaluations and feedback from your attendees. In the next chapter, we are going to go through the preferred solution for evaluation: Dynamics 365 Customer Voice.

Questions

The following are some questions that will help you gauge your understanding of the topics discussed in this chapter. The answers are provided in the *Assessments* section at the end of the book.

1. You can only use Microsoft Teams as your webinar provider.

   A. Yes

   B. No

2. In which marketing form can you register attendees?

   A. Landing page

   B. Forward to a friend

   C. Event registration

   D. Event attendees

3. How is the speaker connected to your event and session?

   A. Directly to the event

   B. Directly to the session

   C. Directly to the session track

   D. Through speaker engagements

4. If you use Microsoft Teams as your webinar provider, you can't change any options – it uses the organization's settings.

   A. True

   B. False

Part 3 – The Microsoft Ecosystem Adding Value

One of the biggest advantages of choosing a Microsoft system is the surrounding environment and the big ecosystem. From extending the marketing system to having an event portal and asking customers for their feedback – there is a solution in the Microsoft world to achieve it. The following chapters are included in this part:

9

Dynamics 365 Customer Voice

Everyone needs a tool for surveys. There are a lot of tools out there, but none are as tightly integrated with Dynamics 365 as Customer Voice. In this chapter, we'll go through what Dynamics 365 Customer Voice is and how you can utilize it in your marketing efforts. For example, we can improve our events by getting information from our attendees, and we can discover what our sales process or customer service is like for customers by sending them a survey.

This chapter will go through the following:

- What is Dynamics 365 Customer Voice?
- Creating and managing surveys
- Adding questions to a survey
- Sending surveys

What is Dynamics 365 Customer Voice?

Before we start going through how to use Customer Voice, let us go through the history of the product.

Until July 01, 2020, there was a survey solution in Dynamics 365 called **Voice of the Customer** (**VoC**). In 2020, this solution was deprecated and removed from all Microsoft solutions, as it was very complex and not widely used. In July 2019, Microsoft decided to create a solution from the Microsoft 365 tool, **Forms**. They called it **Forms Pro** and worked on giving it more functionality than Forms. At Inspire in July 2020, they announced that Forms Pro was now changing – not just the name, but more functionality and where the data was stored. Dynamics 365 Customer Voice was the new name for this product. The evolution of the names and survey tools is shown in *Figure 9.1*:

Figure 9.1 – Surveys tools connected to Dynamics 365 applications

Dynamics 365 Customer Voice has a lot of the same features and functionalities as you will find in Microsoft Forms. In 2020, it was decided that the data from Dynamics 365 Customer Voice should be stored in Dataverse. Customer Voice spans every environment you have on your tenant. This is useful if you have multiple environments, such as development, testing, and production. The fact that it's so tightly connected to multiple environments makes it a lot easier for customers to utilize the responses you get on your surveys. You still have Microsoft Forms connected to your Microsoft 365 subscription, but you will only find some of the more advanced functionality in Dynamics 365 Customer Voice.

Dynamics 365 Customer Voice is tightly integrated with several of the Dynamics 365 applications. Here are some ways you can use Dynamics 365 Customer Voice with other Dynamics 365 applications:

- Send a survey to a new customer asking for feedback on the sales process
- Send a survey to a customer after they have completed a customer service case
- Send a survey after your field technician has completed a work order
- Ask a new employee for feedback on the employment process
- Ask a customer how they thought your latest project went
- Evaluate the latest event

These are just some of the areas where you can utilize Dynamics 365 Customer Voice. In this chapter, we are not going to cover the functionalities of Microsoft Forms; we will just look at the capabilities you can find in Dynamics 365 Customer Voice.

For a deeper dive into Customer Voice and Forms, I highly recommend reading the book *Working with Microsoft Forms and Customer Voice*, available at `https://www.packtpub.com/product/working-with-microsoft-forms-and-customer-voice/9781801070171`.

Now that we've gone through a bit of the history, let us see how we can use Dynamics 365 Customer Voice to manage, create, and send our surveys.

Creating and managing surveys

In this section, we'll go through how you can create and manage your projects and surveys in Dynamics 365 Customer Voice.

To find Dynamics 365 Customer Voice and start creating surveys, you need to go to `https://customervoice.microsoft.com/` and sign in with the same credentials as you use for Dynamics 365 Marketing, as shown in *Figure 9.2*:

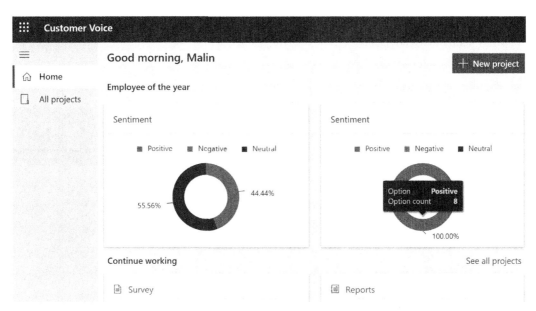

Figure 9.2 – Home page of Customer Voice

Because Dynamics 365 Customer Voice is built on a different tool than the other Dynamics 365 applications, you will not find it in the same area as your other Dynamics 365 applications.

To start creating surveys, you must first create a project. Let's go through projects and how they are used.

Projects

A project is a way of grouping your surveys, satisfaction metrics, email templates, Power Automate flows, and reports. You cannot create a survey without a project. To create a new project, click on the + **New project** button that you can see on the home page, as shown in *Figure 9.3*:

Figure 9.3 – New project button on the home page

The next thing to do is to decide what kind of project you want to create. As you can see in *Figure 9.4*, there are eight different types of projects that you can create:

Figure 9.4 – The eight different projects

The different project templates contain different information and have different purposes:

- **Periodic customer feedback**: This template is used to get your customers' feedback on a regular basis. You can make some changes to the survey and send it to your customers several times to see whether there are any changes in the satisfaction of your customers. It is based on the *Forrester Decisions for Customer Experience* best practices. In this template, you get a survey with questions, an email template, and customer sentiment and satisfaction metrics.

- **Order delivery**: This template is used to get feedback from your customers after an order is delivered. It contains an email template, a Power Automate flow, customer satisfaction metrics, a net promoter score, and product sentiment. The order delivery template is closely connected to Dynamics 365 Sales, and the Power Automate flow is connected to the Order table.

- **Service visit**: This template is tightly connected to Dynamics 365 Field Service and is used to get feedback from your customers after a scheduled visit. This contains an email template, customer satisfaction, and customer sentiment.

- **Support**: If you have Dynamics 365 Customer Service and want to send a survey when a case is resolved, this is the template for you. It contains an email template, customer sentiment and customer satisfaction, and a Power Automate flow.

- **New Patient Survey**: This template is specifically for health organizations and is used for checking in on the patient experience and monitoring their health.

- **Patient Service Center**: This project template is also for health organizations and asks patients about their experience with the Service Center.

- **ACSI® Analytics & Benchmarks**: The **ACSI®** is the **American Customer Satisfaction Index**. It tracks customer satisfaction from more than 400 of the largest corporations in the U.S. marketplace. The survey that follows this project template is used in the banking industry.

- **Blank**: The blank template lets you start from nothing to create your own surveys, email templates, satisfaction metrics, and Power Automate flows. In this chapter, I will use the blank project template to show what you can do when you start blank.

Once you've selected the template you want to create, click **Next** and you will be able to select the survey location, as shown in *Figure 9.5*:

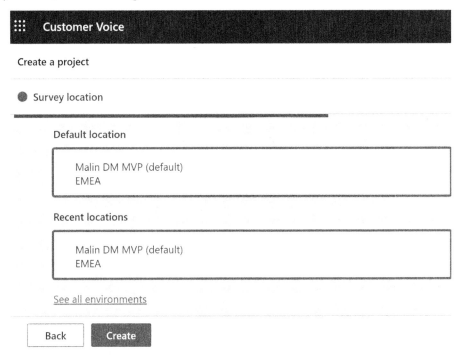

Figure 9.5 – Survey location

If you don't want to use any of the selected environments, you can click **See all environments** to get a list of all your environments, as shown in *Figure 9.6*:

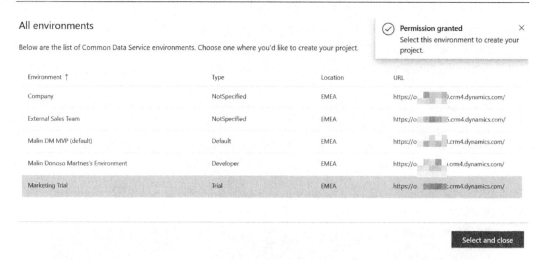

Figure 9.6 – All environments

Why is it important to connect to the right environment? Because you want to make sure that you collect the correct data, and have the data stored and used in your marketing solution. When you select your environment, the system checks that you have access to the environment. You can then click on **Select and close**, and create the project.

You now have a new project with one blank survey, as shown in *Figure 9.7*:

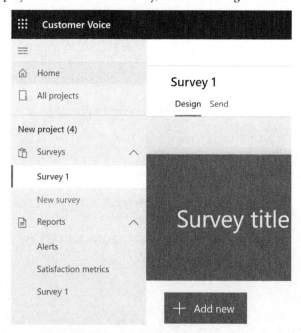

Figure 9.7 – New project with one survey

Now, it's up to you to create good surveys that your customer will want to answer so that you get the answers to the questions you've been wondering about.

As you can see, the project is created with the name **New project**. To change this (as shown in *Figure 9.8*), you must do the following:

1. Click on **All projects**.

2. Select your project.

3. Click on the three dots.

4. Click on **Rename**.

5. Give it a new name and save it:

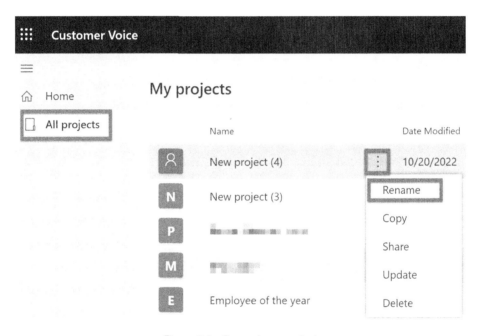

Figure 9.8 – Renaming a project

Renaming projects will make it easier to manage them at a later stage.

One of the benefits of creating projects and potentially having multiple surveys bundled together is that your analytics can also be bundled per project. Let's look at the project analytics.

Analytics

On the home page, you will get some analytics from surveys where you've registered the satisfaction metrics, as shown in *Figure 9.9*:

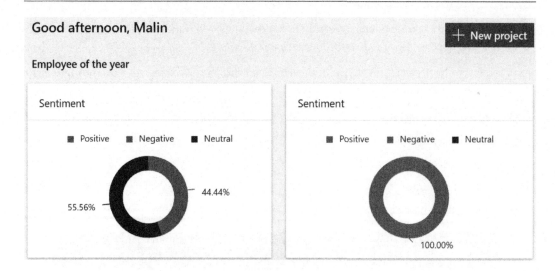

Figure 9.9 – Satisfaction metrics for a project

If you go to a project, you can see the satisfaction metrics and the reports from every survey in the project, as shown in *Figure 9.10*:

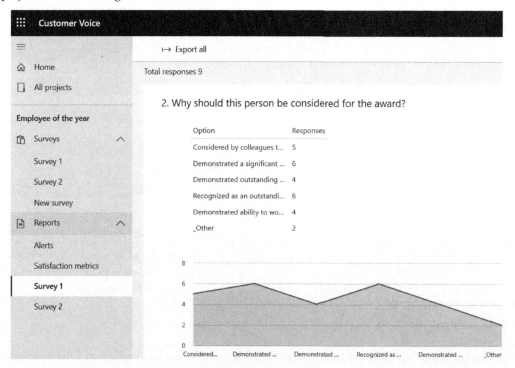

Figure 9.10 – Reports from a survey in a project

The kind of analytics that you get will differ based on the type of questions you ask in your surveys. Let's go through how you create a survey.

Adding questions to a survey

The core of every project in Dynamics 365 Customer Voice is surveys. They are what you create and what you send to your customers.

For all the questions, you can say whether the question is required or optional. You can add subtitles to the questions if you want to describe the question more. You can also add logic to the questions. Let's start by understanding the different question types in a survey.

Question types

These are the different question types in a survey, as shown in *Figure 9.11*:

- **Choice**
- **Text**
- **Rating**
- **Date**
- **Ranking**
- **Likert**
- **File upload**
- **Net Promoter Score** ® (**NPS**)

Figure 9.11 – The different question types

Some users will want to add several pages to their survey – they can have many questions – or may want to separate the type of questions into different pages. You can create different sections in the survey by clicking **Section** as you can see in *Figure 9.11*.

Let's go through all the options and how we can use each of them in the survey.

Choice

Ask a question, and choose an answer from the predefined answers. This is a very popular question type. Let's go through the different options you have, as shown in *Figure 9.12*:

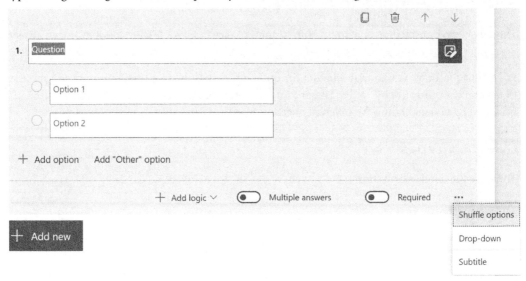

Figure 9.12 – Choice type

You can add more options or use **Add "Other" option**. This way, you can tailor the answers in the way most suited to your company's needs.

With a **Choice** question, you can either have a single-choice answer or multiple answers. You can select whether the question is a multiple-choice question by toggling the **Multiple answers** toggle.

You can shuffle the options so that people don't always select the top answer; this way, you can make sure the answer selections aren't skewed by the order of the answers. If your question is how well you think we performed, and the answers are **Bad**, **Neutral**, and **Good**, then shuffling isn't a good idea.

The **Drop-down** option lets you show the answers as a dropdown, and users can select their answers from the list.

Text

The next question type is the **Text** type, as shown in *Figure 9.13*:

Figure 9.13 – Text type

You can have a short, one-line textbox, or a **Long answer** textbox over several lines. You can also set restrictions, as shown in *Figure 9.14*, where you can specify whether the input should be a number, or an email, or add your own custom regular expression to specify the input:

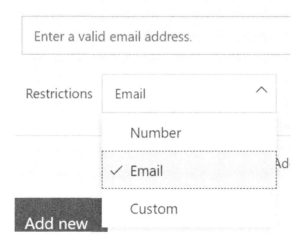

Figure 9.14 – Setting restrictions for a Text answer

Rating

Let's say you want to know how happy attendees are with the event you've just had. You want them to answer on a scale from 1 to 5 about how satisfied they are, where 1 is not satisfied and 5 is very satisfied. **Rating** is the question type that can help you with these types of questions. You can select whether you want to show the scale as numbers, stars, or smileys, as shown in *Figure 9.15*:

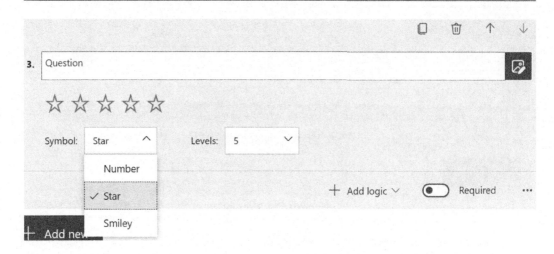

Figure 9.15 – Rating type – choosing the symbol

If you select **Star** or **Number**, you can choose a scale between 2 to 9; if you select **Smiley**, you can choose a scale between 2 to 5.

Date

When do you want the next event to be? When do you want to set up the next sales call? These are both questions for which you can use the **Date** question type, as shown in *Figure 9.16*:

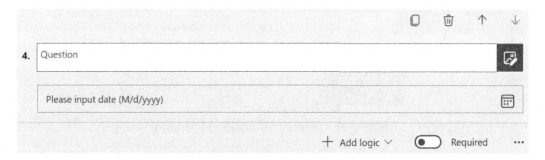

Figure 9.16 – Date type

Ranking

In the **Ranking** question, the customer can drag and drop the different options in their preferred order, as shown in *Figure 9.17*:

Figure 9.17 – Ranking type

Likert

In the **Likert** type, you have several statements that you should select an option for, as shown in *Figure 9.18*:

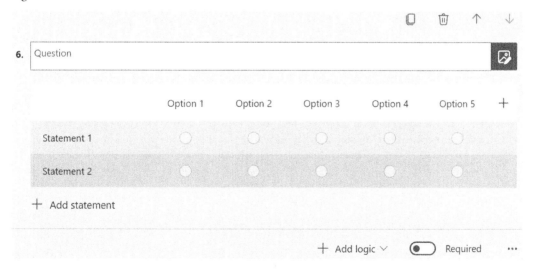

Figure 9.18 – Likert type

Let's say your customer has been to an event, and you want to know how each of the five sessions of the day was, but you don't want them to answer separate questions. You can use a Likert question and have a statement for each session and set the options to **Dissatisfied**, **Neutral**, and **Satisfied**. The customer can then answer for every session and have the same options, without you having to create the same question five times.

File upload

The **File upload** type becomes available if you set the survey to only be internally available. When you set the survey as exclusively internal, only the people in your organization who can log in to your tenant will get access to the survey. All these files will be uploaded to OneDrive, and the names of the people uploading the files will be available. You can restrict how many files can be uploaded, pick a single file size limit, and determine which file types can be uploaded, as shown in *Figure 9.19*:

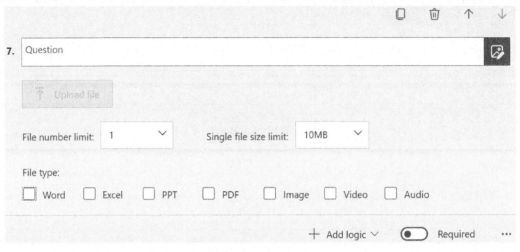

Figure 9.19 – File upload

Net Promoter Score®

Net Promoter Score® is a standardized question to measure customer experience and overall perception. It always has 0 to 10 as options, and the question should always be **How likely are you to recommend us to a friend or colleague?**, as shown in *Figure 9.20*:

Figure 9.20 – Net Promoter Score®

From the answers on the NPS, you have your detractors, passives, and promoters:

- **Detractors** are anyone who answered 0 to 6; they are considered unhappy customers.

- **Passives** are the customers scoring 7 to 8; they are happy but aren't singing your praise.

- **Promoters** are the ones scoring 9 to 10; they are super happy and will talk positively about you to others and are the kind of customers we all hope to have.

Adding logic

Sometimes, you want to ask some questions to unhappy customers or show a section of questions based on what they have previously answered. You can do this by adding logic to each question. You can either add **Display logic** or **Skip logic** to every question.

Display logic

You can choose to display a question based on the response you get from another question, or a variable that you are using in the survey, as shown in *Figure 9.21*:

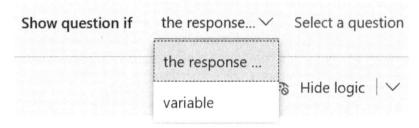

Figure 9.21 – Display logic

You want to further information about why a customer is very satisfied with the work you have done. You can display several extra questions if the customer has responded 9 to 10 (super happy) in the previous question. For any customer that does not respond with 9 to 10, these questions will not be shown.

Skip logic

With the **Skip logic** option, you can have the customer skip to the end of the survey, or skip several questions or several sections, as shown in *Figure 9.22*:

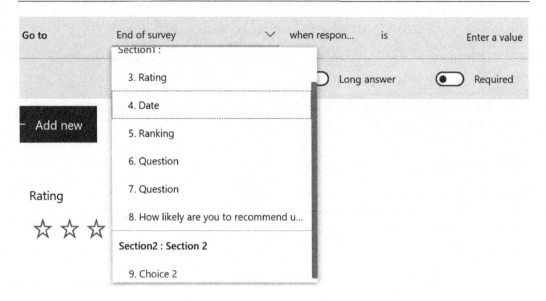

Figure 9.22 – Skip logic

Let's say your first question is **Why did you not attend this event?**. If the customer answers that they were sick, there is no need to ask follow-up questions, so they should be able to skip to the end of the survey. If the customer answers that they didn't feel like going, you can skip to a section where you have questions about what it would take for that customer to join the event.

Now that we have created our survey and added all the questions and all the logic we want to use, it is time to make the survey look and feel like it aligns with your company's design guides.

Customization

To make the survey feel more aligned with your company, you can go into **Customization** on the right-hand side of the screen. You then get six options where you can customize your survey, as shown in *Figure 9.23*:

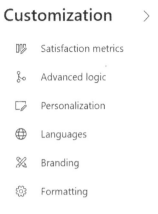

Figure 9.23 – Customization

Let's go through these customizations.

Satisfaction metrics

In **Satisfaction metrics**, you define which questions track your customer satisfaction metrics. As you can see from *Figure 9.24*, you can select **Net Promoter Score**®, **Sentiment**, **CSAT**, and **Custom score**:

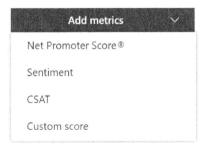

Figure 9.24 – Satisfaction metrics

When you have selected the satisfaction metric, give it a name and add the question that is connected to this metric, as shown in *Figure 9.25*:

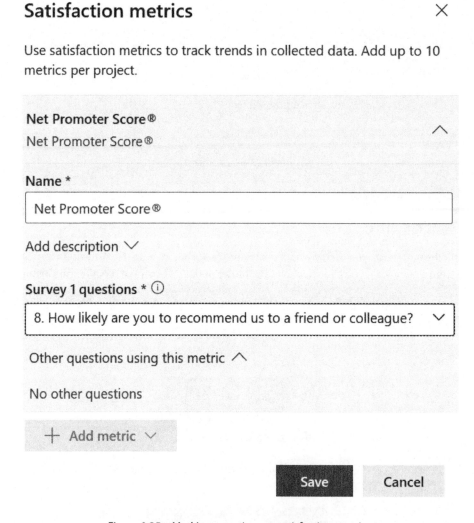

Figure 9.25 – Marking questions as satisfaction metrics

Advanced logic

In each question, you can add simple logic. Sometimes, you have more advanced needs than these simple logics can give you; that is when you use **Advanced logic**, as shown in *Figure 9.26*:

Customize the path people take through this survey

Add simple logic directly on survey questions, or use advanced logic to use more features like creating
links between different surveys and controlling multiple questions from one rule.

Use simple logic   Use advanced logic

Figure 9.26 – Use advanced logic

If you're using some simple logic already in the questions, this will be imported into your advanced logic.

When you are using advanced logic, you can create branching rules, as shown in *Figure 9.27*:

Branching rule

Rule name *

Rule 1

   **Primary rule condition(s)**

+ Add condition

+ Add "If true"

Figure 9.27 – Branching rules in advanced logic

In the branching rules, you can create the condition. You then add the true path – this is what will happen if the customer matches the condition. For example, if a customer has replied negatively to all questions, then it might be a good idea to ask your customer more questions in order to understand why they are so negative.

Personalization

In **Personalization**, you can add variables to create a more personal feeling to the survey, as shown in *Figure 9.28*. You can also use variables where the data comes from Dataverse to create advanced logic.

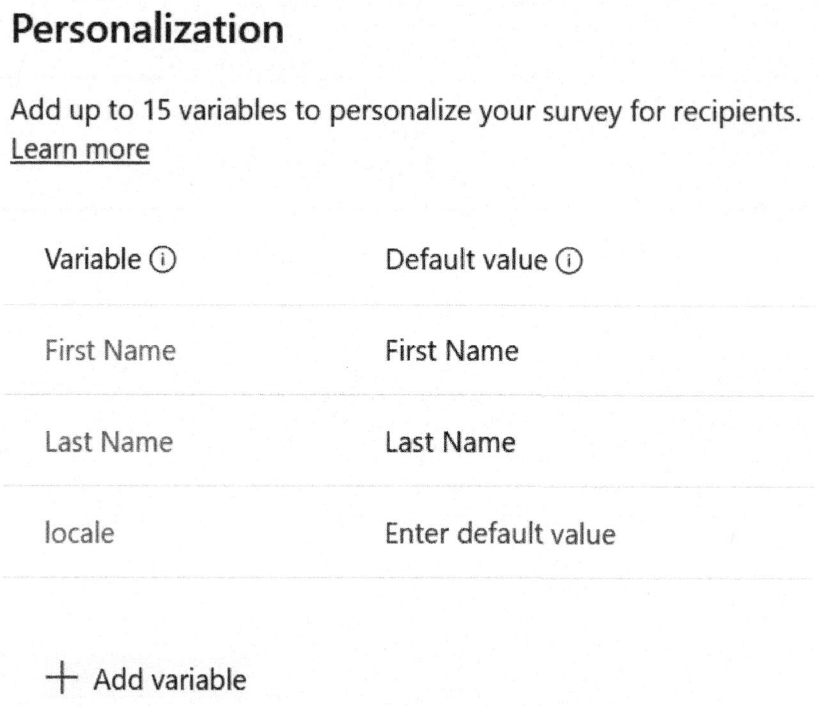

Personalization

Add up to 15 variables to personalize your survey for recipients.
Learn more

Variable ⓘ	Default value ⓘ
First Name	First Name
Last Name	Last Name
locale	Enter default value

\+ Add variable

Figure 9.28 – Personalization with variables

Languages

Some companies have customers who speak different languages and so want to create surveys in different languages. This can be done in the **Languages** section, as shown in *Figure 9.29*:

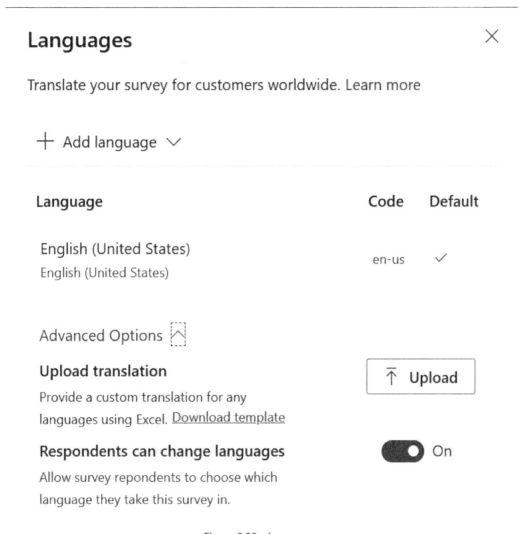

Figure 9.29 – Languages

To add other languages, you need to click on + **Add language**. Once that is done, you can also provide custom translations with the use of Excel. You can also choose whether your respondents can change languages. Be aware that you need to add translations if you want to use multiple languages in your surveys.

Branding

In **Branding**, you can add your own theme color, choose your fonts, and upload the image for your background, as shown in *Figure 9.30*:

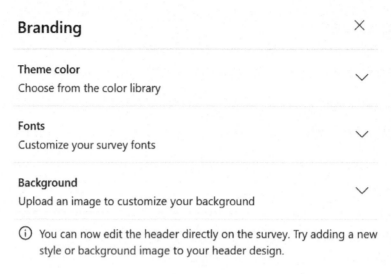

Figure 9.30 – Branding

You can select the theme color by adding the HEX code. You can choose from 1 of 10 fonts, and you can upload a picture from your laptop or OneDrive to use as a background.

Formatting

In **Formatting**, you can choose to show or hide a progress bar if you have multiple sections, show or hide the question numbers, and shuffle questions, as shown in *Figure 9.31*:

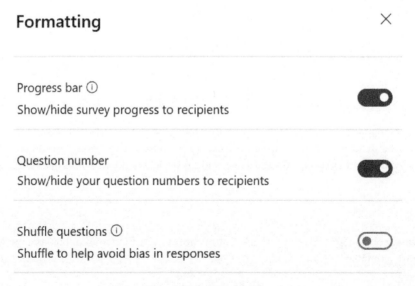

Figure 9.31 – Formatting

Post-survey message

At the end of the survey, you will find the post-survey message, as shown in *Figure 9.32*:

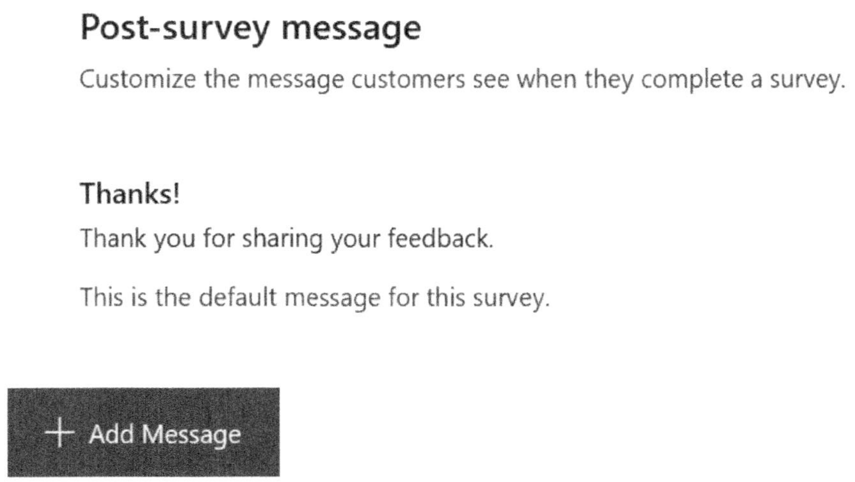

Post-survey message

Customize the message customers see when they complete a survey.

Thanks!

Thank you for sharing your feedback.

This is the default message for this survey.

Figure 9.32 – Post-survey message

Here, you can customize the message you give to your customers after they've completed the survey.

Footer

At the bottom of the survey, you will find the footer. Here, you can customize the footer message for your customers, as shown in *Figure 9.33*:

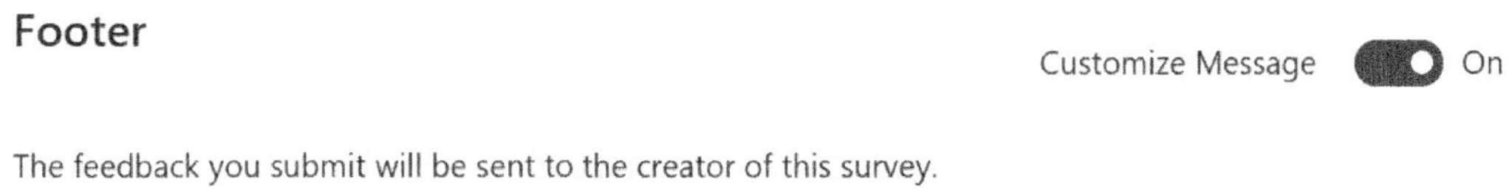

Footer   Customize Message On

The feedback you submit will be sent to the creator of this survey.

Figure 9.33 – Footer

Now, you've completed the survey and you want to share the project with someone else internally to give you feedback. This is done with the **Share** button.

Share

You can share projects with internal users, as shown in *Figure 9.34*:

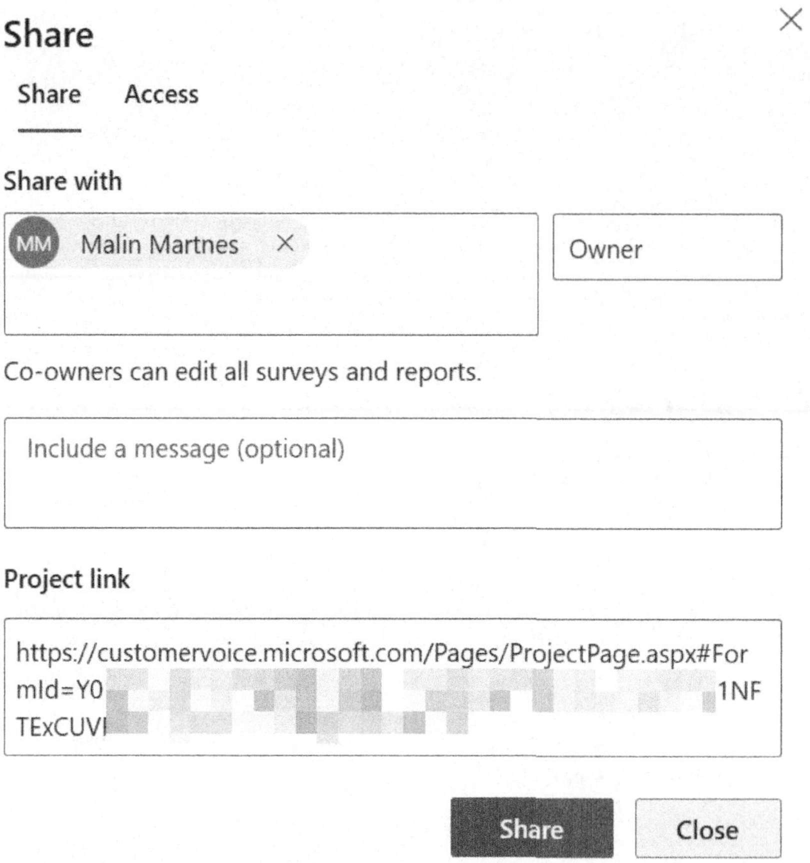

Share   ✕

Share   Access
_____

Share with

| MM Malin Martnes ✕ | | Owner |

Co-owners can edit all surveys and reports.

Include a message (optional)

Project link

https://customervoice.microsoft.com/Pages/ProjectPage.aspx#For
mId=Y0   1NF
TExCUVI

[Share]   [Close]

Figure 9.34 – Sharing a project

When you click on the **Share** button in the top-right corner, you can also see who has access to each project. When everything in the project is done, it's time to send the survey.

Sending surveys

There are several different ways that you can send the survey to your customers. As you can see in *Figure 9.35*, you can have people answer through automation (Power Automate), email, an embedded code, a link, or a QR code:

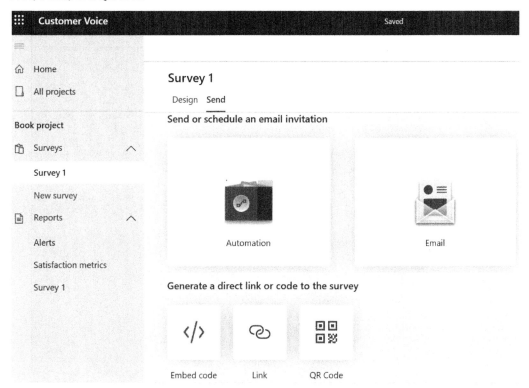

Figure 9.35 – Sending a survey

Before we see how to send the surveys, let's go through the distribution settings.

Distribution settings

When you click on the **Send** tab, other options appear on the right-hand side under **Customization**. Here, you can edit the **Distribution** settings, as shown in *Figure 9.36*. You can set options for **Participants**, **Responses**, **Availability**, **Email**, and **Notifications**:

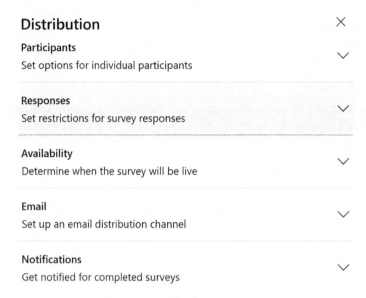

Figure 9.36 – Distribution settings

Under **Participants**, you get a set of options, as shown in *Figure 9.37*:

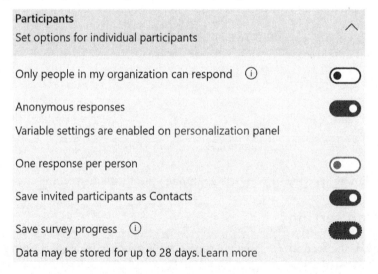

Figure 9.37 – Participants options

You have options for the following:

- Whether internal or external people can respond.

- Whether responses can be anonymous.

- Whether you can have more than one response per person (this cannot be changed if you chose to allow anonymous responses, as you don't know whether they have answered previously).

- Whether you should save invited participants as contacts (this way, they can be reused later).

- Whether to save the survey progress. This is great if you have a long survey that isn't always completed in one go. Users can then come back up to 28 days later and complete the survey.

In **Responses** and **Availability**, you set when the survey is available for customers; if anyone tries to answer the survey outside this time, they will not get access. You can also restrict the response limit so that only a certain amount of responses can be submitted.

In **Email**, you can select who the sender of the surveys should be.

In **Notifications**, you can select whether you want to send a confirmation email to respondents and whether you want to receive an email when a survey is submitted.

Now, let's go through all the different ways you can send a survey from Dynamics 365 Customer Voice.

Automation

When you choose to send a survey through **Automation**, you can either choose from one of many Power Automate templates, or you can start from blank. You can see some of the templates in *Figure 9.38*:

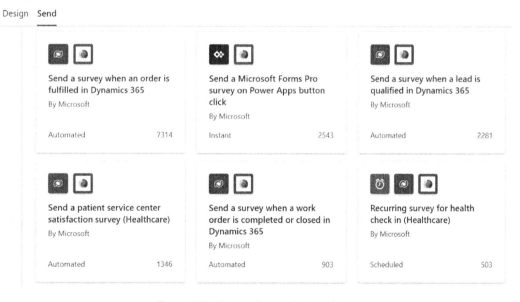

Figure 9.38 – Power Automate templates

I've selected **Send a survey when an order is fulfilled in Dynamics 365**. You can edit the Power Automate template and make it suited to your needs, as shown in *Figure 9.39*:

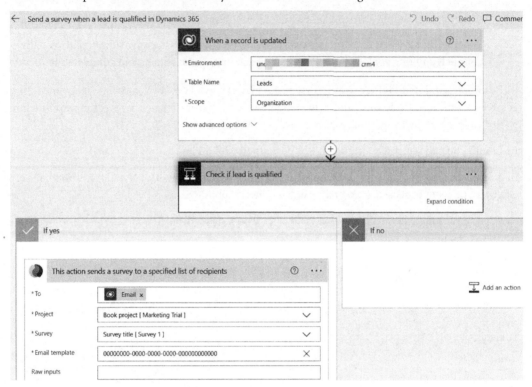

Figure 9.39 – Power Automate template

When the Power Automate flow is configured and ready, then you can go back to your survey, as shown in *Figure 9.40*, and see that everything is ready to start when the Power Automate flow is triggered:

Survey 1

Design **Send**

Figure 9.40 – Survey is ready to send with the Power Automate flow

Now, let's see how we can send it with an email.

Email

When sending with **Email**, you should first decide which email template you should use. You can use the default template and edit it, create a new one, or import one from **Surveys** or **My templates**, as shown in *Figure 9.41*:

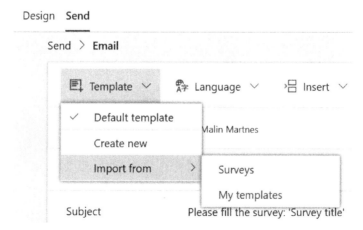

Figure 9.41 – Email templates

As you can also see from *Figure 9.41*, you can set the language of the email.

In addition to this, you can insert different things in the email. As you can see in *Figure 9.42*, you have options to add **Personalized variables**, **First question of the survey**, **Survey link**, and **Unsubscribe link**:

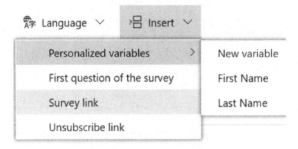

Figure 9.42 – Email insertions

Adding the first survey question is a good way of getting your customers started on the survey; research shows that if you've first started on a survey, it's more likely that you'll complete the survey.

To send the email, you must manually add each recipient or select the upload recipients. As you can see in *Figure 9.43*, there are some guidelines for the upload:

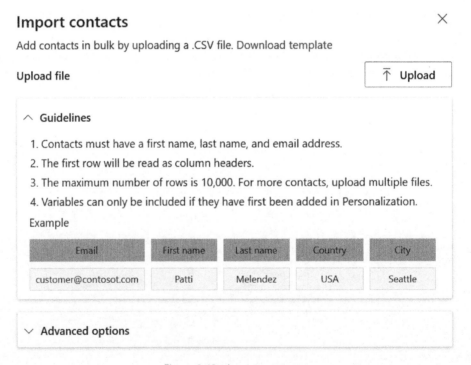

Figure 9.43 – Import contacts

To upload the recipients, you can upload a maximum of 10,000 recipients, and I highly recommend using the template provided; this will make it easier to make sure the data is structured the correct way and you will get all the information about the participants correct.

Let's look at a couple of easier ways if you want to have multiple people answer but you do not have all the information about them.

Embedded code

Some companies want to embed the survey on their website. This can be done in three ways, as shown in *Figure 9.44*:

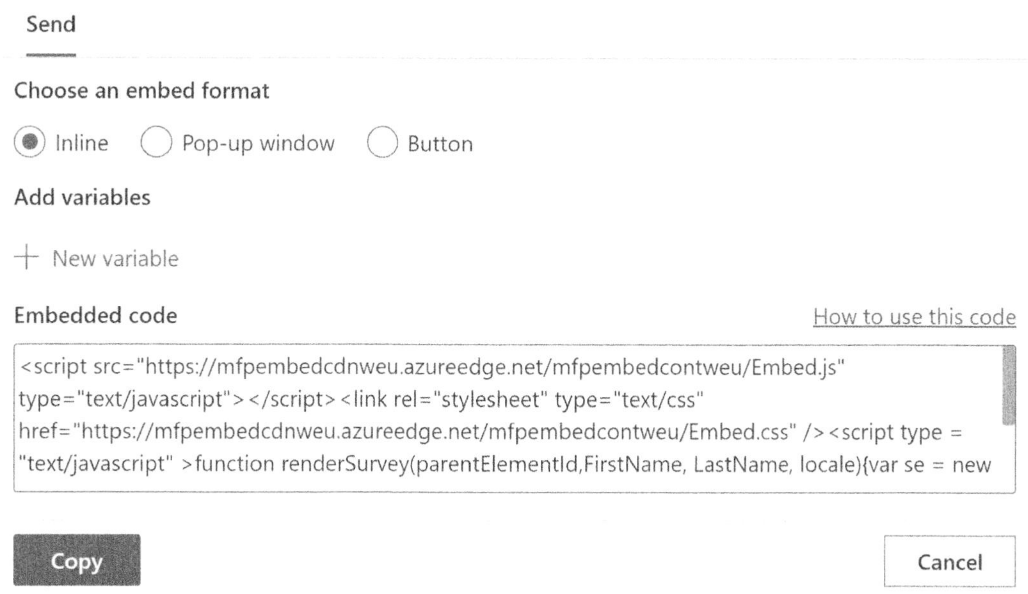

Send

Choose an embed format

(●) Inline   ( ) Pop-up window   ( ) Button

Add variables

+ New variable

Embedded code   How to use this code

```
<script src="https://mfpembedcdnweu.azureedge.net/mfpembedcontweu/Embed.js"
type="text/javascript"></script><link rel="stylesheet" type="text/css"
href="https://mfpembedcdnweu.azureedge.net/mfpembedcontweu/Embed.css" /><script type =
"text/javascript" >function renderSurvey(parentElementId,FirstName, LastName, locale){var se = new
```

Copy   Cancel

Figure 9.44 – Embedded survey

You can choose from **Inline** (where the survey is embedded into your site), **Pop-up window** (which creates a popup on your website), or **Button** (where you open a new page to answer the survey).

Another easy way is to use a link.

Link

The easiest way of getting people to answer your survey is to send them a link to the survey. This will not save any personal information but it is an easy way of sending surveys. When you click on the **Link** option under **Send**, you will get a link that you can copy. You can also create custom links if you want to keep track of where the answers are coming from. All of this is shown in *Figure 9.45*:

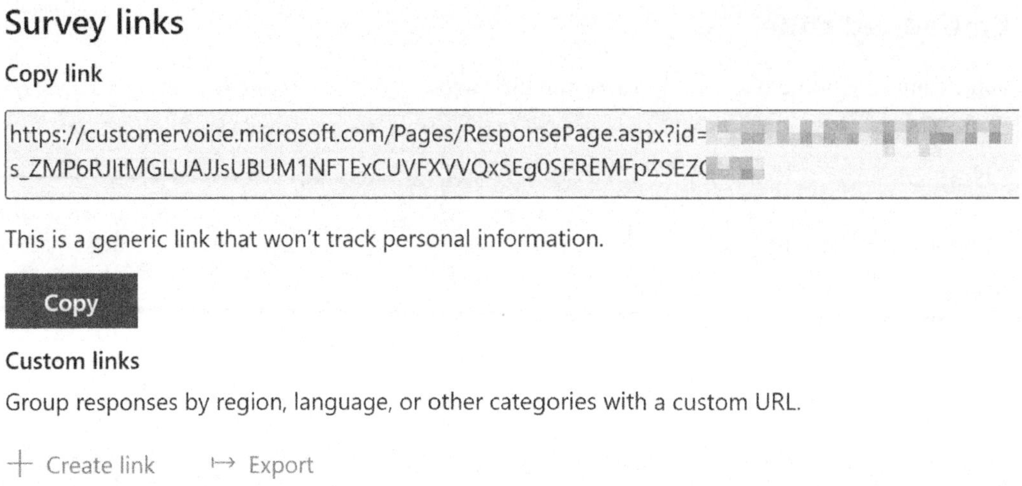

Survey links

Copy link

https://customervoice.microsoft.com/Pages/ResponsePage.aspx?id=
s_ZMP6RJItMGLUAJJsUBUM1NFTExCUVFXVVQxSEg0SFREMFpZSEZ(

This is a generic link that won't track personal information.

Custom links

Group responses by region, language, or other categories with a custom URL.

+ Create link   ↦ Export

Figure 9.45 – Using a survey link

Another way of having anyone answer a survey is by using a QR code.

QR code

A QR code is something almost everyone with a smartphone can read. You scan the code with your phone's camera and you click on the link it provides. As you can see from *Figure 9.46*, you can download the QR code to the survey and use it where you want:

Download a QR Code

Customers can scan this code to fill out the survey.

Download   Cancel

Figure 9.46 – QR code for a survey

Now, let's see how Dynamics 365 Marketing can send surveys.

Dynamics 365 Marketing

In Dynamics 365 Marketing, you can create an email where you link to the survey through a button, as shown in *Figure 9.47*:

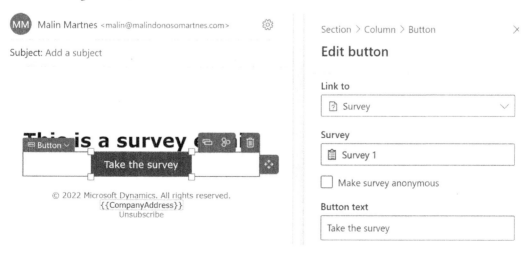

Figure 9.47 – Linking to a Customer Voice survey in an email

This email can be used in a customer journey and sent to your customers. This works both in real-time marketing and outbound marketing.

After a survey is answered, you can use the out-of-the-box triggers for Customer Voice to trigger a new customer journey, as shown in *Figure 9.48*:

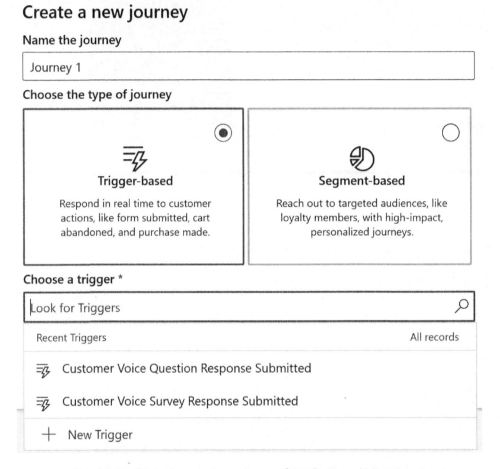

Figure 9.48 – Triggering a customer journey from Customer Voice triggers

You can also automate sending the survey with Power Automate and custom marketing triggers in real-time marketing.

Summary

As you can see from this chapter, Dynamics 365 Customer Voice is a very good survey tool, tightly integrated with Dynamics 365 Marketing.

In this chapter, we have gone through all the different types of questions you can have in a survey. We've gone through how you can use simple and advanced logic, and how you can make customizations to create a survey that is specific to your company's needs and design guides.

We've also gone through how you can best send the surveys. We've seen how you can use automated solutions, such as Power Automate flows, and the use of tools in Dynamics 365 Marketing. We've also seen how you can use more manual methods of sending surveys: emails, links, and QR codes. Finally, we have looked at how you can integrate a survey into your website using embedded code.

Now, you can create surveys that will give you insight from your customers and employees. Gaining insight is the best way you can improve your company or your marketing efforts. Asking customers for their experience with your company is the best way to gain insight.

In the last chapter, we're going to go through how you can use other systems, such as Dataverse, to make changes in your data model and model-driven apps to change your Marketing application.

Questions

The following are some questions that will help you gauge your understanding of the topics discussed in this chapter. The answers are available in the *Assessments* section at the end of the book.

1. Microsoft Forms and Dynamics 365 Customer Voice are identical:

    A. Yes

    B. No

2. Which of these is *not* a type of question you can have in a survey? (There is more than one answer)

    A. Rating

    B. Ranking

    C. Rhetorical

    D. Funnel

    E. CSAT

    F. NPS

3. You can create a single survey not connected to anything in Dynamics 365 Customer Voice:

    A. Yes

    B. No

4.   Embedding the survey on a website can be done in which three ways?

   A.   Inline

   B.   Outline

   C.   Button

   D.   Pop-up window

   E.   Download

5.   How long is the survey progress stored if the setting is turned on?

   A.   1 week

   B.   1 month

   C.   14 days

   D.   28 days

   E.   3 months

   F.   1 year

Further reading

This chapter has just scratched the surface of what is possible with Dynamics 365 Customer Voice. If you want to have a proper deep dive into the possibilities and the logic behind using surveys, then I highly recommend Welly Lee's book, *Working with Microsoft Forms and Customer Voice: Efficiently gather and manage customer feedback, insights, and experiences*: https://www.packtpub.com/product/working-with-microsoft-forms-and-customer-voice/9781801070171.

10
Power Platform

Dynamics 365 Marketing is a very powerful tool on its own, but the real power is in the Microsoft ecosystem. Microsoft Power Platform is a collection of low-code tools to help companies achieve more. You can see the different tools in Power Platform in *Figure 10.1*:

The low-code platform that spans Microsoft 365, Azure, Dynamics 365, and standalone apps.

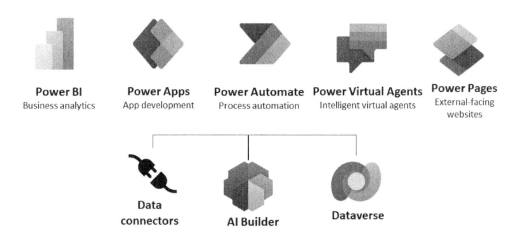

Figure 10.1 – Microsoft Power Platform

We are not going to go through all these applications. In this chapter, we're going to focus on the tools that have the most impact on Dynamics 365 Marketing. We will go through how you can make changes and customizations with Dataverse and Power Apps. For everything you want to automate, you can utilize the capabilities of Power Automate.

In this chapter, we will scratch the surface of the following areas, so make sure you look through the resources in the *Further reading* section for a deeper understanding of them:

- Dataverse

- Power Apps

- Power Automate

- Power Pages

- Customer Insights

By the end of this chapter, you will know how to customize the data model in Dataverse to adhere to your company's needs, how to make changes to model-driven apps to customize your marketing application, and how to use canvas apps to create apps for all of your company's needs. We'll look at how you can make life easier and more automated with Power Automate. The event portal built into Power Pages is something that can help you, as can getting a 360-degree view of your customer with Customer Insights.

Dataverse

Dataverse is the database that all Dynamics 365 **Customer Relationship Management** (**CRM**) applications are built upon. You cannot have a Dynamics 365 solution built on something other than Dataverse. Dynamics 365 Marketing cannot be set up on-premises. Power Pages and model-driven Power Apps also run exclusively on Dataverse. Dataverse is where you make your customizations to the database, and where you can add specific things that are just relevant to your company. This can be a column on the account where you register a local VAT number, or have your own membership number that you want to register.

In Dataverse, everything is stored in tables. A table contains several columns where you add information specific to each row.

In *Figure 10.2*, you can see the following:

1. Table name: **Account**

2. Row: **MaCoTra AS**

3. Column: `https://www.macotra.no/`:

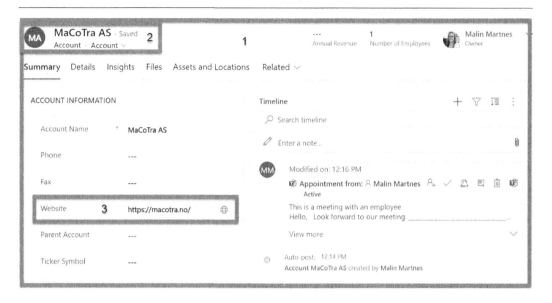

Figure 10.2 – Account table

All of your data is stored in tables, and all of your tables have several columns. The data is stored in separate rows.

But we don't start from a blank canvas when we set up a new Dynamics environment. Let's go through what is behind this.

Microsoft, together with Adobe and SAP, has collaborated and created the **Open Data Initiative** (**ODI**). The ODI is a collection of standard data formats. These companies work together so that every company that uses one of their solutions can easily integrate and have a familiar data structure in their environments. The core of the ODI is the **Common Data Model** (**CDM**), which is the definition of how data should look and how it should interact with other data sources. The CDM is a defined data schema with core tables that you can customize, and you can also add your own tables with your own data but still have the foundation in place. It is a way for you to have a predefined data schema rather than starting from scratch.

Dataverse is built on the CDM and has predefined tables, such as the following:

- **Account**
- **Contact**
- **Activity**
- **Email**
- **Phone Call**
- **Owner**

- **Task**

- **Currency**

In addition to this, when you add one or more of the Dynamics 365 applications, you will get a set of predefined tables.

A very important aspect of using Microsoft technology is its built-in security. Let's look at how this is sorted in Dataverse and Dynamics 365.

Security

For users to have access to Dataverse, they need the following:

- The user must be created in **Azure Active Directory** (**AAD**)

- The correct license

- One or more security roles

Security is a big topic and this is a short chapter, so we cannot cover everything about security here. To learn and understand more about security and how it's set up, I recommend reading the **Learn** module from Microsoft, which specifies security concepts in Dataverse: `https://learn.microsoft.com/en-us/power-platform/admin/wp-security`. In the Microsoft 365 admin center, you can add your users and give them the right licenses so that they have access to your tenant. The next thing to do is go to the Power Platform admin center and give the user the security role. The security role is what gives you access to each table and tells the system what data you should have access to.

Solutions

Every change you make in the system should be made in **Solutions**. You can find your solutions at `https://make.powerapps.com/`, as shown in *Figure 10.3*:

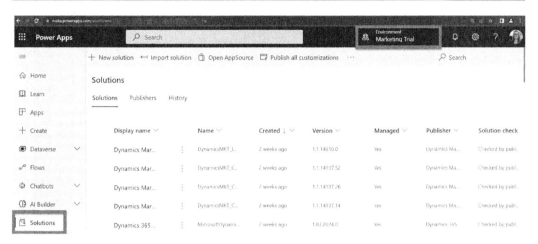

Figure 10.3 – Solutions in make.powerapps.com

As you can see in *Figure 10.3*, you must make sure you're in the right environment, which can be changed at the top right. You must create a solution and do all the customizations and development you want to do to the system. Solutions can be lifted from one environment to the next.

Once you've created your solution, you can fill it with the existing tables to make changes to these. In *Figure 10.4*, you can see that I've added the **Account** and **Contact** tables to my solution:

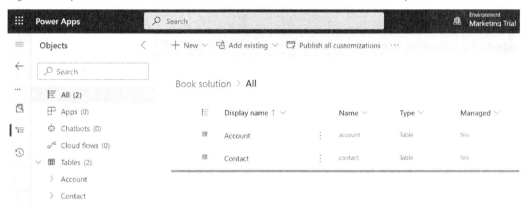

Figure 10.4 – Tables added to a solution

Now, I can make changes to the **Account** and **Contact** tables. I can also create my own tables; let's go through how that's done.

Creating new tables

To create a new table, click + **New** | **Table**, as shown in *Figure 10.5*:

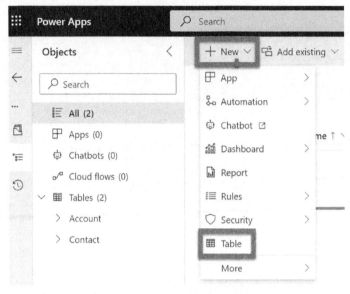

Figure 10.5 – Creating a new table

You will see a window where you can fill in the **Display name** field to give your table a new name, as shown in *Figure 10.6*:

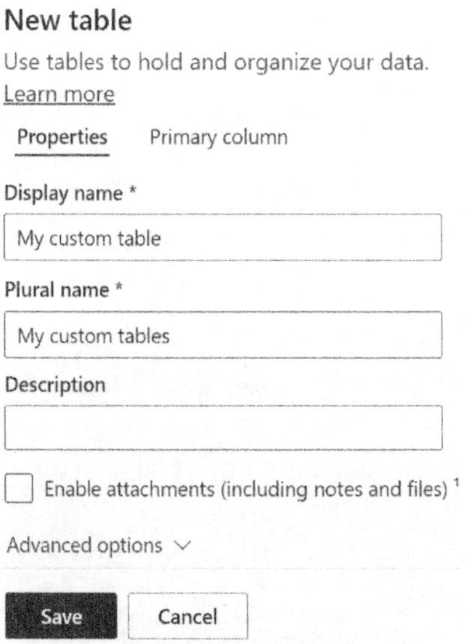

New table

Use tables to hold and organize your data.
Learn more

Properties   Primary column

Display name *

My custom table

Plural name *

My custom tables

Description

☐ Enable attachments (including notes and files) [1]

Advanced options ⌄

Save   Cancel

Figure 10.6 – Naming a new table

Be aware that there are a lot of important options in the **Advanced options** area, so make sure you go through them before clicking **Save**. Once the table has been saved, you can see it in your solution, as shown in *Figure 10.7*:

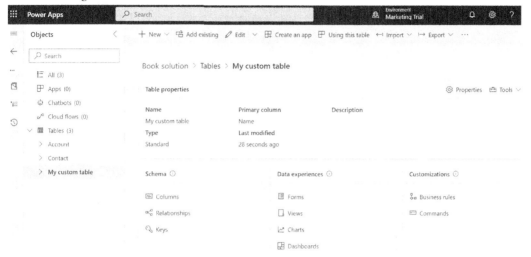

Figure 10.7 – The new table in your solution

Several columns are created when you save the table, but you will also need to create your own columns. Let's go through how you can create new columns for your new table.

Creating new columns

Once your new table has been created, you can add a new column by clicking **+ New | Column**, as shown in *Figure 10.8*:

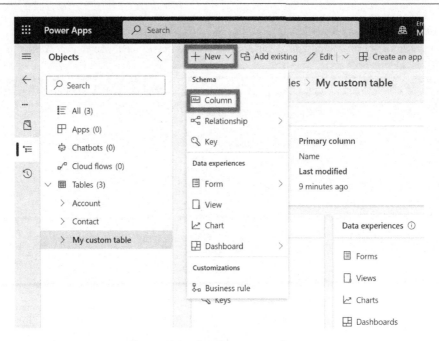

Figure 10.8 – Creating a new column

When you create a new column, you must select a **Data type** option, as shown in *Figure 10.9*:

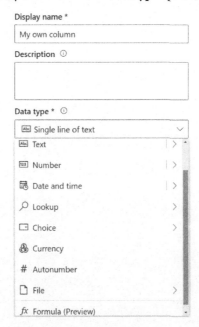

Figure 10.9 – Data type for a new column

The data type cannot be changed after the new column is saved; you must delete and create it again.

When you've saved the column, you can go into **Columns** and check that it's been added, as shown in *Figure 10.10*:

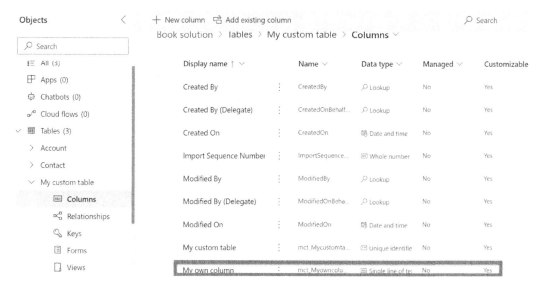

Figure 10.10 – My column

Now that we've created a table with a column, it's time to create our form so that we can see and create rows.

Creating forms

To create a new form, click on + **New** | **Form** and select the type of form you want to create, as shown in *Figure 10.11*:

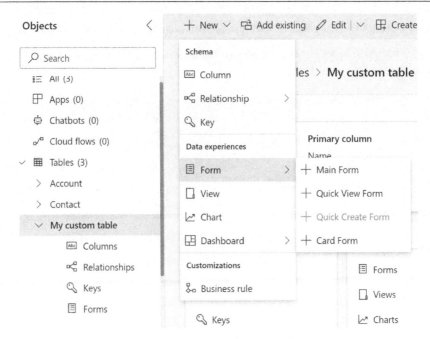

Figure 10.11 – Creating a new form

The most used form is **Main Form**. When you click on + **Main Form**, a new form will be created with the default column (often the **Name** column) and the **Owner** column. As you can see in *Figure 10.12*, the new form is in the middle of the screen and you can see our columns, including the one we just created, on the left-hand side:

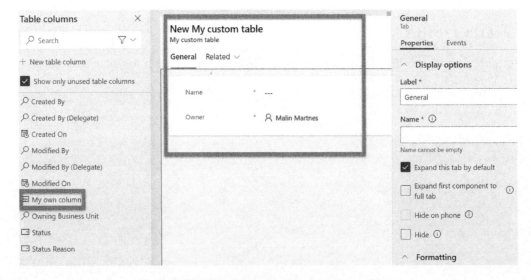

Figure 10.12 – New form with the new column shown

We can now drag the created column into the form, save and publish our form, and start using our new form, which shows our new table with our new column.

We can also add other components, not just columns, to a form – you can see the other components in *Figure 10.13*:

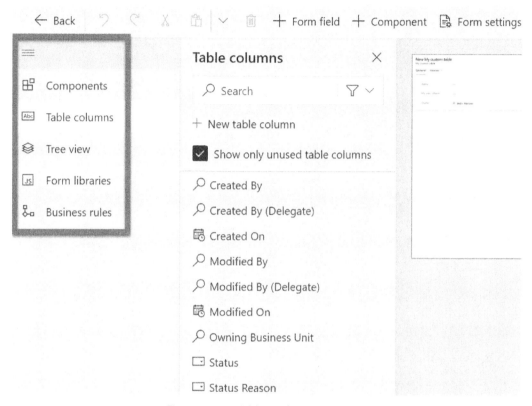

Figure 10.13 – Adding other components

Now that we've created the form for our new table with our new column, how are we going to consume this data? We can create views to do this.

Creating views

Back in the solution, we can click on + **New** again and create a new view by selecting **View**, as shown in *Figure 10.14*:

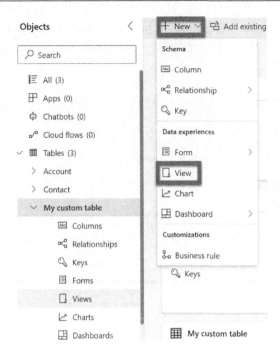

Figure 10.14 – Creating a new view

When we click on **View**, we get a popup in which we can give the view a name, as shown in *Figure 10.15*:

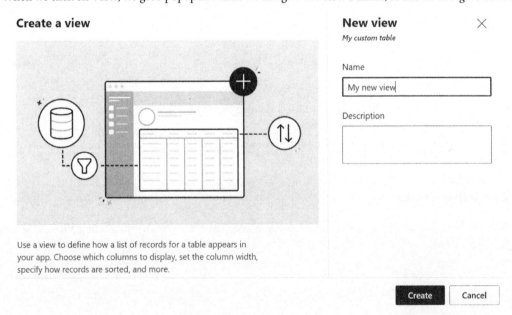

Figure 10.15 – Naming a new view

We can then add the column of our choice to the view. As you can see in *Figure 10.16*, I've added the column we created previously:

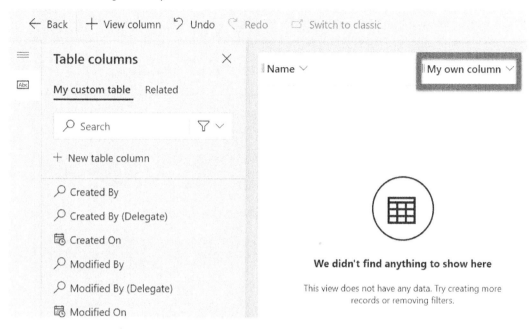

Figure 10.16 – Adding a column to the view

We can now save and publish the view. With that, our new table, with the new column, is ready to be viewed.

Now, let's talk about Power Apps and how you can put all of this together to create your own apps to show the data.

Power Apps

Power Apps consists of two different tools for creating apps:

- Model-driven
- Canvas

There are several templates you can use when creating both model-driven and canvas applications. These are very good for learning purposes, so make sure you check out the templates and learn how they're built.

Let's look at how to use these solutions.

Model-driven

Every CRM application in Dynamics 365 is a model-driven Power Apps app. This means that if you know how to edit and create a model-driven app, you know how to make changes to your Dynamics 365 Marketing solution to customize it to your company's needs. Let's start with how you can edit an existing app.

Editing apps

To be able to edit an existing app, you must first add it to your solution. You can do this by clicking **Add existing | App**, then **Model-driven app**, as shown in *Figure 10.17*:

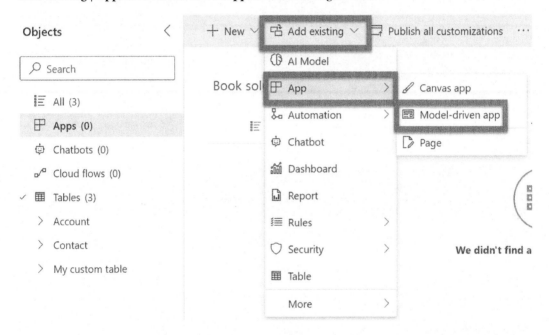

Figure 10.17 – Adding an existing model-driven app

Then, you can select the app you want to edit. The app will now appear in your solution and you can click on it to make changes.

When you open the app, you will see the app on the middle screen, information about the app on the right, and your pages and options on the left-hand side, as shown in *Figure 10.18*:

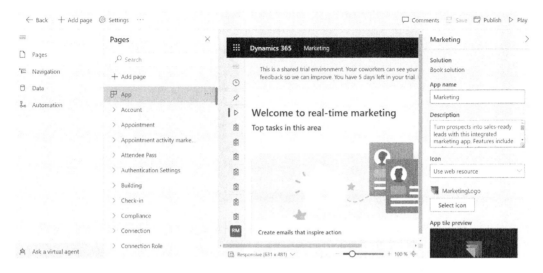

Figure 10.18 – Editing the Marketing application

Let's add the table that we created earlier in this chapter. Click + **Add page**, as shown in *Figure 10.18*; you will get a popup in which you can choose from the following page types:

- **Table based view and form**
- **Dashboard**
- **Custom**

This is shown in *Figure 10.19*:

Add page   ✕

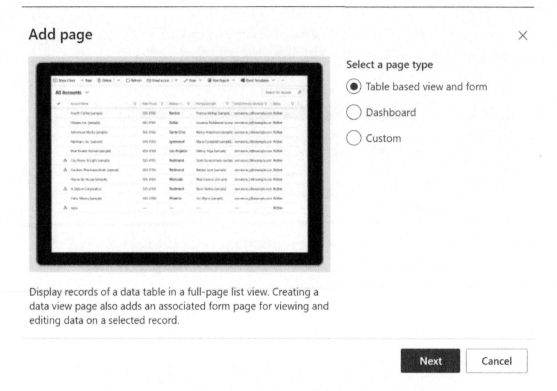

Select a page type

⦿ Table based view and form

◯ Dashboard

◯ Custom

Display records of a data table in a full-page list view. Creating a
data view page also adds an associated form page for viewing and
editing data on a selected record.

| Next | Cancel |

Figure 10.19 – Adding a page to an app

When you click **Next**, you can select the tables you want to add. You can select existing tables or create
new tables. In *Figure 10.20*, you can see that I've searched for and selected the table we created. I've
also checked the checkbox for it to show in the navigation, as shown in *Figure 10.20*:

← **Add table view and form pages**   ✕

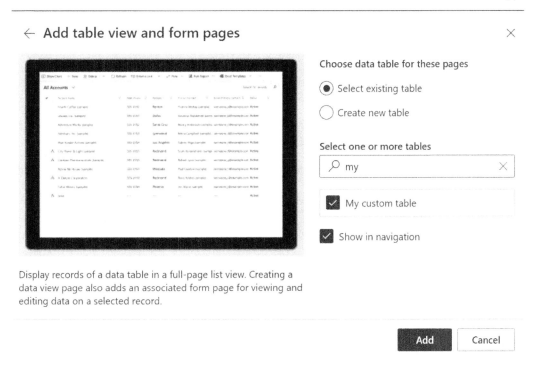

Choose data table for these pages

◉ Select existing table

◯ Create new table

Select one or more tables

🔍 my   ✕

✓ My custom table

✓ Show in navigation

Display records of a data table in a full-page list view. Creating a
data view page also adds an associated form page for viewing and
editing data on a selected record.

Add   Cancel

Figure 10.20 – Selecting the table

When I click **Add**, **My custom table** is added to the solution. I can also see that my new view is
available, and I can immediately see that the app works and that I can add a new row for my custom
table, where **My own column** has already been added to the form, as shown in *Figure 10.21*:

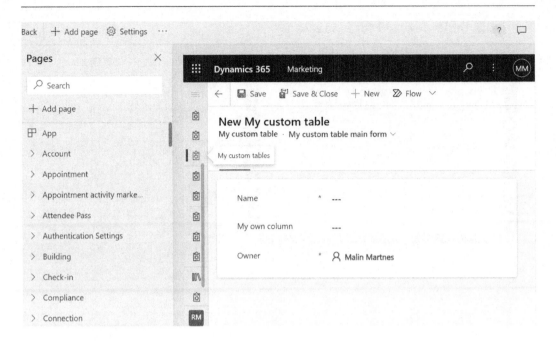

Figure 10.21 – My custom table added to the Marketing app

You can also make changes to **Navigation** if you want to add another subsection or move the different tables around. You can even remove parts of **Navigation** if nobody is using them.

Let's say you want to use the **Real-time marketing** (**RTM**) area, so you want to have everything you need in this area. The **Customer** section is in the **Outbound marketing** area, as of October 2022. By making changes in **Navigation** and clicking on the three dots in the group (where you can find **Accounts**, **Contacts**, and more), you can move the entire section up to the RTM area, as shown in *Figure 10.22*:

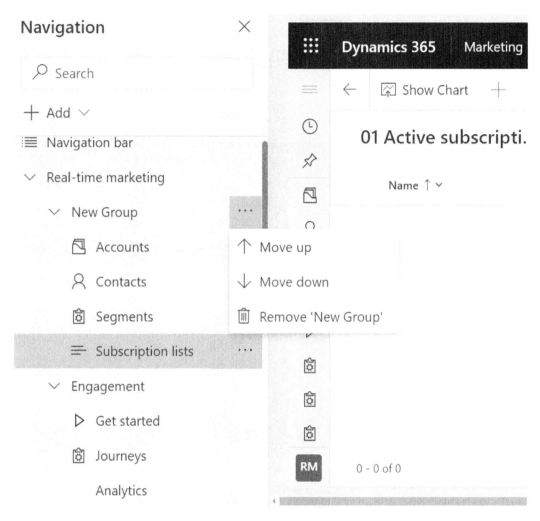

Figure 10.22 – Moving a group up and down

Click **Save** and then **Publish** to go live with the changes. Now, when I open the Marketing app, I will see that this section has moved and is now in the RTM area, as shown in *Figure 10.23*:

Figure 10.23 – Changes in Navigation in the Marketing app

I can also see that **My custom tables** has been added to the solution, and I can start working with this table.

With that, we've made changes to the existing Marketing application, but we can also create our own applications, where we can have much simpler navigation. You can create as many applications as are needed in your environment.

Creating new apps

To create a new app, you go back to your solution and click **+ New | App | Model-driven app**, as shown in *Figure 10.24*:

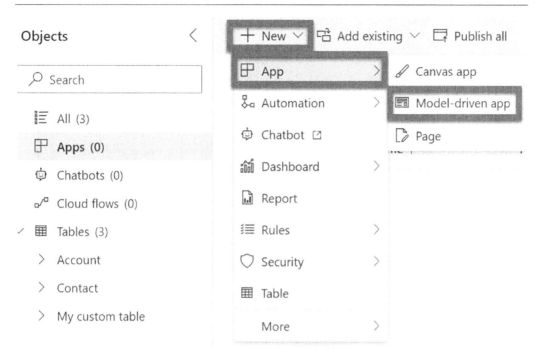

Figure 10.24 – Creating a new model-driven app

Here, you can give your new app a name and start adding pages to your application in the same way that you can make edits to an existing app. In *Figure 10.25*, you can see that I've added **Account**, **Contact**, and **My custom table** to the application:

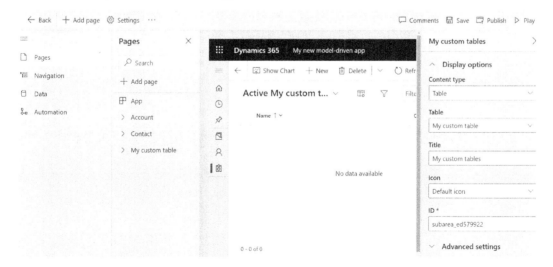

Figure 10.25 – My new model-driven app

The app is now ready to be saved and published and shared with the users that will benefit from this app.

This is the no-code way to create a new application. Now, let's look at the other Power Apps app you can create: the canvas app.

Canvas

There are several ways to create a new canvas app. You can start from the solution and click **+ New | App | Canvas app**, as shown in *Figure 10.26*:

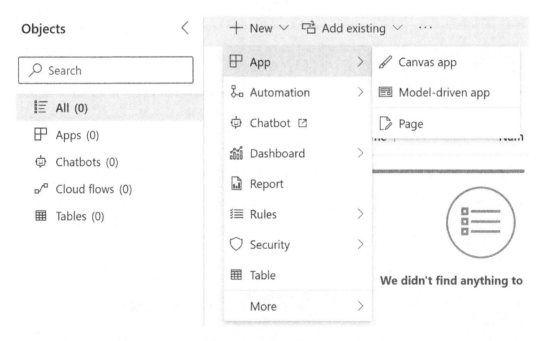

Figure 10.26 – Creating a new canvas app

The first thing you must do is select your format: **Tablet** or **Phone**. This is an important step and cannot be changed later. When you start this way, you will get a blank app, as shown in *Figure 10.27*:

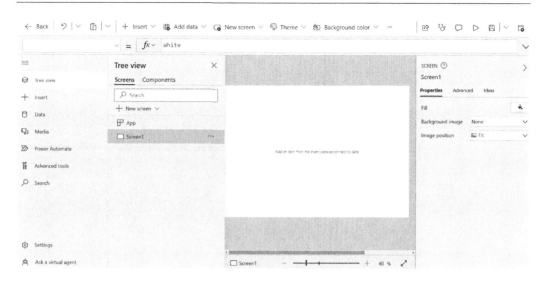

Figure 10.27 – A blank canvas app

Starting from a blank app means that you will have to do all the setup yourself and for this, you will need to know some basics about canvas apps. I have recommended several books in the *Further reading* section of this chapter where you can learn more about creating canvas apps.

The easiest way to create a canvas app when you're using Dataverse is to start from data. As you can see in *Figure 10.28*, you can create your apps from the following options:

- **Blank**
- **Dataverse**
- **SharePoint**
- **Excel**
- **SQL**
- **Image**
- **Figma**

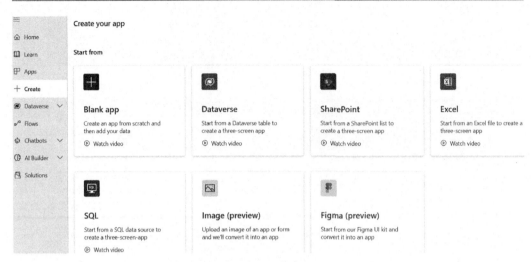

Figure 10.28 – Create your app

I selected Dataverse, so now, I must connect to the right environment and choose a table. In *Figure 10.29*, you can see that I've selected **My custom tables**, which we created earlier in this chapter:

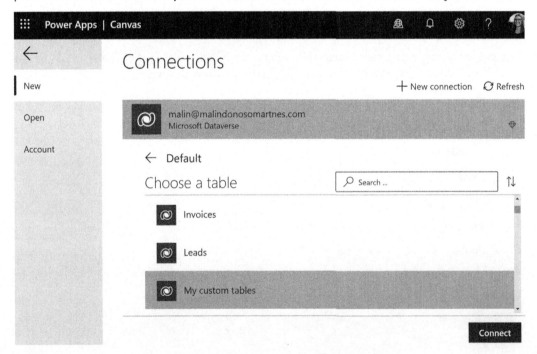

Figure 10.29 – Creating a canvas app from Dataverse

When I click **Connect**, Microsoft creates a three-screen application for me, which I can start using or editing. You can see the app in *Figure 10.30*:

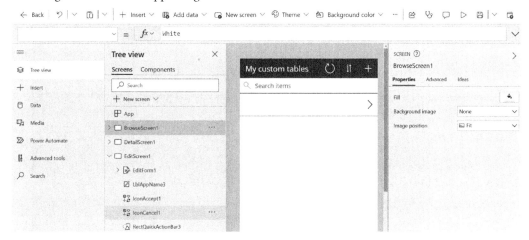

Figure 10.30 – Canvas app based on My custom tables

I can now start using **Power Fx** to create a beautiful application that my users will want to use.

We've very quickly gone through how you can create new applications that you can continue to customize. Now, let's go through how to create *automagic* with Power Automate.

Power Automate

In Power Automate, you can create automations and keep track of processes. These automations are called **flows**. There are different types of flows that you can create:

- **Cloud flows**: These are the types of flows we're going to go through in this chapter. You can create an automated, instant, or scheduled flow.

- **Desktop flows**: These are **robotic process automation** (**RPA**) capabilities where you can automate tasks in an application or on your desktop. These will not be covered in this chapter.

- **Business process flows** (**BPFs**): You can find BPFs in several areas of the CRM applications in Dynamics 365. You can see this in the opportunity in Sales and the event record in Marketing. They are the process bars that you can see on top of the event records. This is where you can add the tasks you want the users to complete before moving to the next stage. We will not cover BPFs in this chapter.

- **Process advisor flow**: With this flow, you make recordings of different people doing tasks, and then get information on how the process has been for the different users and how you can best optimize these processes. We will not cover the process advisor flow in this chapter.

- **Approval flows**: These trigger an approval where a user must approve or deny the request. They can be good to use if you're running a big event and need to have certain speakers approved by your manager. We will not cover approval flows in this chapter.

Now, let's go through how cloud flows can help your company flow better and more automagically.

Cloud flows

We went through a cloud flow in *Chapter 9, Dynamics 365 Customer Voice* (**Send a survey when a lead is qualified in Dynamics 365**), as you can see in *Figure 10.31*:

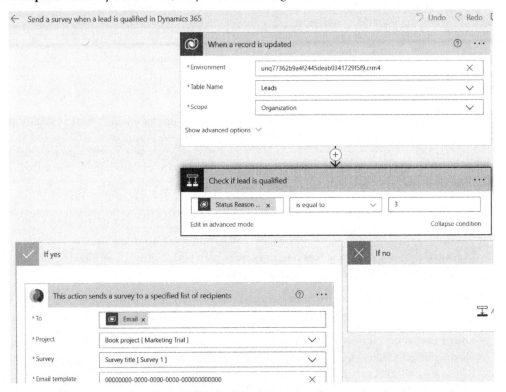

Figure 10.31 – Power Automate flow

Every flow needs to have two things:

- A trigger
- An action

Trigger

The **trigger** is what starts the flow, and the **action** is what happens. In *Figure 10.31*, the trigger is **When a record is updated**, which means the flow will trigger when a row in the Leads table has changed. There is always one trigger for each flow, and a flow can never have more than one trigger. If this flow should be triggered by a row in another table, then you must create another flow.

Action

Check if lead is qualified is the action, as shown in *Figure 10.32*:

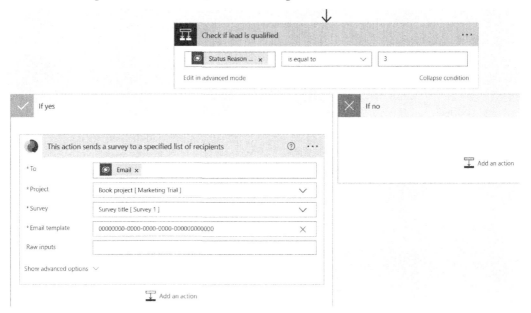

Figure 10.32 – Action of a flow

This will check whether the status reason for the lead is equal to **3** (which is qualified in Dataverse). The flow then has an **If yes** and **If no** path that it sends the customer down, depending on the status reason of the lead. In the **If yes** stage, the customer gets an email where they can complete a Customer Voice survey.

This is just one way of automagic in Dynamics 365 from Power Automate. Let's see how we can use the marketing triggers in real-time marketing with Power Automate.

Custom marketing triggers

You can use Power Automate with custom marketing triggers in many complex ways. You can trigger a cloud flow or an approval flow through a custom trigger in the RTM journey. Let's create a simple journey where we trigger a cloud flow to post about the awesome job the marketing campaign has done of successfully guiding a person through the journey.

To make this work, we need the following:

- A custom trigger
- An RTM journey
- A flow

We went through creating a custom trigger and an RTM journey in *Chapter 7, Real-Time Marketing Journeys*, so we will not repeat how to do this.

In *Figure 10.33*, you can see that I created a journey that sends an email. Based on this email, I have an `if/then` branch that has the condition of opening the email, and in the positive path of this condition I trigger the flow:

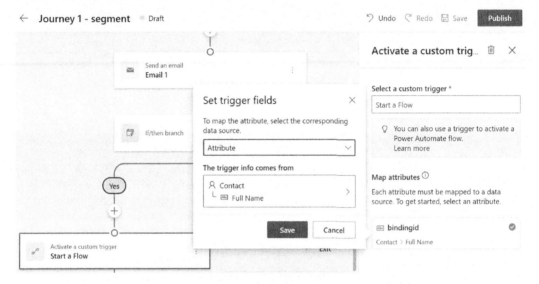

Figure 10.33 – Journey that activates a custom trigger

I've created a trigger called **Start a Flow**, which allows me to start a flow, as the name suggests. Let's see how the flow needs to be set up.

In the flow, I'm using the Dataverse **When an action is performed** option, as you can see in *Figure 10.34*:

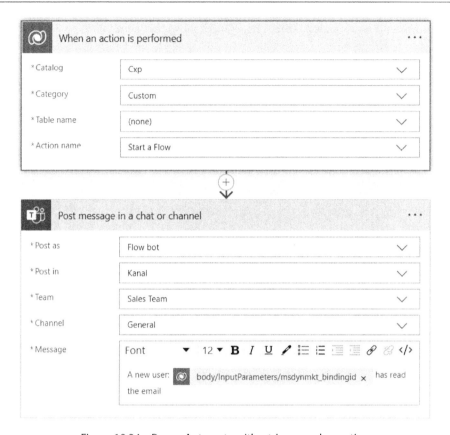

Figure 10.34 – Power Automate with a trigger and an action

In the trigger, I set the options as follows:

- **Catalog**: **Cxp**
- **Category**: **Custom**
- **Table name**: **(none)**
- **Action name**: **Start a Flow**

This is the way you must do the setup to make it work. You can find your custom trigger in your **Action name** dropdown.

The next thing you must do is create the action. This is what you want the flow to do. I've selected **Post message in a chat or channel** from Teams.

Once I've saved my flow, I can go back to Dynamics 365 Marketing and activate my journey. This will cause the email to be sent. If this email has been read, the journey will continue down the positive path and trigger the custom trigger, which again triggers the Power Automate flow.

We can see from the flow that it has been triggered, as shown in *Figure 10.35*:

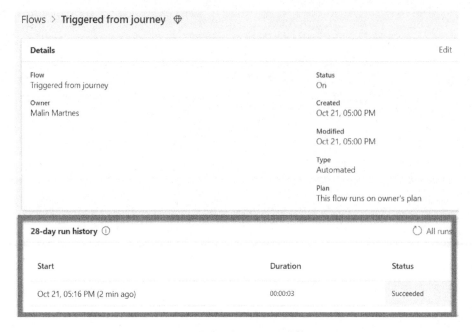

Figure 10.35 – The triggered flow

Now, I can go into Microsoft Teams and see that I have a post in **Sales Team** in the **General** channel, as shown in *Figure 10.36*:

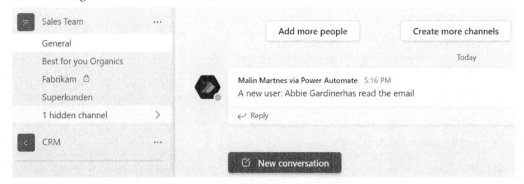

Figure 10.36 – Posted in a channel in Teams

This flow will probably not be something you will be using a lot, but it is a way of showing you how you can combine the custom triggers in Dynamics 365 Marketing with a Power Automate flow.

With that, we've gone through some ways of using Power Automate and hopefully given you some tips on how you can use this amazing tool for a more automated work life. Now, let's see how we can use Power Pages as an addition to Dynamics 365 Marketing.

Power Pages

Power Pages changed names in the fall of 2022; before this, it was called Power Apps Portals.

In *Chapter 8, Managing Events*, we went through a bit about Power Pages and how you can fully integrate it with Dynamics 365 Marketing. Power Pages is a separate product with a separate license. In *Figure 10.37*, you can see the details of a configured Power Pages page:

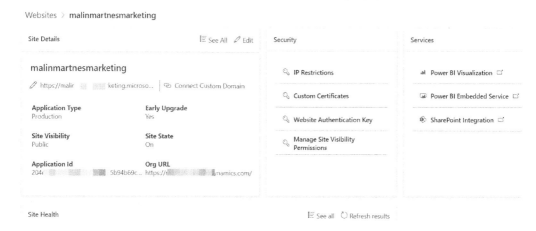

Figure 10.37 – Power Pages setup

From here, I can make edits and do maintenance on my page.

The fall of 2022 is a difficult time to write much about Power Pages, as most of the editing options are changing. The event template is not available in the new interface. For these screenshots, I've selected a generic template to show you how easy it can be to configure the page.

Once we've set up our page, we can make edits. By clicking **Edit**, as shown in *Figure 10.38*, we can start customizing our page:

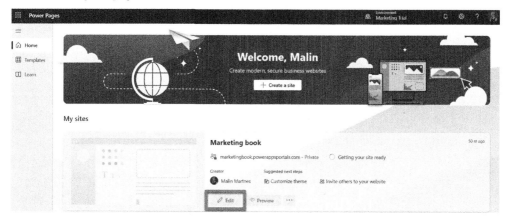

Figure 10.38 – Editing Power Pages

I now have four workspaces:

- A **Pages** workspace: Here, you can make changes to the design with no code, such as adding or changing the text, image, or video and connecting to lists and forms. You can see the **Pages** workspace in *Figure 10.39*:

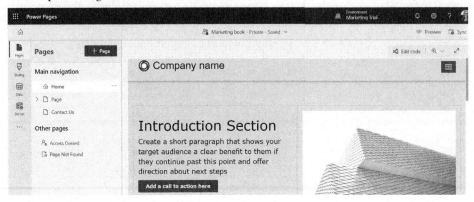

Figure 10.39 – The Pages workspace

- The **Styling** workspace: Here, you can update and apply global styles to your site. You can see the **Styling** workspace in *Figure 10.40*:

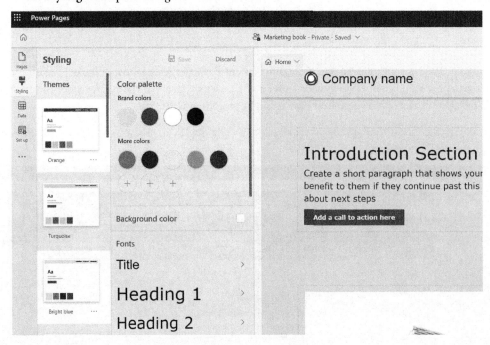

Figure 10.40 – The Styling workspace

- The **Data** workspace: Here, you can work with your data from Dataverse and connect to the model-driven forms and views. You can see the **Data** workspace in *Figure 10.41*:

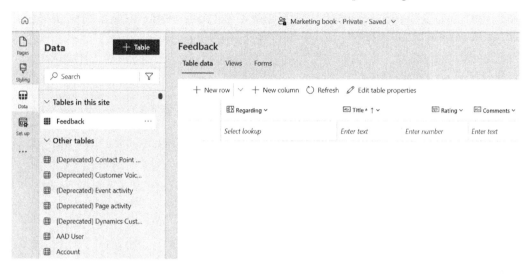

Figure 10.41 – The Data workspace

- The **Set up** workspace: Here, you do administrative tasks such as setting up security and permissions. You can see the **Set up** workspace in *Figure 10.42*:

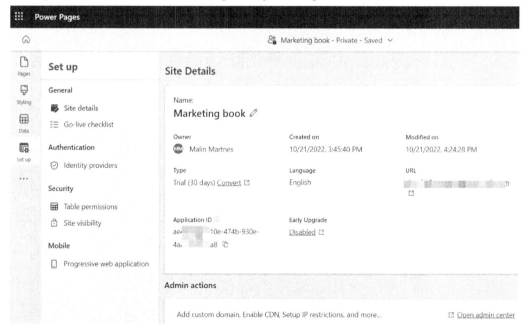

Figure 10.42 – The Set up workspace

As you can see, there are several ways you can customize and utilize Power Pages to work with your Dynamics 365 Marketing application.

Now, let's look at an outsider: Customer Insights isn't part of Power Platform but it is a Dynamics 365 application that is tightly connected to Dynamics 365 Marketing.

Customer Insights

Dynamics 365 **CI** is Microsoft's **customer data platform** (**CDP**). It will help you, with the use of AI, to get an overview of your customers based on several data sources and in real time. CI is tightly integrated with Dynamics 365 Marketing and can create segments with the use of AI, which you can then use in your journeys.

As you can see in *Figure 10.43*, a lot of information about your customer is potentially stored in CI:

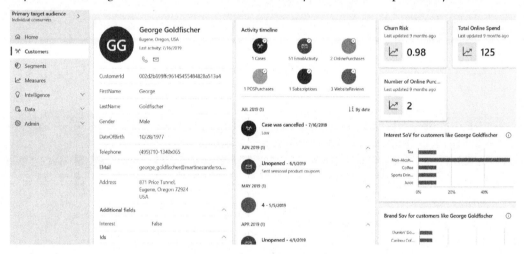

Figure 10.43 – Customer information

As you can see in *Figure 10.44*, there are several segments in my CI environment, and any of these can be updated with data from multiple data sources and automatically transferred to Marketing as a segment:

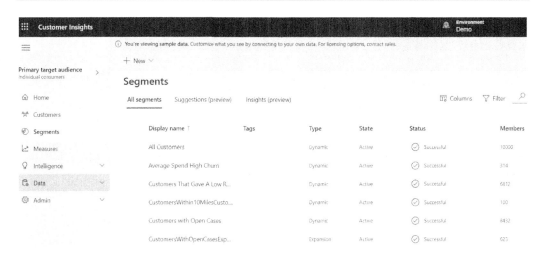

Figure 10.44 – Segments in Customer Insights

A segment coming from CI will always be static and will be updated by CI every time synchronization runs. You should never make changes to these segments. These segments are always created as drafts, so you must activate them to use them in a journey.

CI will never create new contacts in Dynamics 365 Marketing, it will just work with the ones you already have in the system.

Summary

As you saw, there is a lot of functionality in Microsoft Power Platform. Your marketing solution is built on top of Dataverse, where you can create new tables, columns, forms, and views. This way, you can create a solution that is tailored to you and your company's needs. With the use of Power Apps, you can either edit your Marketing application or create new applications that are custom-tailored for you. With canvas apps, you can create beautiful applications that help your company with the help of Power Fx.

To make your life easier and to make it automagic, you have Power Automate. This can be integrated into your marketing solution, and you can integrate it with other applications in your portfolio.

We ended this chapter with Power Pages and Customer Insights – two solutions that can help expand your marketing solution and give your company everything they need to have a complete holistic overview of your customers.

We've now been through the core functionality of Dynamics 365 Marketing and solutions that can help you in your marketing efforts. Congratulations on completing this book. I hope you've learned a lot and will now go and learn even more by testing Dynamics 365 Marketing and using it for your company's marketing automation efforts. Thank you for reading this book!

Questions

The following are some questions that will help you gauge your understanding of the topics discussed in this chapter. The answers are available in the *Assessments* section at the end of the books:.

1. You must bring your own safety to Dataverse.

    A. No

    B. Yes

2. You can only create new **Text** columns in Dataverse.

    A. No

    B. Yes

3. Model-driven and canvas apps are edited with the same functionality.

    A. No

    B. Yes

4. You cannot edit the out-of-the-box Dynamics 365 Marketing application.

    A. No

    B. Yes

5. In which ways can you create a canvas app?

    A. Blank

    B. From model-driven

    C. From data

    D. Image

    E. Figma

    F. UI

6. What does a Power Automate Flow always consist of?

    A. An action

    B. An app

    C. A trigger

    D. A consequence

    E. Data

Further reading

- **Power Platform and Dynamics 365/Customer Engagement/CRM**:

  - *Microsoft Power Platform Functional Consultant: PL-200 Exam Guide: Learn how to customize and configure Microsoft Power Platform and prepare for the PL-200 exam*: https://www.amazon.com/Microsoft-Power-Platform-Functional-Consultant-ebook/dp/B08KQKQ22W/ref=pd_rhf_d_dp_s_pd_crcd_sccl_1_1/143-1488019-8399560?pd_rd_w=3V8GJ&content-id=amzn1.sym.cee83ff1-8fc1-4533-a3f5-bf3d998f4558&pf_rd_p=cee83ff1-8fc1-4533-a3f5-bf3d998f4558&pf_rd_r=C5KSYVSFR7139E03J3VQ&pd_rd_wg=dAtDl&pd_rd_r=9a05d0a8-5825-4045-a0ea-828d5664f16a&pd_rd_i=B08KQKQ22W&psc=1

  - *Fundamentals of CRM with Dynamics 365 and Power Platform: Enhance your customer relationship management by extending Dynamics 365 using a no-code approach*: https://www.amazon.com/Fundamentals-CRM-Dynamics-Power-Platform-ebook/dp/B08HYWX6VL/ref=d_reads_cwrtbar_sccl_2_37/143-1488019-8399560?pd_rd_w=6rQel&content-id=amzn1.sym.c3636f1d-aab3-4576-85e3-007dd638fbde&pf_rd_p=c3636f1d-aab3-4576-85e3-007dd638fbde&pf_rd_r=9SR96CB8T26Z4QH-3N633&pd_rd_wg=pEJwX&pd_rd_r=c40b2e99-6e24-41ca-be15-d9176df-278b7&pd_rd_i=B08HYWX6VL&psc=1

  - *Mastering Microsoft Dynamics 365 Customer Engagement: An advanced guide to developing and customizing CRM solutions to improve your business applications, 2nd Edition*: https://www.amazon.com/Mastering-Dynamics-365-customization-develop-ment-ebook/dp/B07G1B7TB8/ref=d_reads_cwrtbar_sccl_2_38/143-1488019-8399560?pd_rd_w=6rQel&content-id=amzn1.sym.c3636f1d-aab3-4576-85e3-007dd638fbde&pf_rd_p=c3636f1d-aab3-4576-85e3-007dd638fbde&pf_rd_r=9SR96CB8T26Z4QH3N633&pd_rd_wg=pE-JwX&pd_rd_r=c40b2e99-6e24-41ca-be15-d9176df278b7&pd_rd_i=B07G-1B7TB8&psc=1

  - *Power Platform and Dynamics 365 CE for Absolute Beginners: Configure and Customize Your Business Needs*: https://www.amazon.com/Power-Platform-Dynamics-Ab-solute-Beginners/dp/1484285999/

  - ref=sr_1_10?crid=129M36R5NWNSJ&keywords=dataverse&-qid=1666284749&qu=eyJxc2MiOiIyLjQ0IiwicXNhIjoiMi40NyIsInFzc-CI6IjIuNDkifQ%3D%3D&s=books&sprefix=dataverse%2Cstripbooks-in-tl-ship%2C154&sr=1-10

- **Dataverse**:

  Microsoft Dataverse: The Power Platform Series: Leveraging Microsoft Dataverse to build real world business solutions: `https://www.amazon.com/Microsoft-Dataverse-Platform-Leveraging-solutions-ebook/dp/B08S37P2JW/ref=sr_1_1?crid=129M36R5NWNSJ&keywords=dataverse&qid=1666284749&qu=eyJxc2MiOiIyLjQ0IiwicXNhIjoiMi40NyIsInFzcCI6IjIuNDkifQ%3D%3D&s=books&sprefix=dataverse%2Cstripbooks-intl-ship%2C154&sr=1-1`

- **Power Apps**:

  - *Beginning Power Apps: The Non-Developer's Guide to Building Business Applications*: `https://www.amazon.com/Beginning-Power-Apps-Non-Developers-Applications-ebook/dp/B08YXC29DW/ref=d_reads_cwrtbar_sccl_2_8/143-1488019-8399560?pd_rd_w=6rQel&content-id=amzn1.sym.c3636f1d-aab3-4576-85e3-007dd638fbde&pf_rd_p=c3636f1d-aab3-4576-85e3-007dd638fbde&pf_rd_r=9SR96CB8T26Z4QH3N633&pd_rd_wg=pEJwX&pd_rd_r=c40b2e99-6e24-41ca-be15-d9176df278b7&pd_rd_i=B08YXC29DW&psc=1`

  - *Microsoft Power Apps Cookbook: Apply low-code recipes to solve everyday business challenges and become a Power Apps pro, 2nd Edition*: `https://www.amazon.com/Microsoft-Power-Apps-Cookbook-challenges-dp-180323802X/dp/180323802X/ref=dp_ob_title_bk`

  - *Learn Microsoft Power Apps: The definitive handbook for building solutions with Power Apps to solve your business needs, 2nd Edition*: `https://www.amazon.com/Learn-Microsoft-Power-Apps-definitive-dp-1801070644/dp/1801070644/ref=dp_ob_title_bk`

- **Power Automate**:

  Workflow Automation with Microsoft Power Automate: Use business process automation to achieve digital transformation with minimal code, 2nd Edition: `https://www.amazon.com/Workflow-Automation-Microsoft-Power-Automate/dp/1803237678/ref=sr_1_1?crid=3FGP733IBLHJM&keywords=power+automate&qid=1666284904&qu=eyJxc2MiOiIzLjg5IiwicXNhIjoiMy40OCIsInFzcCI6IjMuMTcifQ%3D%3D&s=books&sprefix=power+automate%2Cstripbooks-intl-ship%2C142&sr=1-1`

- **Developer**:

  Pro Microsoft Power Platform: Solution Building for the Citizen Developer: https://www. amazon.com/Pro-Microsoft-Power-Platform-Developer-ebook/dp/ B08KVRRVVN/ref=d_reads_cwrtbar_sccl_2_2/143-1488019-8399560?pd_ rd_w=6rQel&content-id=amzn1.sym.c3636f1d-aab3-4576-85e3- 007dd638fbde&pf_rd_p=c3636f1d-aab3-4576-85e3-007dd638fbde&pf_ rd_r=9SR96CB8T26Z4QH3N633&pd_rd_wg=pEJwX&pd_rd_r=c40b2e99-6e24- 41ca-be15-d9176df278b7&pd_rd_i=B08KVRRVVN&psc=1

Assessments

Chapter 1

1. Can you turn off the tables you don't need for synchronization on data tables?

    A. Yes

    B. **No**

2. What are the different types of templates in outbound marketing?

    A. **Email**

    B. **Form**

    C. **Pages**

    D. **Websites**

    E. Event

    F. **Segment**

    G. **Customer journeys**

3. What tables can a landing page update?

    A. Contacts

    B. Leads

    C. **Contacts and leads**

    D. Contacts, leads, and custom tables

4. Can you send emails from any domains in Dynamics 365 Marketing?

    A. Yes

    B. **Yes, but you need to connect the domain first**

    C. No

5. Do you have one consent center for both outbound and real-time marketing?

    A. Yes

    B. **No**

6. Which social media sites can you connect to?

    A. **Facebook**

    B. Google Plus

    C. Google Ads

    D. **Twitter**

    E. Pinterest

    F. **LinkedIn**

    G. **Instagram**

7. Which third-party webinar provider can you connect to?

    A. **On24**

    B. Microsoft Teams

    C. Zoom

    D. Slack

8. If you have a LinkedIn Lead Gen Form and want to add that to your system, what do you need to do, and in which order?

    A. Sign in to LinkedIn with your company profile, then connect to the correct LinkedIn Lead Gen Form

    B. Sign in to LinkedIn with your profile, then connect to the correct LinkedIn Lead Gen Form

    C. **Sign in to LinkedIn with your profile that's connected to your company's profile and the LinkedIn Lead Gen Form**

Chapter 2

1. Why are leads important?

    A. To generate sales

    B. To have someone to market to

    C. **To have somewhere to register "fussy" interest**

    D. To know your customers

    E. To know your companies

2. Which contact type is considered in licensing?

   A. Sales-ready contact

   B. Marketing-ready contact

   C. Regular contact

   D. **Marketing contact**

   E. Event contact

   F. No contacts are relevant to licensing

3. What type of relationship do contacts and accounts have out of the box?

   A. **1:N**

   B. N:N

   C. They're not related

4. If you want to do lead scoring based on "If a lead has clicked on an email," what type of lead scoring model will that be?

   A. **Behavior**

   B. Demographic

   C. Firmographic

5. Can a lead be scored with multiple lead scoring models?

   A. **Yes**

   B. No

Chapter 3

1. What are the three different blocks you can use in segments?

   A. Demographic

   B. **Query**

   C. **Segment**

   D. Contact

   E. **Behavior**

2. Where do you add the subscription list?

   A. Marketing schema

   B. **Marketing forms**

   C. Marketing pages

   D. Marketing subscriptions

3. What are the three operators to combine several blocks in segments?

   A. include

   B. **or**

   C. **but not**

   D. exclude

   E. if else

   F. **and also**

4. Can marketing lists be used in customer journeys?

   A. Yes

   B. No

   C. **Yes, but only subscription lists**

Chapter 4

1. What are the three standard marketing forms?

   A. **A landing page form**

   B. **A subscription form**

   C. A contact information form

   D. An event registration form

   E. **A forward-to-a-friend form**

2. Why are marketing form fields important?

   A. You need them to create your fields in a marketing form

   B. **You need them to connect the fields in a form to your data in Dataverse**

   C. They are the fields shown on your marketing form

3.   Where do videos in a marketing page need to come from?

A.   A real-time marketing asset library

B.   **An outbound marketing library**

4.   4. What are marketing websites used for?

A.   Creating new websites

B.   Connecting Power Pages to Dynamics 365 Marketing

C.   **Connecting websites to Dynamics 365 Marketing**

D.   Connecting marketing pages to websites

Chapter 5

1.   To start using Litmus integration, you first must do what?

A.   Sign in to Litmus

B.   Create a Litmus account

C.   **Activate Litmus integration in the settings**

D.   Activate Litmus integration in the settings and on the Litmus page

2.   Which two elements are only available in **Outbound marketing**?

A.   Text

B.   Images

C.   Personalization

D.   **Videos**

E.   Dividers

F.   **Code**

G.   QR codes

3.   In **Send now**, you can send an email to a maximum of how many people?

A.   10

B.   20

C.   **30**

D.   40

E.   50

4. Can a marketing form be embedded into a marketing email?

    A. Yes

    B. **No**

Chapter 6

1. How can you use outbound customer journeys?

    A. To send emails to customers

    B. To reply to your customers

    C. **To say how you interact with customers**

2. How many times will a contact go through a customer journey by default?

    A. **1**

    B. 10

    C. Unlimited

3. You can use either a suppression segment or an excluding segment audience; they both do the same thing.

    A. True

    B. **False**

4. In the Send an email tile, you can make changes to what?

    A. The design of the email

    B. **The send time of the email**

    C. The content settings of the email

    D. **The expiration of the email**

5. What always needs to be done before you can start using the customer journey?

    A. Saving

    B. Publishing

    C. **Going live**

Chapter 7

1. When creating a custom trigger, it must be embedded as code on a website?

    A. Yes

    B. **No**

2. What two options are there to activating a journey?

    A. Audience

    B. **Trigger**

    C. Custom trigger

    D. Manually

    E. **Segment**

3. A goal for the journey is set out-of-the-box

    A. Yes

    B. **No**

4. You can always use AI to use the right channel to the audience?

    A. Yes

    B. **No (if the audience hasn't gone through any channels, then it won't know where to send the audience)**

Chapter 8

1. You can only use Microsoft Teams as your webinar provider.

    A. Yes

    B. **No**

2. In which marketing form can you register attendees?

    A. Landing page

    B. Forward to a Friend

    C. **Event registration**

    D. Event attendees

3. How is the speaker connected to your event and session?

   A. Directly to the event

   B. Directly to the session

   C. Directly to the session track

   D. **Through speaker engagements**

4. If you use Microsoft Teams as your webinar provider, you can't change any options – it uses the organization's settings.

5. True

6. **False**

Chapter 9

1. Microsoft Forms and Dynamics 365 Customer Voice are identical:

   A. Yes

   B. **No**

2. Which of these is not a type of question you can have in a survey? (There is more than one answer)

   A. Rating

   B. Ranking

   C. **Rhetorical**

   D. **Funnel**

   E. **CSAT**

   F. NPS

3. You can create a single survey not connected to anything in Dynamics 365 Customer Voice:

   A. Yes

   B. **No**

4. Embedding the survey on a website can be done in which three ways?

   A. **Inline**

   B. Outline

   C. **Button**

   D. **Pop-up window**

   E. Download

5. How long is the survey progress stored if the setting is turned on?

    A.   1 week

    B.   1 month

    C.   14 days

    D.   **28 days**

    E.   3 months

    F.   1 year

Chapter 10

1. You must bring your own safety to Dataverse.

    A.   **No**

    B.   Yes

2. You can only create new **Text** columns in Dataverse.

    A.   **No**

    B.   Yes

3. Model-driven and canvas apps are edited with the same functionality.

    A.   **No**

    B.   Yes

4. You can edit the out-of-the-box Dynamics 365 Marketing application.

    A.   No

    B.   **Yes**

5. In which ways can you create a canvas app?

    A.   **Blank**

    B.   From model-driven

    C.   **From data**

    D.   **Image**

    E.   **Figma**

    F.   UI

6. What does a Power Automate Flow always consist of?

    A. **An action**

    B. An app

    C. **A trigger**

    D. A consequence

    E. Data

Index

Packt.com

Subscribe to our online digital library for full access to over 7,000 books and videos, as well as industry leading tools to help you plan your personal development and advance your career. For more information, please visit our website.

Why subscribe?

- Spend less time learning and more time coding with practical eBooks and Videos from over 4,000 industry professionals

- Improve your learning with Skill Plans built especially for you

- Get a free eBook or video every month

- Fully searchable for easy access to vital information

- Copy and paste, print, and bookmark content

Did you know that Packt offers eBook versions of every book published, with PDF and ePub files available? You can upgrade to the eBook version at packt.com and as a print book customer, you are entitled to a discount on the eBook copy. Get in touch with us at customercare@packtpub.com for more details.

At www.packt.com, you can also read a collection of free technical articles, sign up for a range of free newsletters, and receive exclusive discounts and offers on Packt books and eBooks.

Other Books You May Enjoy

If you enjoyed this book, you may be interested in these other books by Packt:

Empowering Marketing and Sales with HubSpot

Resa Gooding

ISBN: 9781838987145

- Explore essential steps involved in implementing HubSpot correctly
- Build ideal marketing and sales campaigns for your organization
- Manage your sales process and empower your sales teams using HubSpot
- Get buy-in from your management and colleagues by setting up useful reports
- Use Flywheel strategies to increase sales for your business
- Apply the inbound methodology to scale your marketing
- Re-engage your existing database using the HubSpot retargeting ads tool
- Understand how to use HubSpot for any B2B industry in which you operate

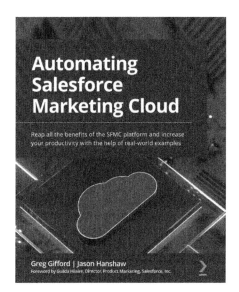

Automating Salesforce Marketing Cloud

Greg Gifford, Jason Hanshaw

ISBN: 9781803237190

- Understand automation to make the most of the SFMC platform
- Optimize ETL activities, data import integrations, data segmentations, email sends, and more
- Explore different ways to use scripting and API calls to increase Automation Studio efficiency
- Identify opportunities for automation with custom integrations and third-party solutions
- Optimize usage of SFMC by building on the core concepts of custom integrations and third-party tools
- Maximize utilization of employee skills and capabilities and reduce operational costs while increasing output

Packt is searching for authors like you

If you're interested in becoming an author for Packt, please visit `authors.packtpub.com` and apply today. We have worked with thousands of developers and tech professionals, just like you, to help them share their insight with the global tech community. You can make a general application, apply for a specific hot topic that we are recruiting an author for, or submit your own idea.

Share Your Thoughts

Now you've finished *Becoming a Microsoft Dynamics 365 Marketing Functional Consultant*, we'd love to hear your thoughts! Scan the QR code below to go straight to the Amazon review page for this book and share your feedback or leave a review on the site that you purchased it from.

`https://packt.link/r/1803234601`

Your review is important to us and the tech community and will help us make sure we're delivering excellent quality content.

Download a free PDF copy of this book

Thanks for purchasing this book!

Do you like to read on the go but are unable to carry your print books everywhere?

Is your eBook purchase not compatible with the device of your choice?

Don't worry, now with every Packt book you get a DRM-free PDF version of that book at no cost.

Read anywhere, any place, on any device. Search, copy, and paste code from your favorite technical books directly into your application.

The perks don't stop there, you can get exclusive access to discounts, newsletters, and great free content in your inbox daily

Follow these simple steps to get the benefits:

1. Scan the QR code or visit the link below

https://packt.link/free-ebook/9781803234601

2. Submit your proof of purchase
3. That's it! We'll send your free PDF and other benefits to your email directly

Printed in Great Britain
by Amazon

21364730R00215